THIS TIGER'S TALE

A Southern Tier Football Odyssey (1957-1992)

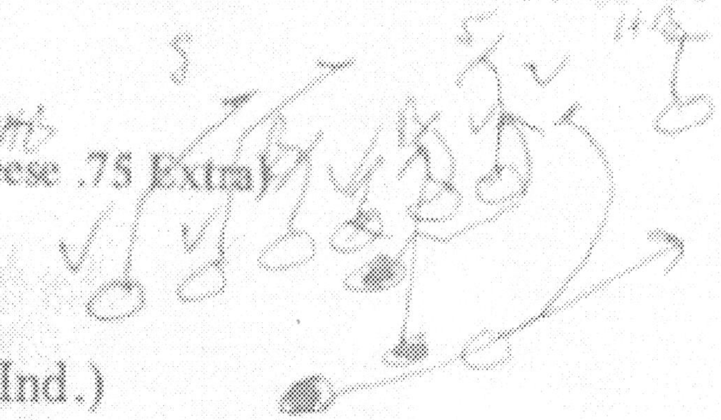

BY **FRAN ANGELINE**

This Tiger's Tale

by

Fran Angeline

FIRST EDITION

Printed in the United States of America

10 9 8 7 6 5 4 3 2 1

ISBN: 1-57087-306-2
LC: 96-72416

Published by

Brundage Publishing
102 State Street, Suite 600
Binghamton, New York

Design and Graphics by
The Graphorium, Inc. of Endicott, New York

Produced by
Professional Press of Chapel Hill, North Carolina

To Pat and the Children

— and to my "Adopted Families":
the Players and the First Team *(staff)*

ACKNOWLEDGMENTS

It is a pleasure to acknowledge the assistance I received while writing this book. My daughter, Vaun, encouraged me and made several positive suggestions from the very beginning. Nino Samiani provided invaluable assistance in the computer world. There is no way I can ever repay my colleague and good friend, Bob Gallagher, the master of the spoken and written word, for his expertise, diligence, and patience throughout. Wayne Davison, neighbor and graphic designer, rendered his professional advice, guidance, and considerable talent during the entire project.

A very special thanks to my best friend and wife, Pat, who scrutinized each chapter, and inspired and assisted me every step of the way.

These good people helped me stay the course during the sometimes lonely journey of writing this story. In their wisdom, they never tried to change the integrity or message of my narrative. They made it look and read better.

CONTENTS

FOREWORD

To understand Fran Angeline it is necessary to know that perhaps from as early as his teen years he knew what to pursue as a career. Football was his bliss. The late Joseph Campbell said that we should follow our bliss. By this he meant that we should stay with our hearts' desire because it leads to happiness. And, if ever a person became a devotee of this advice, it was and is Fran Angeline.

At age 16 he demonstrated his discipline and work ethic by making the Union-Endicott High School starting lineup and by earning *Southern Tier Conference All Star* honors as an end. Then, as a senior, he captained the *Tigers* and also was named captain of the *Binghamton Press All Southern Tier Conference* team.

Staying true to his bliss, Fran accepted a scholarship and took his talents and dedication to Colgate University. His leadership recognized, he became a Red Raider captain. He wrapped up his career at Colgate by serving as an assistant coach while earning his master's degree.

Fran returned to the Triple Cities area in 1957 as a 22-year-old head football coach at Johnson City High School.

This was and remains today a record young age for a head football coach in the Triple Cities. And, in just his second year he produced a champion, serving notice that this young man would make his mark in coaching.

The return to his alma mater in the fall of 1960 heralded a 33-season span, the Angeline era. It started with building (or rebuilding) a program that would return U-E to its glory as a powerhouse. Victories were needed and wanted by a community that would become an avid legion of followers. Once the Angeline engine was cranked, that is.

Victories came. Crowds at Ty Cobb Stadium became enormous. Angeline, who started as the youngest, with 216 triumphs, became the winningest coach in Triple Cities history.

One might ask how this came about. Well, Angeline's being a stickler for detail combined with his indefatigability probably had much to do with it. His attention to detail in this book is simply an extension of his habits in coaching. The world of theater has a word: run-through. It means to go over and over a scene — to get it as near perfect as possible. This is vintage Angeline in coaching AND writing. The man labors assiduously to get things right. It was thus in coaching and now in the telling of this 36-year odyssey.

In the chapters that follow, Fran details what Tiger football was all about both at Ty Cobb Stadium (oh, those Saturday nights!) and on the road. Highlighted are the crowds, electrifying plays, upsets, heartbreaks, incredible team and individual performances, and post-game hugs and happiness. But, actually, there is more — more than the on-the-field excitement. And even more than the daily grind of preparation. We read about the factors involving a coach's dealings with the players and with the players' parents. That is, Fran shares what he experienced off the field with confused players and with the father-son relationship. Also, he gives huge credit to those truly unsung heroines — the encouraging Rock of Gibraltar mothers who arrange dinner schedules to accommodate the occasionally bruised and late-arriving gridders with their gargantuan appetites.

Not everyone who played for or against U-E during Angeline's career is listed. An enormous number are, however. Receiving ample coverage and praise are the great coaching rivals, Dick Hoover of Vestal and Joe Moresco of Ithaca. The loyal and able assistant coaches receive their due. And since Fran and his staffs were always hungry literally as well as figuratively, some favorite restaurants and their specialties are part of their journeys. Also interwoven are many interesting anecdotes about and actual conversations with not only U-E players and such, but also opposing coaches, players, and officials.

Finally, Fran includes and has appreciative words for a loving and supportive family. The lady-behind-the-man here is wife Pat. She could write pages about sharing parental and other duties with a man whose "season never ends" during a 12-month year. Sons Chris and Larry became football Tigers who would make any parent glow with pride. Daughter Vaun, an acting and singing phenom at U-E, achieved the highest level of academic excellence at Syracuse University, where, naturally, she also worked for Coach Dick MacPherson in the football office.

Football. Angeline. The words seem synonymous. From the youngest to the winningest the man followed his bliss. Now he tells us all about it in *This Tiger's Tale.*

Bob Gallagher
Binghamton, New York
1996

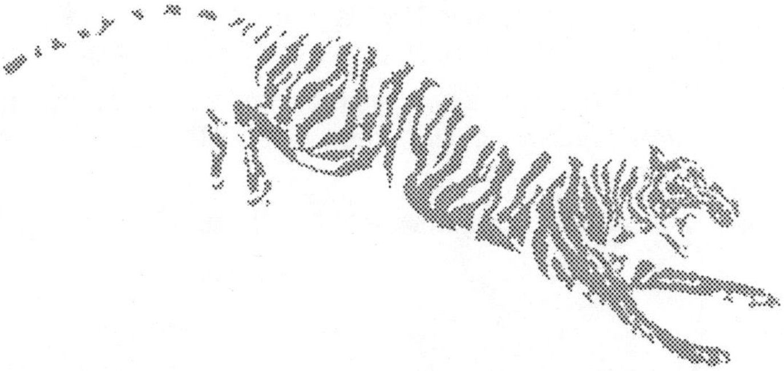

INTRODUCTION

Since my retirement from football after the 1992 season, three former coaching rivals have been meeting over lunch, at least once annually: *"The Golden Bear"* himself, Vestal's Dick Hoover; the *Little Red's* (Ithaca's) dynamic Joe Moresco; and I. Often these sessions have lasted almost all day. Most area football fans would readily agree that we three old warriors had an extremely intense, exemplary rivalry — one that spanned four decades. As this veteran coaching triumvirate reminisces and relates ancient "war stories" (which get better with each passing year, naturally), there is obviously a common thread, a bond — PRIDE — in having been participants in this league, and perhaps, in having put our signatures on a sizeable portion of its glorious history.

Another "regular" at these gatherings has been the esteemed athletic director at Johnson City, Paul Munley. Although a relative "youngster" with this crowd, having lined up opposite all of us for a brief stint as JC's coach, Paul has added much to our discussions, and he is called upon to act as mediator upon occasion.

Most of the members of my coaching staff had been players in the splendor of this league, during the 1960's. Therefore, they have shared in many of these happenings directly, or have been subjected to hearing about them indirectly.

These luncheons, along with the constant urging of my staff and family, have prompted me to share these anecdotes, this rich history, with everyone in the Southern Tier.

What follows now, is the story as seen through the eyes of this *Tiger.*

The Man in the Glass

"When you get what you want in your struggle for self;
And the world makes you a king for a day,
Just go to a mirror and look at yourself,
And see what THAT man has to say.

For it isn't your father or mother or wife,
Who judgement upon you must pass;
The fellow whose verdict counts most in your life
Is the one staring back from the glass.

Some people may think you a straight-shootin' chum
And call you a wonderful guy —
But the man in the glass says you're only a BUM
If you can't look him straight in the eye.

He's the fellow to please, never mind all the rest,
For he's with you clear up to the end
And you've passed your most difficult test:
If the man in the glass is your friend.

You may fool the whole world down the pathway of life
And get pats on your back as you pass,
But your final reward will be headaches and tears,
If you've CHEATED the MAN IN THE GLASS."

— author unknown

Chapter One

"A ship is safe in its harbor,
but is that what a ship is for?"

QUALITY OF SOUTHERN TIER FOOTBALL

"How good is the football around here?" is a frequently asked question. While we recognize that, under the current *Section IV* structure with its eight divisions, there are some consistently strong teams in all the divisions, these reflections deal mostly with the original *Southern Tier Conference (STC)* rivalries (plus any other schools that may have crossed our path frequently). The old *STC*, formed in 1947, consisted of the following teams: Binghamton Central, Binghamton North, Elmira Free Academy, Elmira Southside, Ithaca, Johnson City, Union-Endicott, and Vestal (joined in 1957). Everyone played each other once, plus one non-league opponent, for an eight-game season. (This was the maximum allowed, in those days, by our governing body, the *New York State Public High School Athletic Association* — the *NYSPHSAA*.) Very few leagues anywhere could ever match the old *STC* for intensity and spectator appeal. (Vestal versus U-E drew between 14,000 - 17,000 spectators in the early 60's!) Weekend after weekend any team could upset any other team on a given day. And often did. Therefore, there was plenty of suspense each season, and more often than not, the championship could not be determined until the final game.

I've had the opportunity to attend several football clinics and conventions all over the country, sometimes as a speaker and sometimes as a "student." One has an opportunity to observe game films of the most prestigious high schools from different areas at these conventions. Having studied a copious number of these films and having discussed our sport with all of these coaches, we had come to certain conclusions about the quality of football around here: First, our *STC* coaches were as dedicated and knowledgeable as those in any other area of the country. Second, although certain sections of our state and country may have produced more "quality" teams, our best teams, over the years, could have played with anyone.

Intermittently, a well-meaning sports writer or a few other skeptics (There are always a few, aren't there?) have wondered, "What about the paucity of our alumni who have gone on to the *National Football League*?" Although we have had some of our young men perform in the *NFL*, who decided that this should be any kind of measuring stick? This area has sent an impressive percentage of her sons (mostly with scholarships) on to the college gridirons across the country, competing in all divisions. If you check the roster of Syracuse University's 1959 *National Champions*, the number of players from the Southern Tier might boggle your mind! Two of the starters came from our own backyard — JC's Jerry Skonieczki and EFA's Ernie Davis.

We could list several inter-sectional and inter-state contests to further substantiate our claim. Just a few of these games and their results, arguably, beg to be reviewed. In sequence: Allentown Catholic, Allentown, Pennsylvania and Erie East, Pennsylvania, both with strong reputations, versus U-E in '63 and '75, respectively. ("What, play those coal miners? *You must be crazy!*"); Brockton, Massachusetts, *"The Toast of the East,"* according to at least one national high school publication, versus Vestal in '75; Berwick, Pennsylvania, a team with a national reputation, a team which has enjoyed the top ranking in the nation (*USA TODAY*) at times, versus Binghamton in '85.

The results? Let's just say that in each game the Southern Tier schools scored "a lot," while the highly touted opposition scored "a little" (if any), and let it go at that.

Names such as Ernie Davis, Bobby Campbell and Steve Webster lead lists of dozens whose deeds are recorded far beyond their Southern Tier roots.

Chapter Two

...There is something beautiful about watching the process of sport. I have spent almost all the autumns of my life moving crowds of young boys across acres of divided grass. Beneath the sun of late August, I have listened to the chants of calisthenics, watched the initial clumsiness of overgrown boys and the eyes of small boys conquering their fear, and I have monitored the violence of blocking sleds and gang tackling. I can measure my life by the teams that I have fielded and I remember by name every player I ever coached. Patiently, I have waited each year for that moment when I had merged all the skills and weaknesses of the boys placed in my care. I have watched for that miraculous synthesis. When it comes I look around my field, I look at my boys, and in a rush of creative omnipotence I want to shout to the sun: "By God, I have created a team."

— Prince of Tides *by Pat Conroy*

PAYING MY DUES

— *THE JOHNSON CITY* WILDCATS, ***1957-1959***

"He's too young for this cutthroat league!" at least one rival coach said of him. The media had announced that Johnson City had hired a new head football coach, and that, at the tender age of 22, he was the youngest head coach in this area, ever. (The media will tell you that this still holds true today.) On opening night, the rival coach's conviction about this rookie's youth might have been true.

I remember my first game, as if it were yesterday. The *Golden Bears* of Vestal would be our guests under the lights at Johnson Field (in reality a converted baseball field; home of the *Binghamton Triplets*). Although this would be Vestal's inaugural season as a member of the *STC*, it had already established itself in the area as a potential power. After an extremely sporadic night's sleep, I was a nervous wreck in school all day Friday. The 8:00 P.M. kickoff couldn't come too soon *for me!*

In those days we dressed at the Main Street school and then had to negotiate a cross-country trek of nearly a mile to reach the ball park. We crossed a field and a creek by way of a large conduit. (*I almost fell in!*) We then had to walk down a couple of blocks through a ready-made cheering section, as our fans in this neighborhood would gather on their porches and shout encouragement. In retrospect, this was quite a pre-game warm-up in itself, although we didn't think so much about it then. (Can you imagine anyone walking through those hazards today, let alone the potential lawsuits?) I never did get used to the low hanging, antiquated plumbing pipes in the *Triplets* dugout or the confining locker room at *Johnson Field*. Those pipes and I must have met at least a dozen times on that first night. (*The pipes won!*) As we hit the field, our band immediately struck up, *"Oh, When the Saints Come Marching In."* I didn't think I could contain myself. I kept silently asking many last-minute questions — especially these two— that I'm sure every coach often asks himself: "Have we covered every possible eventuality? Will the officials give us a decent game?"

On our first play from scrimmage, our swift halfback, Billy "Yelvie" Yelverton, got the call on a straight, quick-hitting *Dive* play. Vestal's Dick Hoover, who would become a coaching legend, has since related his thinking on that night: "Rookie coach (me)...relatively green personnel...brand new offense (Split-T)...opening game.... We'll throw up a *Goal Line-Gap 8* defense at 'em right away and rattle 'em." (Incidentally, had our roles been reversed, I probably would have done the same thing.)

Well, "Yelvie" took the exchange cleanly (thrill number one), popped through the hole (thrill number two), cut across the field against the grain right in front of our bench (thrill number three), and sprinted *all the way!* I was absolutely *ecstatic!* JC 6, Vestal 0 — with only a few minutes expired on the clock.

However, as the game went on, I witnessed first hand what would become a Hoover signature over the next few decades — a ball-control offense, based on speed and deception — and an aggressive, penetrating defense. With its tackle-size quarterback, Dick Stanton, working his magic, Vestal dominated most of the remainder of the game and won. Not having prepared to lose, I was crestfallen. In retrospect, although the initial moment of my coaching career was a peak, I was to begin "paying my dues" by learning there are valleys — as well as peaks — especially in the coaching profession.

There were two unusual occurrences for us in that first season, and both involved Elmira teams:

Because the flu bug had invaded the entire section, and decimated all the teams to different degrees, most of us were forced into making a few scheduling adjustments. Many teams, ourselves included, postponed one weekend's games, and rescheduled them for the following Monday or Tuesday. Because of this, we held a light Sunday practice that raised a few taxpayers' eyebrows. When we visited Elmira Southside, the officials proposed the option of shortening each quarter because everyone was hurting with the flu.

The high point of that initial season for us was easily when the charismatic coach, Marty Harrigan, brought his Elmira Free Academy *Blue Devils* to town. The team featured future *Heisman Trophy* recipient and future top pick of the Cleveland *Browns* of the *NFL* — Ernie Davis. We didn't really belong on the same field with them, but several guys stepped up and allowed us to stay with them. As I recall, guys like our linebacker, Tom Breese, with a real *"nose for the ball"*, were particularly effective in thwarting their advances all night long. (Tom would do a great job with my staff for a few years after his college days.)

The "young" coach reviews strategy with some of his JC champs in 1958.

Quite early in that game you'd know that we were grasping at straws when we called for a *"Statue of Liberty"* play off a fake punt. (By doing this, we were taking advantage of their aggressive defensive end play.) It worked. Our diminutive, speedy halfback, Artie May, took the ball from behind our punter's back and didn't stop until he had hit pay dirt 44 yards later. Artie kept them off balance with a 132-yard rushing performance, including two TDs. Unfortunately, we couldn't convert. But neither could they and the game ended up in a 12-12 tie.

It was a unique, awkward feeling on our visit to my alma mater, Union-Endicott, that first season. We were across the field from my own (and my brother's, and my father's) former high school coach and good friend. He was the revered Harold *"Ty"* Cobb after whom the U-E stadium would be named upon his imminent retirement. A steady deluge didn't allow either team to do much offensively. We were lucky to "out-mud" the *Tigers* in a low scoring victory.

Under the outstanding tutelage of Robert *"Bud"* Deyo, the Binghamton Central *Bulldogs* had been on the brink of big things in the mid 50's. Led by their big, strong tackle, Bob *"Moose"* Ward, and very talented halfback, Billy Harrison, they dominated 1957 with a perfect 7-0-0 conference record, while scoring almost twice as many points as the opposition.

Vestal was close behind, losing only to Central in a game marked by controversy. As I recall, Vestal protested a key play by questioning the referee's whistle. (Did he blow it, or didn't he?) The controversy cannot detract from an auspicious debut by Vestal in the *STC* with a 6-1-0 record, and a superlative effort by two great football teams.

— 1958

The 1958 season ushered in a new coach — Tom Hurley, at ESS. He introduced the league to an innovative *"Side Saddle"* formation — the quarterback would not line up directly behind his center, but rather at a 45 degree angle to either side. He was still in position to take the snap, but a direct snap to his all-conference back, Bobby MacBlaine, was also possible. This formation incorporated the principles of both the *"T"* and the *"Single Wing"* formations. Coach Hurley's *Green Hornets* became a team to be reckoned with over the years.

After struggling early in the season, we developed into a formidable team, and at the end, found ourselves traveling, as contenders, to Ithaca to meet Joe Moresco's once-beaten *Little Red*. Very few people gave us much of a chance against Ithaca's vaunted *"Single Wing,"* led by its first-rate tackle, Joe Spano, and giant quarterback, Carmen DiGiacomo. In fact, one local paper predicted something like a 38-0 blowout by Ithaca. Naturally, we taped this to the door for our players to see before boarding the bus for the trip. Can you imagine being told by anyone that the other team is 38 points better than you in any game— let alone a game of such stature? I can still hear our halfback, Richie Donlick, grumbling, "That's ridiculous!", in reference to the prediction. Richie would join me eventually for a brief stint as an assistant in later years before changing careers.

My dedicated chief assistant, Joe Ciesielski, turned in a thorough scouting report on Ithaca, and incorporated a brilliant defensive strategy by keying totally on DiGiacomo and crashing our tenacious strong-side end, Bob Hnat. Our young men played beyond their ability, the ball kept bouncing their way, and *they shocked the entire league!* To win that first crown was a genuine thrill, and is certainly a memory we shall cherish. However, let's interject at this point that Coach Moresco would get his licks in, down the road, and would establish himself as a coaching legend, with a trademark of rock-ribbed, hard-nosed defense.

Only two of our JC boys were selected on the *All-Conference* team that season — Maurice *"Moe"* Sterner, halfback, and Bobby Hart, quarterback. Perhaps this small number of selections points up the parity of the league. Dave Lutsic, our sure-handed end and kicker, gave us solid leadership as our captain-elect. Incidentally, North's fine tackle, Gary *"Barney"* Barnaba, would face us again, several years later, as the head coach of Syracuse Christian Brothers Academy. Our Dino Paparella would join his brother, Al (a high school and college teammate of mine), in the coaching ranks after college.

— 1959

In '59 the Binghamton North *Indians* turned a difficult '58 season completely around, under the sterling leadership and guidance of Coach Gordie O'Reilly (*"Gordie O"*). With all-purpose athlete, Dick King, at quarterback, they achieved an undefeated season. Another standout on this squad was Ralph Muro, who would continue to face us as a long-time valued assistant at Binghamton.

The leading rusher in the *STC* that season was a little Vestal scatback, by the name of Steve Mahon. He would become the head football (and track) coach at his alma mater. Our captain-elect that year was our fine halfback, Doug Clark. An outstanding junior-teammate of his (and an equally outstanding Latin student) was Bill Baker, one of the toughest ever, who would one day face us across the field at Susquehanna Valley.

Southern Tier East-West Optimist All-Star Game

Before we leave the rookie years behind, the summer games, sponsored by the *Endicott Optimist Club*, deserve mention. Three of these took place — in the summer of '58, '59, and '60. This coach felt quite honored to have been hired to coach the East squad for the first two games. These games were absolutely first-class in every respect. The selection of the best players at each position from the entire *Section IV* area was done by a neutral committee. (There was no quota system.) Both teams were housed and practiced at separate camp facilities outside the Triple Cities for ten days. The camaraderie was outstanding. What an opportunity for these young men — former opponents — most of whom were about to further their education and football in just a few weeks. Here was a chance to really get to know each other not only by practicing side-by-side, but by *actually living together*!

Naturally, a few incidents took place that I can share with you:

For a diversion, we had a skit night. The mock wedding between a couple of our larger linemen (with all the proper "bridal attire" a football camp could provide) is one of the more memorable skits. The little town of Lisle (affectionately pronounced *"Lizzly"* by our players), the site of our camp, had a bell tower. One night *Moose* Ward of

Binghamton Central decided to climb the tower to see if the bell really worked. (Linemen are "curious creatures" by nature, you know.) It *worked!* The good villagers were aroused from their peaceful slumber and Old Lizzly has never *been the same!* After assessing Ward the penalty of some extra laps at the end of the next morning's practice, we renamed him *"Quasi Modo"* for the remainder of camp.

On another occasion, the entire squad was invited to nearby Glen Aubrey, as the guests of the stock car races. The boys were introduced individually, during a break in the action. As each player took his introductory lap, we coaches marveled at how a few of the "walking wounded" suddenly became "healthy" again. Our trip to get there though, was a real harrowing experience. We jumped on an old school bus, which was at our disposal. Anyone familiar with the Whitney Point "hill" will appreciate the challenge we faced in trying to get that old, tired machine even halfway up. But, T.R. Roberts from Binghamton North came *to the rescue!* Not even failing brakes could prevent T.R. from driving that thing and us, somehow, to safety.

The positive interaction between the coaches and opposing players from other schools was a thing of beauty, also. One evening after supper and a meeting, one of the coaches (the only bachelor among the coaches) departed to visit his lady friend. Upon his return to camp in the wee hours of the morning (never a curfew for bachelor-coaches), his attempt at a stealthy entry into the dormitory was marred by an intricate booby trap, consisting of empty cans and other noise makers, rigged by the players. Those *rascals!* After much laughter, giggling, and snickering, everyone settled back to sleep.

The exposure these *Optimist* all star games provided for some players was very beneficial. Ramie Seager, a rough, tough linebacker from Homer comes to mind immediately. One year, I realized that Ben Schwartzwalder, head coach of Syracuse University, would be in attendance to observe his already-signed prize, Ernie Davis. So I mentioned to Ben that he might want to look over Seager while he was at it. It sure didn't take long. Ben signed Seager to a full football scholarship before leaving Endicott that day. Obviously, Ben liked what he saw.

The camaraderie of the players spilled over to the coaches. How excited this rookie coach was to be working with, living with, and learning from the veterans Gordie O, Bud Deyo, Jack Halloran (future basketball coaching legend at Whitney Point and beyond), and Merritt Klumpp (the popular Mayor, as well as football coach at Windsor). Each squad had cheerleaders, baton twirlers, and even queen candidates. The day before the game, a slow motorcade took place, with all the participants in uniform, sitting up on the back of a fleet of convertibles. These games enjoyed huge crowds, and were usually closely contested.

I would feel remiss if I did not conclude this discussion of my rookie years at Johnson City with a sincere thank you to the fine folks there. I shall forever be grateful to JC's administrators (Ken Myers, superintendent; Lyle Young, principal; Ken Kintner, athletic director) and to the JC Board of Education for deciding to take a chance on a 22-year old. I shall always remember the *Wildcats* and the community with fondness.

ALL STARS

Listed here, and at the end of each subsequent chapter (era), are the *All-Stars* of all the *STC* teams through 1966, and of the early *STAC* (*Southern Tier Athletic Conference*) teams of 1967 through 1969. Beginning with the early 70's, however, only the *All-Stars* of the more prominent teams of the different divisions covered in each chapter will be listed. These lists are the official league *All-Stars* selected by the coaches, unless otherwise noted.

ALL STARS from the Late 50's (1957-1959)

1957

School	*Position*	*Player*	*School*	*Position*	*Player*
BN	G	JOE CARBO	UE	G	DAVE BURAN
EFA	HB	ERNIE DAVIS	IHS	FB	WILLIE YOUNG
VHS	QB	DICK STANTON	VHS	E	JERRY HILL
VHS	T	PHIL DAILEY	BC	E	JOE MANKUS
BC	C	DICK LYNN	BC	T	BOB WARD
BC	HB	BILL HARRISON			

1958

BN	E	JOHN VAUGHN	UE	C	JIM HAICK
ESS	G	CLARENCE FLEMING	ESS	HB	BOB MacBLAINE
IHS	G	ED MICHAEL	IHS	T	JOE SPANO
JC	QB	BOB HART	JC	HB	MOE STERNER
BC	E	BARRY SCHUMAN	BC	FB	DAVE GOULDIN
BC	T	BILL FUSCO			

1959

IHS	G	ED MICHAEL	UE	T	DAVE HOSPODOR
JC	E	BOB HNAT	VHS	T	AL PLYMALE
VHS	HB	STEVE MAHON	EFA	G	STEVE GOLDFARB
EFA	HB	HENRY GREENE	BN	E	GARY KING
BN	QB	DICK KING	BN	C	ART TESTANI
BN	FB	BOB CUNNINGHAM			

A future coach's mentors: Coach Ty Cobb and his 1951 Tiger *captain at U-E High School (top); Coach Harold Lahar of the Colgate University* Red Raiders *and his 1955 captain (bottom).*

Chapter Three

"To love what you do and feel that it matters — how could anything be more fun?"

— Katherine Graham

STRIVING TO BELONG

— *THE UNION-ENDICOTT* TIGERS, ***1960-1963***

A phone call suddenly changed my life. It came during a faculty meeting at Johnson City in the early spring of 1960. I can still see the stern stare of JC principal, Lyle Young, as he personally handed me the message. It was urgent that I return a call to Robert Agone, superintendent at U-E. After assuring me there was an opening for the position of head football coach at U-E (since I refused to be responsible for anyone's ouster), Mr. Agone asked if I would consider meeting with him to discuss the opportunity.

I really enjoyed my eventual interview with him and the U-E Board of Education. They knew what they wanted, but weren't sure how to get it. It was immediately evident that they were very hungry for two goals. I considered both goals realistic: first, to restore pride in U-E football; second, to attract more fans. They informed me that both goals had been suffering lately. (Can you imagine only a few hundred U-E fans — *maybe* — in the latter 50's?)

I was offered the position, and immediately faced the toughest decision of my early professional career. Although I had become quite attached to JC's warmth (and looked forward to a wealth of returning football starters), I felt even more strongly about the challenge that U-E presented. As a native of Endicott, I wanted to try to do something for my home town.

Moreover, a wedding date was set for summer. I would marry Pat Hanley, a U-E alumna and former co-captain of the cheerleaders and we planned to live in Endicott.

It might be interesting to some that I never made a formal application to U-E. I accepted the position of head football coach and Latin teacher, and never looked back.

In the remaining few weeks of the spring semester, before my new position was official, I met with my JC squad. Several JC players approached me about their strong desire to transfer to U-E. Ethics dictated that I discourage them (*although my heart wanted them badly!*). Ethics won.

I feel that the cooperation which I received from the U-E Administration and Board of Education at that time was significant. Not only did we secure the necessary equipment, but we also brought in a new staff of assistants — starting at the junior high level — right up through the junior varsity and varsity programs.

— 1960

As I recall, the biggest job that confronted us immediately at U-E was trying to change the attitude of the faculty and community, through the players themselves. We really worked at it. One teacher said, typical of the U-E climate at the time, "We're happy to have you here, Fran, but you had it made up there [JC]. Why would you want to come down to this *hell hole*?"

The student body, and to a lesser degree some of the faculty and fans in the community, did not take too kindly to our switching "spectator-seating" sides (home and visitors) at our stadium. Today it is hard to imagine the U-E faithful of the 50's sitting in the small, riverside bleachers (rickety, wooden slats, at that time), with the team sitting only a few yards away. Meanwhile, the visitors sat in the spacious, relatively new stadium side, with its superior vantage, and their team in full view several yards below.

Of course, nothing made these attitudes go away faster than a few wins. With U-E coming off two consecutive seasons ('58 and '59) with a combined STC record of 3-11-0, our opening win over North (first time since '54), and some more victories along the way, had a way of making concerns disappear. We also planted the possibility of lights at U-E for the future. Incidentally, our courageous quarterback and captain in 1960 was Dave Sammon. Dave would eventually take his leadership to great heights as Vestal's head football and lacrosse coach before his accidental and untimely death.

Elmira Southside, led by its dangerous quarterback, Jerry Reagan, shared the championship with Hank Diller's outstanding JC team led by its nifty quarterback, Phil Dembowski. Both teams wound up with 6-1-0 *STC* records. This season would mark the beginning of Coach Diller's impressive decade of tenure as JC's coach. *What a way to break into the ranks!* Incidentally, Vestal's field general was a real magician as the quarterback executing the deceptive, innovative *"Short Punt"* formation that season. He was Dick Hoover's oldest of three sons — Glenn.

— 1961

We were blessed with our first child that spring — a son, Christopher. Pat and I were so elated! (Naturally, I began making football plans for him right away.)

U-E football embarked on two brand new ventures in 1961: Summer camp and night football.

After several money-raising projects, and with the support of the U-E Booster Club, we spent our pre-season training at Camp Susquehannock in Brackney, Pennsylvania for the next dozen years. This was probably the single most important — most valuable — undertaking in those early years in our attempt to build U-E football into something that might become very important to the entire community. Since the merits of camp (with the *Optimist All-Stars)* were already discussed in the last chapter, we'll only supplement here.

As a speaker at various high school football conventions, I was often asked to address the topic of "camp". This is exactly what I told them, and I would feel the same way about taking a squad away to camp today. If you are a young coach just taking over the reins, or if you are in a situation needing a complete overhaul, take your squad out of town to a camp. It takes much organization and effort, particularly during the off season, but it will pay big dividends in the long run. Nothing else can quite match eating, sleeping, practicing football for a week or so — *WITHOUT ANY DISTRACTIONS.* (We always said, "When the trees at camp start talking back, *we're getting ready!"*)

Whenever we have any kind of alumni gathering today, if they were "campers" from the years 1961 until 1973, it is one of the very first, and very last things about which they reminisce. Especially the various extra-curricular activities....

They love to tell about the coach calling for midnight calisthenics because a certain cabin was playing "ghost games" one night. We had them report to an open area (I can still see the main culprits yawning and feigning "sleep"), where they exercised under our flashlights and the headlights of the coach's car for approximately a half hour. When my car wouldn't start up the next morning due to a dead battery, the players had their revenge (and *the last laugh!*)

Another "coach" story they love to tell involved two of our assistants, Dick Hover (*"Hovie"* would become our athletic director) and Joe Marzo (who would become our assistant superintendent). One early afternoon, during a recreation period down at the waterfront at placid Tripp Lake, Hovie and Joe set out by canoe, to test their nautical prowess. After they were quite a way from shore, a sudden storm came up, accompanied by torrents of rain (much to the delight of the many "spectators" on shore). It was quite a sight — these two (not the smallest guys ever to man a canoe) paddling with all their might and then, trying to beach the canoe on a very slippery landing dock.

We held some "organized" diversions, too. We had some memorable skit nights. Dan Consol, who would become a long-time dedicated assistant with us, is still called *"Rosy"* by some, in reference to his act as a *"Dancing Lady of Easy Virtue"* on one of these nights. His partner was big John *"Bubba"* Schaffer, who would become the father of some outstanding Vestal athletes, president of its Booster Club, and a football official. We also held a movie night, and usually showed *"On The Waterfront."* (The coach has long been a big Marlon Brando fan.)

We always took the squad into the tiny, quaint village of Montrose, Pennsylvania on Sunday morning. Most of the players eagerly attended the various services available (although I'm afraid religion might not always have been the motivation). It became something that both the community and our players looked forward to each September.

We also had a "family day" — an open house on Sunday afternoon. Several "care packages" of food were always smuggled in at this time, even though the players had all the nutritious, high quality food they wanted at every meal. I eagerly awaited seeing Pat and the kids at this function. I missed them more than they'll ever realize. As my children became older, they would really get into this camp visit.

The other U-E venture of 1961 was our experiment with night football — by renting a portable lighting system. This innovative concept was heartily embraced by the community. Vestal, JC, and Elmira already had *permanent* lights.

We struggled through the '61 season without much experience or size. We had our share of injuries, too, including our gritty captain, Mike Ciotoli. But we always kept plugging, with our eyes to the future.

The highlights of our season involved both Elmira teams, although at opposite ends of the scoreboard: We achieved our first shutout — over EFA — on the road — 20-0, and flirted with a major upset of the eventual *STC* champion, ESS, before losing at home, 6-0.

I believe that it was in '61 when an innovative adjustment took place at Binghamton's *North Field.* As I recall, North was hosting EFA. Due to very rainy weather conditions, the Binghamton field was under water, especially at one end. The officials decided to go ahead with the game, but with the stipulation that it was to be played at *only one end!* The mechanics of its administration were as follows: anytime one team would cross the 50-yard line, the officials would "cross it back over" and head the other way, at the end of the play. Certainly neither team gained any edge by defending a certain "end" that night. My recollection is that, fortunately there were no long, breakaway runs, and that it was a very well-played game. I have never heard of anything like this happening again.

Although an outstanding Vestal team had scored almost twice as many points as the opposition (a bunch of them against us), it was just nipped in the championship game by an equally strong ESS team. This allowed the *Green Hornets* to finish undefeated, with a 6-0-1 record. Aside from some controversy involving a last-ditch goal line stand by ESS, an unusual punt took place in this exciting game. The *Hornets* had a tremendous punter, mammoth P.J. Richards, who consistently hit *NFL*-type boomers (both in direction, as well as in hang time). Those who watched in awe, say that P.J. uncorked one that night in Elmira that went so high it hit the guide wires stretching way over the *top of the stadium!*

Southside was led, for the second year in a row, by its superb quarterback, Jerry Reagan. The *Hornets* also had a hard-running back who had provided the winning margin in our game. That "back" would go on to provide Elmira fans with many more winning margins as "coach" Dick Senko — producing exciting EFA *Blue Devil* football teams for several years.

The *Golden Bears* had their share of talent, too. One of their players was a tenacious linebacker, referred to as their *"trick or treat man"* — Frank Hoyt. We're happy to say that Frank would eventually "cross the river" and do some great work for us (and provide us with some light moments) as our head frosh coach for a long, loyal tenure.

— 1962

Pat gave birth to our second son, Laurence, in June. Some people accused us of trying to produce our own team. Larry's arrival was an exciting time although initially, Chris felt threatened. It was a given that one day both sons would proudly wear the *Orange and Black*.

At U-E, our football "calendar,"— our time table — had arrived ahead of schedule. We had been building our program from the ground up, with our sights set on the 1964 or 1965 season for some big things to happen. Halfway through the '62 season, it was obvious that if we kept improving, we might have a shot at the championship.

We found ourselves entering the final game against undefeated Vestal with only one blemish on our record. The mark was a tie versus an inspired JC team in a game that had been postponed by JC officials due to unplayable conditions at a very soggy *Johnson Field*.

This Vestal versus U-E matchup was the first of many barn-burners in this nascent rivalry. It was played at U-E on a Friday night (before we switched permanently to Saturday night action at home). They say that several spectators were "staking out their claims" for good seats even before school let out *at 2:45 P.M.!* Game time in those days was 8:00 P.M. These fans even had their suppers packed in boxes and had spread out their blankets just like the beach. The crowd was estimated at an unheard of *14,000!*

Vestal's unparalleled Bobby Campbell, just a sopomore then, proved his advance publicity was deserved. He caught two long bombs from his quarterback, Joe Mushock (who would eventually join Auburn's football staff, and make his mark as its very successful head baseball coach). We didn't have anyone to catch Bobby, and Vestal shut us out, 13-0. This Vestal team's hard-working fullback, Jim Hoover (Dick's second son), would go on to an exemplary coaching and administrative career at Walton. Our squad was led by our captain, Ken Pacioni, and John Dellos and tough Bobby Atkinson.

This was the first time a few overly-jubilant adult fans from Vestal began to fuel the flames of an already intense rivalry by driving around Endicott after the game with their windows lowered and loudly belting out their Barney impersonation from *"The Flintstones"*: *"Yabba, Dabba, Doo!"* And they kept it up for a couple of years. Unfortunately, there are always a few adult-jerks in every community (and Endicott is no exception) who sometimes get too involved in a game played by teenagers — for teenagers.

— 1963

It has often been said that a tie score is like "kissing your sister." Since I never had a sister, I can't use this comparison. I can only tell you that it is an empty feeling — I don't know how else to describe it. However, when it happens in the opener of the season against an evenly matched team, as it did with us versus Ithaca in '63, it can give a team a foundation on which to build.

I don't know if our coaching staff ever completely recovered from an event that took place later that day. Upon our arrival back in Endicott, we were completely spent by the heat and the tie. Realizing that we intended to immediately turn around and scout a game at ESS later in the day, our athletic director, Hank Vetter, offered to let us relax. He said that he would gladly drive us to Elmira. We jumped at the offer.

However, — *relax?!?* Talk about a *lead foot on the accelerator!* We arrived at the Elmira stadium within *forty-seven* minutes after departure from the U-E locker room. (A normal one-hour drive.) Hank always wondered why we refused his future offers. Thanks, but no thanks, Hank.

I learned a coaching lesson later in the season. We had scheduled a huge Allentown, Pennsylvania team — Allentown Catholic — at home. (Some of our Pennsylvania transplants thought we were crazy to schedule those "coal miners.") They stuffed our running game, but had difficulty defending against the pass. Behind the golden arm of our gutsy, diminutive quarterback, Fred *"Zapp"* Zappia, Jr., we had built up an insurmountable lead, 32 - 0. Zapp's back-up, Mickey Murtha, and the rest of the substitutes finished the game, with instructions from me not to *"put it up on top"*. We did not want to embarrass our guests. First Murtha was angry at me, and afterwards, their coach accused me of *"rolling it up"*.

For those "thanks," I vowed on-the-spot that if we ever had a similar situation for substituting at will (and we would have several opportunities down the road), I would never restrain my quarterback or any other reserves from doing what we had trained them to do.

The '63 road to the championship was very closely contested. In truth, the only thing that separated the eventual champion, Vestal, with a 6-1-0 *STC* record, from Ithaca with 5-1-1, was Ithaca's opening day tie with U-E. We finished at 4-2-1.

Coach Bill Plimpton's EFA club at 5-2-0 was right behind the leaders with a smooth-passing quarterback, Dom Rainey, and one of the most relentless high school runners ever — reckless, rambling Ray Fratarcangelo. I can still envision the dust flying when *"Frat"* started those piston-like legs churning, while the train's wail echoed through *Parker Field* from the nearby tracks. The train and *Frat* made for an eerie combination.

Our colleague, Gordie O, retired from North. One of his fine players, Bob *"Scottie"* Scott would become an integral part of the merged Binghamton (Central and North) football staff for many years.

We almost made the race really exciting at mid-season, but it was not meant to be. A crowd at Vestal, estimated at 9,000, watched Vestal come from behind our fired-up *Tigers* to win, 18-13. Led by our hard-nosed captain, Ron Ciotoli, a guard and defensive corner, we almost pulled it off. The game ended in an end zone controversy, with the *Tigers* knocking on the *Bears'* door inside their 10-yard line. Suffice to say, on the final whistle, Joe Moresco and his Ithaca assistants (who had been scouting from behind that end zone) sprinted out on the field. They confronted the official who had ignored the controversial infraction at such a crucial time.

However, none of this memory can erase a great effort — a hard-hitting, clean game between two fine teams. You can't hold down a talent like Bobby Campbell forever.... He eventually would go on to a brilliant career at Pennsylvania State University, and a brief stint with the Pittsburgh *Steelers* of the *NFL*. Later, Bobby enjoyed an outstanding high school coaching career in the Syracuse area and Frederick, Maryland.

Talk about a *one-man show*! Bobby Campbell was the *only all-star pick* from Vestal that season!

Until we had our own permanent lighting system, we had several memorable mid-week practices under the lights at *Page Avenue Field* (*Peewee*), compliments of the *Endicott Boys' Club*. The alumni from those days remind me of some very tough sessions there, with the dust rising up to almost snuff out the lights. They like to relate how *Jo-Jo* McBride kicked off one night and the ball landed on a neighbor's rooftop. Joe's comment? "If I get a foot into it, it's good-bye Jack."

At the end of the season, the Angeline household increased again. I rushed Pat to the delivery room at Wilson Memorial Hospital in the middle of the night. The remainder of the night and morning were spent anxiously in the "waiting room" (the *"Fathers' Room"* in those days). I dozed off intermittently, but with a new baby on the way, and an important game versus JC pending, I was "wired." After what seemed an eternity (you'd think that I would have been a relaxed, seasoned veteran by then!), Pat's gynecologist, Dr. Ted Nowicki, entered. As a football fan, he started right off talking ball. He wanted me to know he agreed completely with a recent article in the local paper in which I had taken a few football officials to task by publicly blasting their incompetence. (Who — *me??*). As soon as I had a chance, I asked, "By the way, Doc, how is Pat?" He responded very casually, "Oh yeah, you have a baby girl. Both she and Pat are doing fine."

Wow! A baby girl?! Honestly, I had never considered *that* possibility. Vaun Marie has given us much joy and has grown up to be quite a lady.

Although I was walking on air at our JC game that night, we managed to win it. The players had dedicated the game to Baby Vaun. To this day, some of them ask me how the "JC Baby" is doing?

I was really tired after the game that night — I went straight home and collapsed into bed. But, that hectic weekend wasn't quite over yet. After my first solid sleep in the past 48 hours, the telephone's ring screamed at me around 12:30 A.M. The adult caller brayed, "Vestal won a second straight championship...."

All I could muster up was, "Thank you." Had I been a little more alert, I might have said a few other things to this midnight-caller jackass. I hung up and removed the phone from its hook for the remainder of the night.

To this day, long after the proud pop brought Pat and baby Vaun home from the hospital, I don't know how Pat managed three babies — all still in diapers — and managed a household as well. But she did. And *did it well*!

— Ernie Davis

Before we move on to the mid 60's, I must share this with you. It's well recorded that Ernie Davis was a tremendous talent on the field. Ultimately, he wound up his sparkling career at Syracuse University as the recipient of the very prestigious *Heisman Trophy*, presented annually to the best college football player in the country. However, those who knew Ernie well, will tell you that he was even more than a *"Most Valuable Player"* off the field — a gentleman in every sense of the word, a humanitarian, a young man with a very strong moral fiber. Ernie Davis was everything a parent would want in a son. What a role model for young, aspiring athletes he was!

Ernie happened to be visiting in his home town of Elmira and came to our game at EFA. He paid us a very welcomed surprise visit in our locker room just before the game. The timing of this visit is the most important factor of all — because in retrospect, Ernie, Paul Brown (coach of the Cleveland *Browns*), his family, and very few others would have known that Ernie's days were numbered by leukemia at that time. After exchanging a few pleasantries, he asked me if he could say a few words to our squad.

Just think about that gesture for a moment. I wonder how many young men, given his exact circumstances, would have done the same thing?

Ernie spoke for just a brief moment or two, and basically was extolling the virtues of football and what an opportunity we all had. This "football giant" was merely saying, "Hello". What none of us knew at the time, however, was that this was his way of saying, "Good-bye."

The entire football world was shocked to learn of Ernie Davis' untimely death a short time later...without ever having stepped on an *NFL* field. Is it any wonder that a school in the Elmira school district bears his name, as does the current, annual post-season *Exceptional Senior All-Star Game*?

I shall never forget this young man, and I know that there are legions who feel the same way.

ALL STARS — The Early 60's (1960-1963)

1960

School	Position	Player	School	Position	Player
UE	C	RICH VIVONA	VHS	HB	TONY LENKIEWICZ
IHS	G	STEVE SHIPPOS	IHS	HB	MEL ROBINSON
EFA	E	LEE ROPELEWSKI	EFA	FB	LONNIE MOSS
JC	E	LARRY VIRGILIO	JC	T	BILL MISATA
JC	QB	PHIL DEMBOWSKI	ESS	T	GARY COUNSELMAN
ESS	T	RON LOWE	ESS	G	ROCKY EMMICK

1961

IHS	HB	MEL ROBINSON	BN	C	DOUG MAINS
BC	G	JOHN NUZZELA	ESS	T	P.J. RICHARDS
ESS	QB	JERRY REAGAN	JC	E	TONY FUSCO
JC	G	BILL ARMSTRONG	VHS	E	DICK POST
VHS	HB	DAVE GUSTIN	VHS	T	MIKE MINNICH
VHS	FB	AL ANDERSON			

1962

JC	T	JOHN MINCHIK	EFA	HB	RAY FRATARCANGELO
IHS	T	BILL KOHM	ESS	E	TOM HURD
BN	E	MARTY KORSAK	ESS	QB	DICK SENKO
BN	G	KARL MICALIZZI	ESS	FB	TOM STUART
UE	T	KEN PACIONI	VHS	G	BOB YUHAS
UE	G	RON CIOTOLI	VHS	E	JIM LUCAS
UE	C	MARIO AMORESE	VHS	HB	BOB CAMPBELL

1963

VHS	HB	BOB CAMPBELL	ESS	C	GARY WILBER
JC	E	DENNY RITLINGER	EFA	HB	RAY FRATARCANGELO
JC	G	DAVE WILCOX	EFA	QB	DOM RAINEY
IHS	T	JERRY BEACH	UE	E	FRAN PILARCEK
IHS	E	DAVE BONNEY	UE	T	MARK SELIGA
IHS	FB	PAUL LISSECK	UE	G	RON CIOTOLI

To Mom:
Thank you for everything
you have done for me. You
have made my four years
Love
Mom,
Thanks for putting up with
me. I know I'm tough to put
up with during football.
I Love you with all my heart!
Mom-
This is it!
My last game as a
tiger. Thanks for all
your support + love
the past years. I love
you and Dad both.
Rob
Mom,
you're really very
special. Thanks
for everything you've
done for me. You've had
a whole lot of troubled times
and you've always come through.
I really Love you.
Mom,
Although we have
had many problems and many disagreements
lately. I just wanted to say.
I love you,
thanks for
everythin
I Love you,
Steve

Chapter Four

"Lo, the man whom adversity neglects for he has no chance to prove himself."

— Seneca

PARENTS as PARTNERS ... or PROBLEMS?

"I can't do anything with this kid," the parent lamented. This comment is heard all too frequently by coaches and teachers. As much as we want to say, "Have you tried?", most of us listen patiently and try to make discreet suggestions, especially if given an opening. A coach gets to know many parents in thirty-six years. Parents, like kids, come in all shapes and sizes (so to speak). Allow me to introduce you to some of these various parent-types:

The "*Wannabe*" Parent

Occasionally I have encountered a parent who is living vicariously through his son — perhaps he was a non-athlete himself. Unfortunately, he intrudes into his son's progress without realizing it and his intrusion can become counterproductive. His entire life revolves around junior's athletic progress. Some common concerns of his usually encompass whether or not his son should be getting more playing time, or perhaps whether or not he should be a starter. Let me ask something: Does anyone honestly think that any coach would intentionally sit a "better" player on the bench (unless other factors are involved)? C'mon, get real. I'll share a few examples of this "wannabe" type of parent.

Early in my career, a father accused me of all kinds of negative things. He informed our athletic director, Bob "Wurt" Wurtenberg, that I physically abused kids — that after a recent loss I had tied them up and beaten them — that I always smacked them around, constantly punched them, and that I had been particularly abusive and unfair with his son. He stated further that he had become aware of these atrocities because his son had told him. You'd have to agree that these were very serious allegations.

Wurt, of course, knew his coach well enough to realize that these accusations were unfounded without even asking me. There's virtue in a long relationship based on trust, honesty, loyalty and friendship between an administrator and coach. He handled the situation perfectly. He asked all the principal parties to meet with him in his office — father, son, and me.

The first thing Wurt asked was for the father to repeat all of his accusations. The father deferred to his son. The boy (who recently had lost his starting position on the team) stated categorically that everything his dad had been saying was a trumped-up charge. He went on to say that his coach was not only fair, but that he loved the man. Finally the real "problem", in his father's eyes, surfaced when the boy stated that he wanted to quit school and get married, and that he had lost all interest in football. The son was calling his father a liar. And worse.

What a sight ensued! Certainly one which I'll never forget. The sobbing father embraced me, admitted that everything had been invented, and apologized for any anguish he had caused me. He finally faced the fact that he had "just wanted his son to play so badly." He begged for my forgiveness. I felt sorry for the man — and for his son, as well. Of course I forgave him, but can you believe to what lengths a parent will go just because his son doesn't really want to play ball? It is a sad commentary, indeed.

Another episode involves an injury to a starter. Dealing with injuries is one of the most difficult things any coach has to face. It's always the delicate line between "playing with pain" versus taking care of injuries so they don't cause further problems. The challenge comes in trying to be a mindreader with fifty kids and trying to keep track of their hurts.

We deal mostly with two opposite personalities — some who are spoiled and whine at every little cut and bruise, and feel that even a little sniffle should keep them out. At the other end we have some who won't admit to injury because they can't bear to miss a practice or a quarter of playing time, much less a game. The dilemma is in trying to strike a balance.

Now, this particular injury (a sprained ankle, wrist or something similar, as I recall) wasn't serious, but it was severe enough to put this starter on the shelf for a game or two. We have always had this policy about injuries, depending on their severity: We wanted a doctor's opinion — especially if the injury was going to last a while. (Incidentally, this policy is now a mandate by the *NYSPHSAA*.) As soon as the injured player was given the green light by the doctor, we gave him the opportunity to gradually work his way back into the starting line-up.

We did this for two reasons: First and foremost, we wanted to make sure that the player's injury and general conditioning would gradually improve — we certainly didn't want to rush a player's return (relying more on heart and emotion than the mind) nor did we want to jeopardize his entire season. The other reason was that we didn't want to abruptly tell his back-up (who had been busting his hump!) that he was back on the bench.

So, after this particular boy had been medically cleared for participation, we broke him in gradually in practices and in the next game. We also had an unwritten understanding that if a boy was not ready on Thursday, he wouldn't be ready on Saturday. Well, this particular boy didn't start, but played approximately a half. The phone was ringing early Sunday morning. It was the injured boy's father. One would think that a serious catastrophe had taken place. The father's exact words were, "What's the matter — isn't my kid good enough for you?"

We discussed the situation thoroughly. After his emotions had died down somewhat, he finally conceded, although reluctantly, that we coaches only wanted what we all wanted — that which was best for his son — and ultimately, what was in the team's best interest. I think he finally realized that we actually knew what we were doing.

The Over-Protective Parent

Parents sometimes have difficulty in allowing their boys to become men. Some actually "baby" their kids and cater to their every whim. They try to rescue their sons from any real pain or hardship. A few incidents which took place at pre-season camp, and a personal reference, come immediately to mind.

First, we must understand a few things about the camp scenario. Here are a few givens: Camp is tough (so is this sport we love!). It is approximately 25 miles from home and "civilization." Football is not for everybody — nor is camp.

Here was our policy if a boy wanted to quit: He had to pack up and call home for someone to pick him up. I'm sure several of our boys thought about leaving camp over the years, but it's surprising how few followed through with it.

I can still see one of these boys, sitting on his luggage awaiting his ride home, after calling his parents. It always amazed me how quickly these parents would drop everything at home (almost as if they were waiting for a call) and rush out to camp. The parents of this particular boy must have set a record (and must have broken the speed limit) in getting to camp. It seemed as if they had collected their son and his luggage and were gone within seconds.

Later that year, this same boy also left school. Perhaps quitting had become a pattern for him. I do not know what has become of him.

I also remember some other young men who had packed and called home, but had a change of heart while waiting. I don't think any were sorry they stayed.

I can't tell you how many times I saw parents at camp — especially moms — carrying their sons' luggage while their sons were walking around with their girlfriends or just standing around socializing. I know that I brought it to the attention of more than one big, strong lug and their appreciative mother. It always made one wonder what went on at home.

The parents of another sophomore boy, who showed a lot of desire and potential but lack of experience, approached me at camp. They felt that their son should be starting, that I was being unfair, and that he ought to quit. I don't know how other coaches handle this common confrontation, but here's exactly what I told them: "If I had a son in the same situation, I would pull him — I would not allow him to play for someone who was so unfair."

Obviously, this was hardly what this particular mom and dad expected to hear. They were no doubt looking for some kind of guarantee. I'll bet you already know the outcome. The boy decided to sever the umbilical cord — he stopped whining to his parents (that's how it usually starts) — and stuck with the "unfair" coach. His maturity and determination eventually paid big dividends for him. He had an enjoyable football career and his self esteem had risen considerably. He was happy, his parents were happy, and his coaches were happy.

Another time, a mother called my wife to complain that her son was "lonely" at camp. Can you believe that? What was my wife's reaction? She informed this mother that the coach was lonely, too. (*Way to go, Pat!*) This lonely boy "stuck it out" and went on to have his college education completely paid through his football prowess.

Yes, I can appreciate parents' concerns and anxieties. And I promised you a personal reference:

The scene took place in the mid-50's. It was Colgate University playing Syracuse University and their ace, Jimmy Brown, who would become, arguably, the greatest running back in *NFL* history. We always played at Syracuse in front of a capacity crowd. In those days, this rivalry and the Army versus Navy rivalry were _the_ games in this part of the country.

Sometime during the first half, while playing defensive end, I received a small gash beneath my eye from a cleat (probably Jimmy's) during an attempted tackle from behind. It was one of those fleshy cuts that looked a lot worse than it was — blood covering most of my face. (Face-masks hadn't been perfected yet.)

Well, my mom (*God bless all moms!*) came marching right down to the sideline where our team physician was administering to me. Remember, this was in front of a crowd of 50,000 or so — whatever *Archbold Stadium* held before the current *Carrier Dome* was built on the same site. Was I embarrassed? *Wow — I'll say!!*

I'm told that my mother, herself an implacable fighter when facing opposition, charged through variously dismayed, shocked officials and placating coaches. "My son will never play football again," she stated emphatically.

I can remember the Colgate coaches, some of whom were from Oklahoma, trying to soothe her with their slow, Okie drawl. Hal Lahar, our head coach, put his arm around her shoulders and assured her that everything was going to be "aw-raaaght." After cleaning up my face, the Doc put a butterfly or two on my cut at halftime. I played the entire second half...and many more games.

The Apathetic, Non-Supportive Parent

I'm happy to say, there have been very few non-suportive parents, but they still exist. They are the opposite of the over-protective parents. They don't really care about much of anything, except perhaps, their own selfish agenda.

I think it was Hank Diller of JC who initiated some form of a senior/parent ceremony in the early 60's. We began honoring our seniors and their parents annually during the mid-60's. It was an emotional pre-game ceremony on the field at the last home game. We started with the dads wearing their sons' away-game jerseys, and eventually added the moms.

One father-son relationship from many years ago jumps out at me today. This ceremony magnified it. This particular father had never come around, never really taken any interest whatsoever in his son's football, nor in anything else his son did for that matter. I don't think he saw many of his son's games over the years, even after his boy had established himself as one of the premier players in the entire league. However, upon the coach's written invitation and encouragement to the father to participate in the ceremony, he showed up. He even came for the practice-run during the week. As they were introduced, father and son embraced in a "mesh" at mid-field. (Our photographer always took pictures of each "mesh.")

The following week this player came to my office. He was beaming. I don't think I've ever seen a wider grin on a kid's face, even after winning a championship. It was immediately obvious to me that he was elated about something special — and that it was related to the contents of a bag he was carrying. "Coach, I want to show you something," he uttered excitedly. He then removed an enlarged picture of himself and his dad embracing at the ceremony. What a *poignant* moment! He was so proud, happy, and filled with self-esteem. If he could have, I'm sure he would have raised that picture high enough for the entire world to see. He confided that it was the only time he could ever remember that his father had hugged him (although he had knocked him around plenty, after several drunken bouts).

Although this athlete accepted a full *NCAA* football scholarship at a major university, he unfortunately left after a brief stay. I can't help wondering if those years of neglect and physical abuse by his father were reflected in his decision to drop out.

For one brief moment in time, however, on that day when he dropped in to show me that precious picture, he knew what the top of the mountain looked like. I know that I'll always remember hugging him and thanking him for showing me his treasure, — and I'll never forget that we both shed enough happy tears to fill a bucket.

The Unappreciative Parent

The subject of college recruiting is covered in the next chapter, *"Time-constraints,"* but here are some brief anecdotes relating to parents in particular. Most of the players and parents sincerely appreciated our guidance and effort toward helping them realize their dreams of college and the possibility of attaining a scholarship. We are not in this profession for thanks, but anyone who goes that extra mile would be lying if he said he didn't care whether it was appreciated or not.

However, as time went on, we were placing an ever-increasing percentage of our seniors in college. A few of our parents (perhaps their sons to an extent, too) became slightly spoiled. They began taking too much for granted.

Here are a couple of occurrences that substantiate this claim:

We were winding-up our annual post-season college-informational meeting for parents of seniors (another perk/courtesy we extended to team parents). During our question-answer period, one mother, a single parent, hit me with this loud zinger: "What am I supposed to do with all these questionnaires which keep pouring in from college football offices all over the country — there must be over 200?"

Can you imagine a question like that? The answer seemed obvious: "You shouldn't do anything. Your son should fill out each and every one, or at least those in which he has some interest — as he has already been advised by us. All it will cost is a little time on his part, and a stamp on those few that are not already stamped. — That's a mighty inexpensive investment [*i.e.*, time and a few stamps] for a possible huge return, Mom."

Before I let her completely off the hook, I couldn't resist adding a question of my own: "Isn't it nice that your son has so many opportunities — so many colleges *interested in him?!*"

Case closed. Her son accepted a full football scholarship at a *Division I* university a month later (after returning some questionnaires!)...and that's all that really matters, I guess. Today, he is a very successful salesman. Perhaps, somewhere along the way he and his mother have learned how to say, "Thank you."

Another grievance dealt with the quality of football in a particular division. We felt that this young man was an outstanding college prospect — he had it all, including *All-State* credentials as well as an impressive academic profile. His only shortcoming, by *college* gridiron standards, was his lack of size. Realizing that the *Division I* colleges would consider him too small, we pursued the *Ivy-League* colleges and similar schools very aggressively. His parents, he and I were all on the same page — we were excited about the possibilities. However, the Ivies were less enthusiastic than any of us had anticipated. I argued, pleaded, and cajoled the Ivies almost daily by phone (kept Ma Bell in business). In the end, they all would welcome him as a "walk-on" (Naturally...who wouldn't?), but "could not offer because of his size."

We were extremely disappointed. To this day I'm convinced that those schools missed the boat on this outstanding student-athlete, regardless of his size. He ended up accepting a fairly substantial scholarship to a small, prestigious college playing *Division III* football. Although athletics were not a priority there, he received an excellent education and made quite a name for himself for his athletic exploits.

Shortly after he began his college career, word arrived back to me from several sources that his parents, and in particular his mother, were quite vociferous in bad-mouthing me. "I had let their son down — I hadn't done anything for him," *etc., etc., ... ad nauseam, ad infinitum.*

To this day they have never confronted me with these ridiculous statements, nor have they or their son ever given a hint of appreciation for the extra hours of effort on their behalf. Perhaps the overwhelming appreciation of "outsiders," as well as that of most of our own, serves to magnify the attitude of these few ingrates.

Let me explain, *"outsiders"*. We have always been willing to help any neighbor (opponent). Several used to contact me for assistance and advice about college. (Many still do.) Over the years, we were happy to have helped some athletes and their families from not only the Triple Cities area, but from other parts of the Tier and beyond.

Here's yet another story about another *Wannabe* — an unappreciative and over-protective set of parents with a slightly different twist. It is about another *"Blue-Chipper"* (*i.e.*, full football scholarship to a *Division I* college). During his freshman year of college his mother asked me if I would see to it that the squad would all sign a birthday card (supplied by her) for her "little" boy (235 pounds!) because he was "so lonely, so far away."

I absolutely refused. This was another unappreciative family, including the player, who apparently felt all along that we owed them that full scholarship, a birthday card, and everything else. *Amazing!* This family could easily have afforded to finance a college education many times over, but it *didn't cost them a cent* as things turned out. This athlete definitely had ability, but do you suppose we ever received any thanks for all the time we spent helping this boy and his family realize their dream?...Yeah, right.

Is it any wonder that a very close friend of mine — an extremely caring, sensitive man — resigned from a very successful tenure as the boys' head basketball coach at one of the largest, most prestigious upstate high schools "because of the parents?" When I pressed him for more clarification, all he would tell me was that the kids were great — that he loved to coach — but that the parents had gotten to him. That happened years ago — in his prime. Unfortunately, the student-athletes in that school and the entire community lost a gem, a positive influence, and a rare role model. Our coaching profession lost a heck of a coach — and we can't afford that. What a price was exacted because of the interference of *some* parents!

Remember, the anecdotes which I have shared with you are exceptions — but they are all true. Other coaches will have similar stories. I'm also happy to say, the parent-types I described above are in the minority.

Ideal Parents — the Majority

I guess that the ideal parents and adoring fans are those adults who are able to strike the proper balance between interest and encouragement, and do not feel the need to live vicariously through children. My experience tells me that these *ideal* parents represent the vast majority whom I have had the pleasure of knowing and working with. So many positive, supportive parents come to mind, that I could write a book on that subject alone. No high school football program could exist without them.

One father was so appreciative of our efforts in trying to find a college match for his son that he sent us a check "to help defray all the postage and telephone expenses incurred in his son's behalf." This certainly wasn't necessary or expected. I have never forgotten this tangible means of thanks — especially because it was from a family with an average income.

Here are a couple of other pre-season camp stories, but with a little different slant:

You remember our policy about any player who wished to quit camp? Well, as with the young lad we mentioned earlier whose parents had rushed right up to pick him up, another boy, in another year, had packed up his belongings and placed his call home. He was convinced that football was no longer for him.

His dad answered the "distress" call, and proceeded to tell his son that he had no intention of picking him up, and that if he wanted to quit, he'd have to bum a ride home (this was early 60's, remember), or walk the 25 miles.

Was this father un-caring? On the contrary — it was a form of *"tough love."* Knowing this father, as I do, I'm sure that it killed him to refuse his son's request, but it was his way of supporting and loving him. The boy stayed, became a starter, and was chosen by his teammates as the most improved player at the end of the season. I'll bet he has occasionally looked back on that seemingly bleak day and drawn upon its experience in his very successful, everyday business.

Another year, a distraught father (for whom I had a great deal of respect as a person, and as a tough ex-gridder) called me upon our return from camp. He apologized for the call and for his son quitting so early at camp. Apparently he had been "working on" his son, and the boy was having second thoughts. The father wondered if there was any way the boy could be reinstated.

This was one of those difficult decisions for me — and to this day I don't know if it was the correct one. Although I appreciated this friend's sincere request, I did not feel it would have been fair to the other fifty young men who had "graduated" from all the rigors of a one-week *Tiger*-camp, to reinstate this boy, no matter how sincere his intentions. I took into account that the boy had already made a decision, and had been relaxing at home for the previous week. For that reason, I denied the father's request...and he accepted it as a man. Even now, I'm sure that neither the father nor son realizes that my decision pained me as much as it did them. I only hope an important lesson about irrevocable decisions was learned at a young age. In any event, despite this temporary setback, I'm happy to say that the boy has become an exemplary citizen and, together with his handsome family, contributes a great deal to this community. Coincidentally, his younger brother joined our squad in later years, stuck with it, and became a vital ingredient in the foundation of a *Tiger* team which went on to achieve state-wide prominence.

Once I remember sharing a concern with a few parents and team leaders immediately following a rare, disappointing season. I felt that we had lacked a vital ingredient on that particular team which is so essential for the success of any team — *UNITY*. We addressed this issue for hours, and exchanged ideas that we felt might alleviate this situation for future teams. Much positive dialogue took place. I believe it was the parents of our captain-elect that year who suggested having a pre-season, covered-dish picnic at one of the area parks. All the players and their families would be invited. The idea was enthusiastically endorsed by all, and obviously emerged as the winner over many solid suggestions.

We didn't want it to be another one of those committee-ideas that "looks good on paper," but stays there (on paper). How to implement it? These same parents initiated and organized the first of these picnics many years ago, and it quickly became a tradition. It provided a rare opportunity for fellowship away from the field and locker room. Sometimes there was some impromptu entertainment by some family members. Parents, coaches and their families, players and their siblings all intermingled, became better acquainted, and formed an invisible bond. The evening usually culminated with the squad singing the *Alma Mater*. (A wide variety of vocal talent was in evidence from year to year, but, whether in pitch or not, they always sang with gusto.)

A couple of area football coaches attended these dinners with their families. Their sons were U-E players. I remember that these men were impressed and they commented about the effect of the picnic on everyone — one big, happy family. One of them stated, "Is it any wonder that U-E does as well as it does? We need to do something like this in our program."

The traditional *Senior-Parent* ceremony mentioned earlier, conjures up many images of positive, supportive parents. It was Dr. John Hudock who planted a seed in my mind about a possible adjustment in the ceremony many years ago. It happened as he joined his twin sons, Mike and Steve (themselves successful doctors today), on the field. The good doctor wondered why his wife couldn't be there, too? I've never forgotten his reason: "She's the one who has had more to do with raising them than I have."

After the season, when I always tried to analyze and evaluate the entire program "from head-to-toe," I gave his concern a great deal of thought. It wouldn't really be a precedent. Although this was a rarity in those early years, we had already had a few mothers "stand in" for deceased or absent fathers. I ran it by Pat (my assistant head coach, you know). She endorsed the idea without hesitation or reservation.

But, what would we have the mothers wear? (Both sets of jerseys were already committed.) It was decided that each senior would present his mom with a small corsage (after all, as the son of a florist I was somewhat florally orientated) accompanied by a personal note. We adopted this as policy the next year, and are happy we did.

As I reflect, I can't understand why the mothers weren't included from the start. I have never thought of myself as a male chauvinist. I am embarrassed to admit this now, but I had just never even thought about including mothers down on the field. (I should have remembered my own *"uninvited"* mom down on the field at Syracuse University....)

I could tell you about some mighty supportive sisters, brothers, aunts, uncles, guardians, grandparents, and godparents who have "stood in" for a deceased, divorced, separated, or absent parent on this night. At times, the adult and the boy would even consult me on some very difficult, sensitive family decisions regarding representation. We usually agreed that, in any "close" vote, the player himself should make the final decision. There will always be a special place in my heart for these very courageous single-parents who gave their sons full support...whatever his decision. It was not always an easy thing to do. As the athletes become adults, most realize that this ceremony is an important memory of their growing, formative years. Eventually, as TV began covering some games, a few tube-watching fans from different areas of the state called or wrote to say how impressed they were with the concept of our *Senior-Parent* ceremony.

Mothers are a strong breed — I'm convinced of that. I have known a few who have chosen to temporarily remain "in-town" when their husbands' jobs forced them to relocate. Although this separation caused a real hardship, they felt that it was of paramount importance that their sons complete their senior year of football at U-E. *And we're happy they did!*

Several parents have been most cooperative and supportive of our program over the years. Whenever we asked for their help, in any endeavor, we could count on them.

I would feel remiss if I didn't mention the following unique group of parents and friends who gave willingly and unselfishly of their time and energy (and in some cases, of their finances). They did this not only while their sons were participating, but also for many years before, and more significantly, afterwards. They shared a common thread: They were loyal; generous; indefatigable workers. These were parents-as-partners, in the truest sense. We shall forever be in their debt:

Anne Bennett, John and Peggy Villanti, and Margot Ketrick — initiated and organized all facets of our exquisite game programs (which many have considered superior to several college game programs).

Joe Pisani (*The Endwell House*) and *"Bucky"* Picciano (*Banquet Masters*) — restaurateurs who annually invited our squads to their establishments as their guests. This became our traditional football banquet where individual and team awards were presented. The team captain for the coming year was always elected at this affair.

Bill Gargano, Sr., Mike Wesko, Sr., and Fred Zappia, Sr. — entrepreneurs who served on most of our football committees, especially those dealing with the large money-raising projects for championship jackets, banners, scholarships, and needs outside the athletic budget. They also donated individual and team trophies, and game-socks annually.

Fran Crooks and *"Shorty"* Bowen — a charter member of our Booster Club and a jack-of-all-trades respectively, were always willing to help us at a moment's notice. They helped immeasurably with football equipment and, basically, anything we needed.

Bob Gallagher and Dave Decker — colleagues who don't qualify as parents of players, but who gave willingly of their time over the years. Bob produced and narrated three memorable highlight films ('64, '74, '79); Dave kept impeccable statistics for us year after year.

The above list does not, by any means, purport to be exhaustive. Thank you, everyone whose name has not been listed. You know who you are. We couldn't have done it without any of you.

Parent-Coach, a Dual Role

"Was it hard coaching your own kid?"

Some fans or colleagues have asked me this question from time to time. It's a fair question, and I'll try to answer as best I can. Of course, the fact that Chris and Larry were good athletes didn't hurt. Both sons became solid starters on teams ('76-'79) that achieved an aggregate record of 29-5-1. This included three championship teams, one of which ('79) received an unprecedented designation as *Number One* in the state.

These guys were two entirely different personalities:

Chris was quite shy, and still is, to some degree. At 6 feet 3 inches and 190 pounds, he became a steady, cerebral quarterback who understood the intricacy of the offense. Most fans would probably say that his forte was passing. He's still in the U-E record books in two different passing categories. However, from our viewpoint as coaches, his contributions of leadership, play-selection, and deceptive execution were much more significant. Although he never said it, I know that Chris was very proud and happy to have his brother as a teammate.

Larry, at 5 feet 9 inches and 205 pounds, was extremely quick, strong, agile, and physically aggressive. These traits served him well as noseman on our defense. In his senior year ('79), this defense allowed but 26 points for the *entire season*. Larry has always been an unusual person — very outgoing, extremely caring and sensitive. In one incident, a poem surfaced, allegedly written by an opposing center whom he would be facing that week. The poem made reference to Larry's "chubby little forearms." Mistake. Larry didn't talk about it. All I remember is that this poet-center was only in the game for the initial snap, and was physically unable to continue for the remainder of the game. Might this give new meaning to *"poetic justice?!?"*

Naturally, Pat and I were as proud as any parents would be, when they both made *All-Conference*. One achieved *All- State* status, and even was named to an *All-American* team. I think that Vaun enjoyed the fame of being their little sister (although I'm not so sure how much of each game she and her girlfriends actually watched). Eventually, as her vocal and acting talents blossomed, the boys became very proud of Vaun (although, as with most siblings close in age, they never admitted their pride in each other).

As sons of the coach I'm sure that it was hard on them at times. Although we never discussed it then, I asked them about it recently. They informed me that there was a lot more positive about it (*i.e.*, the relationship) than negative. They said they remember feeling they had to go beyond their potential, to reach beyond their grasp, to always give 100% for me and for themselves — perhaps to eliminate any possible accusations of favoritism. They both noticed that comments between some teammates — complaints after a particularly tough practice, or perhaps grousing about lack of playing time — would die down when Chris or Larry would enter the locker room. Larry said that he remembered feeling so much pressure during the summer prior to his first year with the varsity, that he had a difficult time sleeping. When I asked him what kind of pressure, he said that he was scared to fail — scared for me and for himself.

I noticed that Chris, in his shyness, never addressed me as "Dad," "Coach," or "Mr." on the field, in the Latin classroom, or even at home for that matter. He may be the only quarterback who never addressed his coach as *anything* in three varsity seasons! I don't mean that he was disrespectful, or that we never had dialogue — it was just unique. On the other hand, to Larry I was always "Dad" — whether we were on the field, at school, or at home. As a matter of fact, my mother-in-law Grace Hanley, was his teacher in elementary school and always enjoyed her appellation of "Grandma" from Larry in or out of the classroom. In spite of some good-natured ribbing by his little classmates because of this, to him she always was his grandma.

I can remember some very quiet dinners on those rare occasions when we all ate together during the season. There wasn't a peep — especially after a particularly poor, or perhaps an extra-grueling practice that is a part of football. On these occasions, when Pat or Vaun might ask them about practice, or something football-related, the boys remained mum. I'm sure they would have liked to say plenty, but perhaps didn't dare, since their coach was at the dinner table. (For the record, I don't recall any loss of appetite at the table by any of us — *anytime*.)

From my perspective, although I know that I strayed from this philosophy occasionally, I tried to make it a policy to never discuss "shop" at the dinner table. Believe me, there were times when I wanted to get to the bottom of some team-related incident or other (commonplace on any football team) — but I did not feel that it would be fair to ask my sons for detailed information about a teammate or incident in the privacy of our home or anyplace else. I felt that it would have put undue pressure on them. I didn't want to make them have to choose between their loyalty to their father or to their teammates.

On the field, I can honestly say that I was not even aware of the fact that my own sons were out there. I had a squad of fifty or so, "sons." The only exceptions to this related to injury or illness — fortunately nothing serious. Both of my guys were forced to miss some practices and games. They knew how concerned Pat and Vaun were. I'm sure they realized that I, too, was concerned — but as their coach, not as their father. Now they'll know that it ran much deeper. I hope they'll never have to experience the anguish a parent feels when his son "goes down" right in front of him.

It happened to Chris on a drill during practice. Football is a contact sport — injuries come with the territory. Even with all of my experience, however, I never thought that my own sons would, or could ever be injured. It had never even entered my mind.

I went over and tried to comfort Chris verbally, as I would with any player. However, it was difficult to hold back my tears as our trainer took Chris to meet Pat at the hospital emergency-room. My heart was in my mouth. I tried to mask my emotions for the remainder of practice — but I was devastated. My heart was with my son — not my quarterback.

At the end of practice, I rushed up to the hospital directly from the field. Without showering.

As I recall with Larry, he had come down with an acute case of pleurisy some days prior to his first game. Our family doctor laid it on the line to him explicitly: "Either rest, take your medication, and miss this one game — or keep going and miss the entire season." Again, I grieved inside for my number two son, but disguised it as best I could.

Up in the stands, Pat had some trying experiences in her dual role as the coach's wife, as well as the mother of two of the players. Obviously some fans are always oblivious to this fact, or not very sensitive if they are aware of it. Several years ago, a colleague shared with me this brief pearl about spectators, taken from some magazine. I've never forgotten it:

> *"Every athletic team could use a man who plays every position, never makes an error, and knows just what the opposition is planning.... But so far there's been no way to get him to put down his hot dog and come out of the stands."*

Well, as is the case at any stadium, U-E has had its share of "experts" in the stands — and lots of delicious hot dogs. Ironically, this scenario was almost a mirror of the CV upset at U-E ten years earlier ('69). It was '78 now, and a struggling M-E team, with an outstanding back, Mark Sarrica, was visiting the undefeated *Tigers* in their den. Coach Joe Bramante's troops had never performed so heroically. The *Spartans* led at the half: 16-0. We didn't get untracked until the 4th-quarter, when we finally decided to play some defense, and Chris, via both land and air, accounted for our meager 12 points. However, Chris had experienced a severe, sub-par first-half (as did our entire squad). He was hearing personal boos from some "professional" home-town spectators. Pat stayed through it all and somehow maintained her "lady-like demeanor" in public. She's a toughie. However, that doesn't mean that she wasn't hurt over the caustic remarks about her son, and the booing that night. Later, she confided to me that she went down to the car and bawled her eyes out while waiting for me.

Our 4th-quarter effort proved too late. Our next-door neighbor (M-E) had secured, arguably, their sweetest victory ever: 24-12. It should be noted, moreover, that a few loyal U-E fans, and even a couple of sports reporters were offended, too. They visited Pat and Chris to apologize for the "boo-birds" and to say how embarrassed they were.

It's amazing sometimes, how friendships evolve. During his college years, Chris and the same Mark Sarrica who had punctured our defense for 141 yards on 30 carries for M-E that night, became fast friends. In fact, along with another former opponent from the same era, Ithaca's ace fullback, George Stiles, Mark was a guest here at the house for a cook-out one hot summer night a few years ago. This crew must have been starved that evening. They proceeded to eat me out of house, home and several pounds of spiedis. (Of course, I managed to devour a few, too.)

On the occasion of Larry's marriage to Susan Armstrong, two of his ushers were Mike Cappellett and Mike Rotondi, Jr. — a couple of guys who once donned the hateful *Green and Gold* as fierce rivals from Vestal before the three became bosom buddies in college.

A couple of other incidents developed which I'm sure wouldn't have happened except in this dual role of father/coach with his sons. Having been steeped in the tradition of U-E football since they had been toddlers, something came up that jolted the boys' "comfort zone" temporarily.

About the time when they were to enter high school, a couple of colleges had contacted me about the position of head football coach. I don't want you to think that my children monitored my calls, but our phone was located in the kitchen — and these calls happened to come in while they were eating there. When the kids were younger, perhaps they were aware of a few other opportunities for their dad to pursue his career at the college level, but hadn't given it much thought. After all, — we were still here.

This particular call was different, however — they were older now and much more aware of the implications. After arrangements for air-travel, the itinerary, and other details had been firmed up to end one of these calls, Chris stated that, if we moved, he would prefer to stay here with Grandma and play football for U-E. It was then that I realized, perhaps for the first time, what kind of "monster" we had created here with the U-E football program. Although I was flattered at the invitations, and met some great people during my visits to a couple of campuses, my trips to and from the interviews were fraught with mental conflicts and anxieties. I stayed with U-E and have never looked back.

Another time demonstrates the strong loyalty and bond between a father/coach and his son. I'm not sure exactly in which year this took place, but somewhere along the line Larry felt that a particular sports writer — fairly new to the area — was giving me a hard time. I don't even remember the specifics of the "hard time" — after all, coaches must accept that as part of our profession. I learned, long after the fact, that Larry had confronted this reporter. Larry wanted to know exactly what this man had against his father. (Not his *coach* — his *father*.)

After learning about this episode, my initial reaction was one of shock. I didn't know what to think. After all, it's not something which I would have encouraged or condoned. Once hearing the story, other coaches and colleagues who were familiar with this reporter's style had a big chuckle over it. They almost unanimously said, "*Good for Larry!*" I must admit that eventually I had a warm feeling of appreciation for my son's loyalty and *chutzpa*.

Joe Moresco, in discussing how much he had enjoyed having his sons play for him, confided to me that he felt he had lost a little spark, that perhaps he wasn't quite as hungry after his last son had graduated. (*It sure didn't show, Joe!*)

I don't know about Dick Hoover's experience with this (never discussed it), but I don't remember any loss of any "fire in the belly" after my sons had graduated. I think my squads after '79 would agree with me although, eventually, my knees did not allow me to do as much "demonstrating" in the early '90's.

I shall conclude this chapter with my reaction to that common concern about the difficulty (?) of "coaching your own kid": How many other jobs can you name where a father is with his sons almost all day, every day, including weekends, for approximately a quarter of each year during those pivotal teen-age years?

...Unequivocally, *I—loved—every—minute—of—it!*

Larry, as noseguard (left), and Chris, as quarterback (right), teamed with Dad as coach from 1976 to 1979; playing together in 1977 and 1978.

Chapter Five

"I cannot change yesterday,
I can only make the most of today,
and look with hope toward tomorrow."

REFLECTIONS:

TIGER BALL / SCOUTING / TIME CONSTRAINTS and FAMILY

Tiger Ball

"I love that *'race horse'* football," remarked a U-E fan..."but I bet they [opponents] don't like it." Although we have been credited with these innovative approaches to football in this area, we certainly didn't invent them. Each one is really a philosophy, a way of life in our football world.

The first approach was of total (or as close to total as possible) two-platoon football, and even beyond — to the extent of substituting an entire offense or defense at times. Without realizing it at the time, Ben Schwartzwalder of Syracuse University influenced me about this long ago. He planted a seed in my mind then, even though I was on the short end of it. (I thanked him many years later.)

Here's what took place: We found ourselves (Colgate University) in the rare role of dominating our arch rival (Syracuse) in one of our usual slugfests of the mid-50's. Our opening drive was every coach's dream — a sustained, clock-eating possession that methodically took us almost the length of the field. When we reached first and goal with all kinds of momentum and steadily building confidence, Coach Schwartzwalder used two ploys: First, he called a timeout, thus interrupting our momentum. Next, as soon as the timeout had ended, he sent completely new defensive personnel sprinting onto the field accompanied by screams and war whoops. What a psychological impact that sight (and possibly that sound, too —) had on us! And it lifted their spirits. Those Syracuse reserves stopped us cold on that crucial series. Syracuse went on to win a closely-contested struggle that day.

At U-E, we began incorporating some aspects of two-platoon football quite early in the 60's. We became convinced that if a boy, although he might not be as talented as a teammate playing the same position, realized that he could win a starting spot on the other side of the ball, he would try even harder. Therefore, although we might have been sacrificing some talent on the bench at times, we felt that we were gaining more by resting eleven men at a time, while developing another eleven to specialize in either offense or defense. We learned that this seemed to improve a player's self esteem, something we always have felt was a big part of our job. Our best effort toward this end was to have twenty starters during some years. (There were always a few who could handle playing on both sides of the ball.)

Eventually, we expanded this to almost a three-platoon system by utilizing players who always gave 100% effort during practice, but who were on the periphery talent-wise. We began to put these diligent players on the various special (kicking) teams, referred to them as starters, and developed some inner-team pride there, too. Although our goal was to field 33 different starters (offense, defense, special teams), we never quite made it. But we did start as many as 27 in some years. We found out that if you had 27 happy, rested players, chances are that they would play well. I've always felt that the key to successful coaching is to get youngsters to perform consistently beyond their ability.

The platooning philosophy lent itself nicely to the next phase we incorporated. Some people call it *"race horse"* football, others refer to it as *"quick huddle"* offense. Like everything else, it took lots of practice (with a stopwatch) and a certain amount of "selling." Of course, this limited sending in plays and necessitated working with the quarterback all week to give him a larger responsibility in play-selection. The more we used it, the more we realized that it was preventing our opponents from making many adjustments, or from doing much shifting on defense. We were definitely running more offensive plays than before. It also seemed to be giving us a big psychological — as well as physical — lift in the second half of most games. This is because we were still sprinting out of our huddle and getting down over the ball quickly.

Our cross country coach, Bob *"Ozzie"* Osborne, a staunch supporter of U-E football, was at our game at EFA in 1965. Arguably, our club that year exemplified this *"race horse"* philosophy more than any other. Ozzie, one of those track guys who always carries a stopwatch, informed us after the game that he had been clocking us from the stands at an average of 13 seconds per play in the second half! (What would the *NFL think of that?!?*) I'm sure this was our best single-game effort of *"race horse"* ever, and we always strove to match it.

The officials hated it. The chain-crew hated it. (You'd better be in shape if you were working a U-E game in those days!) How I used to enjoy reminding officials and chain-crews at the other stadiums that we intended to race, and that we fully expected them to keep up with us. "Don't you *dare* slow us down!"

Of course, those playing defense against us hated it, too. If executed properly, it really took its toll on those three groups. I've run into young adults who had been our opponents in those days. Whenever we reminisce, those who played defense invariably describe how they felt, especially in the latter stages of a game, when our offense would hardly give them a chance to collect their thoughts — or to catch their breath. Our fans loved it. Our players loved it, too — once they saw the results and the look in their opponents' eyes in the fourth quarter. We all took great pride in our brand of *"race horse"* football.

After several years of coaching, we became convinced that the kicking game was the deciding factor in most close games at any level. Nothing has changed my opinion today. Take a look at some closely contested *NFL* contests on a Sunday afternoon, or some of those super-tight college bowl games.

Try this: Keep track of the net yardage (the actual kick yardage less the return yardage) of all kicks over the course of an entire game. (Don't forget to include any turnovers, as a result of a fumbled return, or a blocked kick.) Include all successful PAT's and Field Goals — compare the results of your findings with the results of the game ("close" ones only). You'll appreciate the "kicking" game of "foot"-ball.

Some people have always been amazed by our actual size (*i.e.*, lack of), especially on our better teams. Over the years we would have to be considered on the small-average size by most standards, although we like to think that we "played big." Naturally, there were a few exceptions to this — '64, '72, '79 come immediately to mind — when we were huge, especially defensively.

Why were we usually small-average size? Speed and quickness were always clear-cut priorities for us — on both sides of the ball. Size was our least important asset.

Perhaps, subconsciously, I was drawing upon my high school and college observations, and experiences during my playing days. I must refer to my brother, Rick, who is one year older. He was a strong, courageous and scrappy guard — converted from the backfield. (Two-platoon hadn't been invented yet, and substituting just wasn't done at U-E then.) Day after day as teammates, I watched him beat out his competition on the practice field. However, the other guy always started. Why? The only possible explanation must have been "due to lack of size." My brother was approximately 5 feet 11 inches and165 pounds. The starter "looked better," though, as a solid 190 or 200 pounder. I've never forgotten that.

In college, a particular "under-sized" teammate, Frank Speno (a former rival from Ithaca), comes to mind. Our frosh coach, Dick Offenhamer, called him a "bag of bones" at one practice. This "bag of bones," however, not only had the best kicking leg, but also became a key back for us before our four years were over ("red-shirting" hadn't been invented yet). Frank almost single-handedly won our opener versus Dartmouth with his inspiring, heroic receptions in a remarkable 4th-quarter comeback. Coach Lahar influenced me a great deal at Colgate by winning consistently with small, average-size personnel year after year.

I could tell you a few stories about "big" players who just couldn't get the job done, for one reason or other. But, I could tell you many, many stories about "little" guys — all "too small," "too weak," "too short" — who splattered bodies all over the field because of their quickness, smarts, and most of all, because of their burning desire to excel. We've had lots of 'em start for us. Several *"mini-Tigers"* come immediately to mind. Although I could write a book just about them, I'll introduce you to a few:

Dan Whittaker and Jerry Wolfe were teammates ('77-'78). Dan was a wiry , fearless stick of dynamite as a linebacker. For 165 pounds, he was one of the toughest ever. His teammate Jerry was a gutsy, sure-handed wide receiver. He never let his whopping 148 pounds deter him from catching in a crowd — in fact, he seemed to thrive on it.

Dave Meza and John Barnes ('85-'86) were a pair of short linebackers, both standing just 5 feet 7 inches. Ask Binghamton ('86) about them.

Bill Starring, Jr., ('65-'66), Larry Starchok ('76-'77), Marty Fisher ('81-'82), and Barry *"Oil Can"* Doyle ('86-'87) were a quartet of defensive corners — none over 5 feet 7 inches; 128–141 pounds (maybe). These diminutive packages gave us adequate pass coverage, but their forte was hitting. My, how these guys loved to hit — and they *hit for keeps!*

Ever see a fire hydrant? Matt Palombo ('81-'82) was 5 feet 4 inches and 227 pounds. Some opposing offensive linemen would initially snicker when he'd line up on defense for us. After they had caught a few pops from Matt's forearms, their smirks quickly disappeared. (I recently discovered that a "fire hydrant" can also "pop" a golf ball — a long, long way....)

Saturday nights during the fall have been very special for over thirty years. We had established this "Saturday night" time-slot for our home games. Very few other high school football games in our area ever conflicted with ours. It became a long-standing tradition. Many families, not only from Endicott but from the entire Triple Cities community, felt that Union-Endicott was the place to be on a Saturday night in autumn.

How did our *Tigers* like it? Just ask anyone who has ever donned the proud *Orange and Black*. Better yet, ask our opponents how it felt to enter the *Tigers'* den on a Saturday night. Bobby Campbell will tell you what it was like, especially after an entire new wing, four stories high, had been added to the rear of the school in 1974. It towered above — and seemed to overhang — the entire stadium. He always accused me, kiddingly, of being responsible for adding to this specter by having the lights on the top floor blazing away — as if "eyes of a colossal monster."

I'm afraid I can't take any credit for the illusion — you'd have to talk to the custodians on the night shift....

I'm told that we had a few "rare" rules and regulations — rare especially when our schools, and society, began relaxing and compromising their standards all around us.

For instance, we did not allow our players to wear hats (not even turned-around) inside buildings. This held true even when we were the only ones in the school building during pre-season in mid-August.

We also sat up, rather than lounge, in our seats at all meetings and film sessions. (Of course, my students knew that I expected the same "sacrifices" from them in the classroom.)

Unlike some other sports, our players were never allowed to wear their jerseys in school on game-day — nor were they allowed to wear them anywhere, anytime — except "down in the arena." We informed them that their performance on the field was the way to bring attention to themselves. The only exceptions to this were when we were involved in some community projects or pep rallies.

These rules were non-negotiable. Do you think they were fair? Do you think they made better football players? I can only tell you this: I am convinced that teenagers are "screaming" for discipline. Unfortunately, very few adults "hear" them. Or they choose not to hear.

Scouting (and Eating)

"I have proof that they [a future opponent] took film of our game," a prominent coach stated at a league-meeting way back in the 60's. Although he didn't press charges, almost 30 years later another school in our league "blew the whistle" on a rival coach for the same infraction. It was proven, and the guilty party received an unprecedented (to the best of my knowledge) one-game suspension. Let's explore how the use (or abuse) of film for scouting purposes has evolved.

We have always put a great deal of effort into scouting the opposition — within the legal parameters established by the league. Since, until recently, it was against the rules to scout a team by using a camera of any kind, it was important to assign the entire staff to different games each weekend. We were interested in the basic things: our opponents' personnel, offensive and defensive alignments, offensive plays, kicking game, and especially — tendencies in all situations.

In looking back, we had a rather farcical experience once, although it didn't seem it at the time. We had a team within our division scouted so thoroughly, defensively, that we had jumped out to an insurmountable lead by halftime — mainly because we had shut down their vaunted, high-scoring offense, cold. They were so frustrated by this that one of their coaches made an unprecedented visit to our locker room at halftime. He was extremely emotional and irate when he burst in on us. He accused us of tampering with their communication-system and intercepting their messages and play-selections from it. "Or else, how could you know exactly what we are going to do, before we do it?" he blurted out.

"How about through scouting?" we answered.

Although in reality his tirade was the absolute height of "praise" (in disguise) that our scouts could possibly have received, it was "bush." And a totally unfounded accusation. It just gave our troops even more inspiration in the second-half. We didn't have to say a word. We went out and administered a good, old-fashioned whipping — both physically and on the scoreboard, as well.

Eventually, our adversaries realized that our entire program had always been above reproach, and accepted the fact that they had just plain been buried. The one assistant was totally embarrassed by his blatant, frustrated accusations in front of our squad, and did apologize. We accepted. This isolated incident has never been repeated.

Scouting has changed drastically since the early days — perhaps not necessarily for the better. Sometime during the early *STAC*-years (early 70's), the league proposed, and passed the legality of two teams exchanging game-films. Can you guess what trio of coaches fought this tenaciously?

Messrs. Hoover, Moresco, and Angeline were strongly opposed to it, and refused to participate in any film-exchange in any way. We simply felt that we did not want to exchange our quality film for some inferior film, nor did we feel that we could afford to let it out anytime. We were constantly reviewing it and using it to show to our booster clubs, sometimes weeks later. Unfortunately, we had no control over someone else exchanging their film, with us on it, with a future, mutual opponent. (But we chose to live with this inequity and never compromised our position.)

Anyone can tell you that we, at U-E, have always made an adventure out of a scouting mission. Each August, almost the moment the scouting schedule for the entire season had been posted, one or more of my assistants would list a key restaurant for each outing...and underline it in red. This "pit stop," no matter how far, became just as important to us as any other phase of scouting. We might have had the only bulletin board in any football office that had the distinction of an array of menus from all over our scouting area (and, believe me — that covered quite an area) posted on it, alongside the scouting assignments. It was not unusual for our crew to check a certain menu on the board and make a decision on their order...days in advance of our departure. (Ah, decisions, decisions!)

Many of these restaurants treated us royally. We had built up quite a reputation for our prowess with knife, fork, and spoon. These good people aimed to please...and *we were easy.*

A life-long goal of my staff has been to write some type of *"Dining Guide."* Their eyes will light up with what follows — it will conjure up many pleasant (and tasty) memories. Here are a few of our favorite eating establishments along the scouting trails, including some of their specialties. (If there seems to be an "Italian flavor" in what follows, we make no apology):

ITHACA: *"The CODDINGTON RESTAURANT" — Coddington Road. (Bouillabaisse, and an expansive salad bar in the shape of a huge gondola.)*

ELMIRA: *"BERNIE MURRAY'S"— 500 S. Main Street. (Wings; Ribs.)*

SAYRE, Pennsylvania: *"MANGIALARDO'S." (Minestrone; Veal Scallopini; Garlic Pizza.) Of course, while in the area, there's a great bakery — "SOPRANO'S" — in* ***WAVERLY****. (It even has a delightful "pitch" to its name.)*

HANCOCK: *"The CIRCLE E DINER" — just off Route 17. (Great breakfast; homemade turnovers.)*

AUBURN: *"BALLOON'S" - across from the prison (but don't let that affect your appetite! — Italian Cuisine.)*

ALBANY: *"GRIMALDI'S."*

UTICA: *"GRIMALDI'S."*

SYRACUSE: *"GRIMALDI'S." (Sometimes, I think we should own some stock in the Grimaldi Chain!)*
Their Fettucine Alfredo is excellent, as are all of their offerings.

Getting hungry? — I know I am. Before we leave these three cities, Albany (actually, Colonie) also boasts of "The CRANBERRY BOG" on Wolf Road. (Steak and Cranberry Bread.); Utica has a delightful "FLORENTINE BAKERY"; Syracuse also has "ANGOTTI'S" (same general area as "Grimaldi's" — just off Erie Boulevard — food is excellent — Italian Cuisine).

***ROME:** "The SAVOY" — Dominick Street. (How's that for the name of the main street?!?) (Zuppa di Pesce, lending itself to leisurely "dip-page," as my staff calls it.)*

***MIDDLETOWN (and Downstate):** "The DODGE INN" — off Route 17, the Lake Louise-Marie exit. (Steak-unlimited! — and the biggest Roast Potatoes you've ever seen.)*

***NEWBURGH:** "CHIANTI'S." (Even the name has a certain mellow, cordial ring to it, doesn't it? — Italian Cuisine.)*

***N.Y.CITY:** "MONTE'S" — 97 Macdougal Street. — in The Village. (Pasta e Faggioli; ETC.)*

"Da ROSINA" — W. 46th Street. - "Restaurant Row." (Bruschetta; Pasta e Faggioli; ETC.)

"The FAMILY RESTAURANT" — Queens Boulevard.— Queens. (The most gigantic, succulent Mussels, any style, you've ever had! — Italian Cuisine.)

***PHILADELPHIA, Pennsylvania:** "The DELUXE DINER" —near "Rittenhouse Square." (Unbelievable Breakfast — 24 hours a day.)*

***CHERRY HILL, New Jersey (SOMERDALE):** "PEPPINO'S" — North White Horse Pike. (Every course is exciting, delicious, and plentiful — you'll need a "doggie bag" — guaranteed! You'll want to eat leisurly to do this restaurant — and your appetite — justice. Try their Ciappino.)*

Although it is not a restaurant, per se, *nor is it even out-of-town, no season would be complete for us, without a stop (or two, or three) at the CONCESSION STAND at JOHNSON CITY'S home games. If you haven't tried their Kielbasa (with trimmings), under the watchful eye of Tom Jablonowski, you're missing out on one of the great ethnic delicacies around here. (Incidentally, Tom is a long-time, valued member of the JC Board of Education — a fact which makes his vigilant, volunteer service each fall rather unique, don't you think?)*

To this day, Pat and the children accuse me of inventing an "excuse" to frequent these places. Actually, aside from the delicious food, the real reason for the magnetism of these restaurants is the people. You just won't find finer and friendlier people than the Joe Centini family (*"Coddington"*), Joe Valeant (*"Bernie Murray's"*), Tom Jablonowski (*JC*), Giovanni (*"Monte's"*), Tony (*"Peppino's"*), *"Squeege"* and the whole crew (*"Mangialardo's"*) and everybody at *"Da Rosina."*

Of course, we had to have something to tide us over until we arrived at these restaurants. Thanks to the generosity of our Booster Club, their very understanding popcorn machine, and a series of "master-chefs" — Russ *"Nick"* Nicosia, Bart Guccia, and Shorty Bowen — it was not unusual to see our crew depart for a scouting assignment accompanied by a gigantic box of popcorn. This was not the "jumbo tub" we all know from the movies — I mean an empty *athletic box* that once had housed several shoulder pads or helmets. There was enough 'corn for an army.

This was a ritual — a tradition. We went without, only once that I can remember. Tony Rose had inadvertently placed the 'corn box on top of the van and never realized it until we had blazed down the highway a few miles. I'm certain many creatures of the sky swooped down and had an impromtu banquet that night — at our expense.

Unlike some medical textbooks on the subject, we always felt that our minds were more alert after a sumptuous meal (along with an abundance of exemplary camaraderie, of course). We did eat well...and we consumed a lot. A local business man, Fred Zappia, Sr., one of the most congenial, generous individuals we have ever known, used to say of us (after picking up the dinner tab a few times): "It would be cheaper to buy each of these guys *a new suit of clothes!*"

My staff always said that we were, "undefeated," at the table — any table — over the years. Tony Romeo used to always raise his arms (a TD signal) at the end of each of these meals on the road, accompanied by this one-word utterance that expressed all of our feelings: "VICTORY."

Hey, that was part of the program — we always *"came to play!"*

In retrospect, there were some humorous incidents while scouting (although a few didn't seem so funny at the time).

In the early 60's, two of my assistants were having their usual argument over politics, only this time it had become quite heated. I had to stop the car and order Frank *"Sarge"* Sorochinsky and Bob *"Beef"* Adams to get out of the car and settle their argument outside in the field. We were enroute to Philadelphia to scout JC, and I wasn't about to listen to that loud debate for the next few hours.

In the mid 60's, our car broke down on Route 7 outside Worcester (east of Oneonta) on our return trip from scouting Oneonta at Troy. Steam was pouring out of the hood as we pulled onto the shoulder of the road. Hovie, just awakening from a nap in the back, was startled seeing the steam (as in a dream). You should have seen Hovie, that big bear, scrambling up and over the front seat and out the door. Nick and I bummed a ride to the nearest town for help. A guy in a pickup stopped, and we discovered too late that this good Samaritan was quite inebriated. Since the nearest service station was seven miles away (we were really in the boondocks), those were seven tough, weaving, anxious miles — a real nightmare. We had to leave the car overnight for repairs, forcing us to miss an evening scouting assignment in Vestal. (Naturally, we tried to make the most of a difficult situation by dining at one of Oneonta's fine restaurants.) We stayed at George Matola's house, an old Endicotter and then Oneonta's basketball coach, until my dad (who never missed too many meals, either) came to the rescue. We arrived back home at approximately 4:30 A.M. It was *all in a night's work!*

A few times, we would arrive at our destination, only to find out that the game had been postponed without our knowledge. In the mid 70's a U-E scouting party had traveled all the way downstate to scout Newburgh, only to experience this frustration. Since it was a lost mission, they felt that they would have some fun. Since they were there anyway, they went to another game in the area. They sent me a telegram fabricating some story about their being incarcerated somewhere downstate, but not to worry. As soon as they did get back, they handed me a bogus scouting report. It contained the most detailed information — about the weather conditions, the band ("most valuable

APPETIZERS

Minestrone Soup	.75	Antipasto (Ind.)	2.25
Tomato Juice	.50	Shrimp Cocktail (4)	3.95

DI… S

Filet Mignon	10.95
Porterhouse Steak	9.50
Pork Chops (2)	6.75
Veal Parmigiana	6.95
Italian Sausage	5.25
Ground Round Steak	3.95
Ground Round Parm…	4.75
Ground Round S… …rooms)	4.95
Veal Scaloppine	6.50
Chicken Cacciatore	5.95
Fried Haddock	4.25
Fried Shrimp	6.95
Fried Scallops	6.95
Lobster Tails (2)	.00

Above Include: Bread, Butter & Garlic Sticks

Choice of Two: Salad w/choice of dressing (Blue Cheese .75 Extra)
Spaghetti, French Fries or Vegetable
(Extra Garlic Sticks 1.00)

SALADS (Ind.)

Italian	1.25	Russian	1.25
French	1.25	Blue Cheese	1.75
Anchovies	1.75		

Ice Cream

…	2.00
6 Cups	2.50

"meat" me at
DODGE INN
for steaks
ROCK HILL, NEW YORK

The Tiger bulletin board was the first place to research a good restaurant itinerary for the next scouting mission.

player," and the like), the cheerleaders (with the scouts' own rating scale), and they even included information about some obnoxious spectators. The actual "football" portion of this report had the most ridiculous formations and plays that I've ever seen. *What imaginations!* I still have both the telegram and the "scouting" report among my prized memorabilia.

In the early 80's, we had cut practice short one Friday and drove all the way to Utica to scout Rome. Upon arrival at a desolate stadium, we learned that, an electrical failure at the field had postponed the game until the next night. What to do? I'll bet you can guess. You're right. We "adjusted" with a longer-than-usual repast at *"Grimaldi's."* ...And a stop at *"The Florentine Bakery"* afterwards....

Almost annually, our good friend Barry Weinberg, the trainer of the Oakland *A*'s, visited us toward the end of the season. He would join us on scouting missions, and always marveled at how anyone (the head coach in this case) could sleep (snoring away) and eat popcorn at the same time, while riding to a game.

More recently, while scouting Warwick in post-season playoffs downstate, a tasty surprise greeted me when I opened my scouting case (actually, a portable "desk"). Without my knowledge, some of my guys — I think it was Ed "Fols" Folli or Bart Guccia — had packed several homemade turnovers in my spacious case. These were a specialty-of-the-house from *"The Circle E"* in Hancock (an automatic breakfast stop whenever traveling downstate via Route 17). *Ah, those rascals!* The turnovers tasted just as good outside in the cold as they had back in the diner.

With the use of computers, the tendencies of an opponent and a lot of other pertinent data became much more sophisticated and accurate. When video-tape became vogue in the 80's, most teams jumped on board because of this relatively inexpensive method of shooting game films (with the flexibility of making multiple copies for recruiting purposes). Subsequently, since camcorders were annually becoming more ubiquitous — showing up at stadiums with not only well-meaning relatives of players, but also with a few coaches for illegal scouting purposes — it was just a matter of time before the league passed a resolution that legalized the use of video equipment as a scouting device. This has only been in existence since '93. Personally, I'm glad that it came after I retired. Several coaches have told me that, while it provides a lot of flexibility, it detracts from the overall scouting mission to the extent that it has become a "social gathering" for several coaching staffs (*i.e.*, by allowing the camera to do all the work).

In my opinion, nothing can ever substitute for seeing the opposition with the naked eye, studying them, and getting a feel for them in person....After a delightful meal, of course.

Time Constraints and Family

"*Isn't daddy coming home?* Why does daddy have to stay up there all the time? Is daddy going to be late again?"

A coach's young child asks these questions. Often. If I had anything to do over again, it would be to spend more time with my family. In fact, if I hadn't had "blinders" on in those early years, I would have at least had the boys with me as team ball-boys during their elementary schooling. However, I'll be honest — it never even entered my mind. Because of the time constraints of my dual jobs, teaching and coaching, I didn't have much time to devote to my wife or children, especially during the season. I often didn't get home until after the little ones had been tucked in for the night. In the morning, I often left for work long before they were up. Although I would try to do things with them for the few minutes I was around, it seemed that someone or something outside was always making demands on my time. Or I was too exhausted and faded fast.

During all those years Pat continued to keep an immaculate house, reared our three children virtually alone, and played the role of secretary to the never-ending messages. Yet, she always had a delicious supper warmed up for me, no matter what ridiculous hour, and was always there to listen to my problems. I'll tell you what: Any wife of a high school head football coach should be considered for sainthood. They are a unique breed indeed — and they deserve many more kudos than they get. My hat is off to all of these ladies, *everywhere!*

You ask what time constraints? Would you believe that in the first twenty years on the job I was foolishly (but I didn't realize it at the time) putting in up to 19-hour workdays — seven days a week during the season — year after year?

Doing what?

First of all, teaching a full load of Latin and German, and head coaching, are really two full-time jobs when done properly. It's all those little "extra" things that teachers and coaches do — outside their structured school day and outside the practice field — that disgruntled taxpayers rarely see...or choose not to. Teaching takes plenty of preparation for which a normal school day is not geared, so it's done outside. A head football coach not only has to find time for this preparation, but he also must make time for the many other responsibilities which his job entails. I always said that no school district could have afforded to pay me on an hourly wage, even at minimum wages. I'd be a millionaire today if *this* had been the contract!

Here are just a few of these "extra" jobs which a head coach must deal with, other than the preparation for, and administration of, the entire football program from the modified football level up:

We counsel boys who may be in trouble. This is challenging and at times, an uncomfortable role for which most of us have not really been trained. (It has been said that a head coach's role is often that of a father, doctor, psychologist, and cleric.) What an awesome responsibility, when you think about it! Whoever said that Sunday should be a day of rest? For a football coach, it may be the most important day of the week. This is when the staff meets for most of the day, analyzes yesterday's game film and discusses adjustments in personnel. A lot of time is spent reviewing last year's game film (if you played the upcoming rival) and analyzing the scouting notes before developing a game-plan, a strategy for the next opponent.

The head coach deals with all publicity. Sometimes just that in itself is a full-time job. We don't have the luxury of a public relations person at our disposal. In the beginning, we dealt only with sports writers from the area newspapers. It wasn't too long before this expanded into dealing with the media from our opponents' areas all over the state. Then, along came radio and television — both wanting to broadcast games live, or by video tape delay. Next came state rankings (by the *New York State Sports Writers Association* — the *NYSSWA*, out of Syracuse). They wanted information, beginning around the late 60's. Eventually, *USA TODAY* conducted national rankings out of Chicago...but we didn't have to deal with this every year.

Just ask Pat or the children how often a reporter would interrupt a rare evening at home, or rarer yet, dinner with the entire family. Reporters and announcers wanted (and expected) pre-game scoops, post-game scoops, injury updates, predictions, strategies (the more experienced ones realized that this was a waste of time), line-ups, live interviews, *etc.* — *ad infinitum*.

Some of this took place almost daily during those few precious, "free" minutes during the school day — all year long, but mostly during the season. (I had some very understanding principals and students during my tenure.)

Of course, these media folks had their job to do, and we always respected that. We did not allow interviews with players, however. (As was the philosophy of John Wooden, the UCLA basketball coaching legend, we felt that teenagers had enough pressure on them already, without being quoted, or worse yet being misquoted, in print or on the air.) I realized that most reporters were conscientious and considerate enough to be discreet in using quotes from players. However, there were a few of the other types (reporters) around, too. I just felt I had more important things to do than worry about the dialogue between certain reporters and players — and a responsibility to the team, first and foremost. Thus, the gag-rule. I'm sorry that it infuriated most of the reporters, and hope that someday they will understand where I was coming from. Other than this, we tried to accommodate the media and cooperate with them as best we could. I met some extremely dedicated, industrious, and wonderful people in my association with the media.

Recruiting could be classified as another full-time job. Let me explain: We always felt that we should do everything possible for our seniors who wanted to continue with their education (which we really encouraged) and football. We contacted hundreds of colleges from every section of the country, in our search for the right school and a possible scholarship. We did this each year. There is nothing automatic about it. It takes a lot of work — a lot of man-hours, including numbers of letters, telephone calls, visits, personal interviews and film arrangements. We dealt with these recruiters somewhat during the season, often by telephone, but mostly recruiting took place at the end of the season and then continued all year until the next season.

We built up quite a "clientele" of college recruiters who became interested in the "product" we were turning out at U-E. During the legal period (governed by the *NCAA*) when these recruiters could visit schools, it was not unusual to have visits numbering in the hundreds at U-E after each successful season. Eventually, even after a mediocre season, U-E enjoyed the opportunity of having exposure to several recruiters.

It's surprising how many girls recognized some of these high-profile coaches. When our Mike Crounse was being heavily recruited (after the '85 season) Lou Holtz and Joe Paterno almost brushed shoulders going in opposite directions at U-E. Each was trying to sell Mike on the merits of attending his school. Having seen him in the halls, some

For all the hype and excitement, the selection process for "Blue-Chip" prospects can be a drain on the player and his "families" — on and off the field.

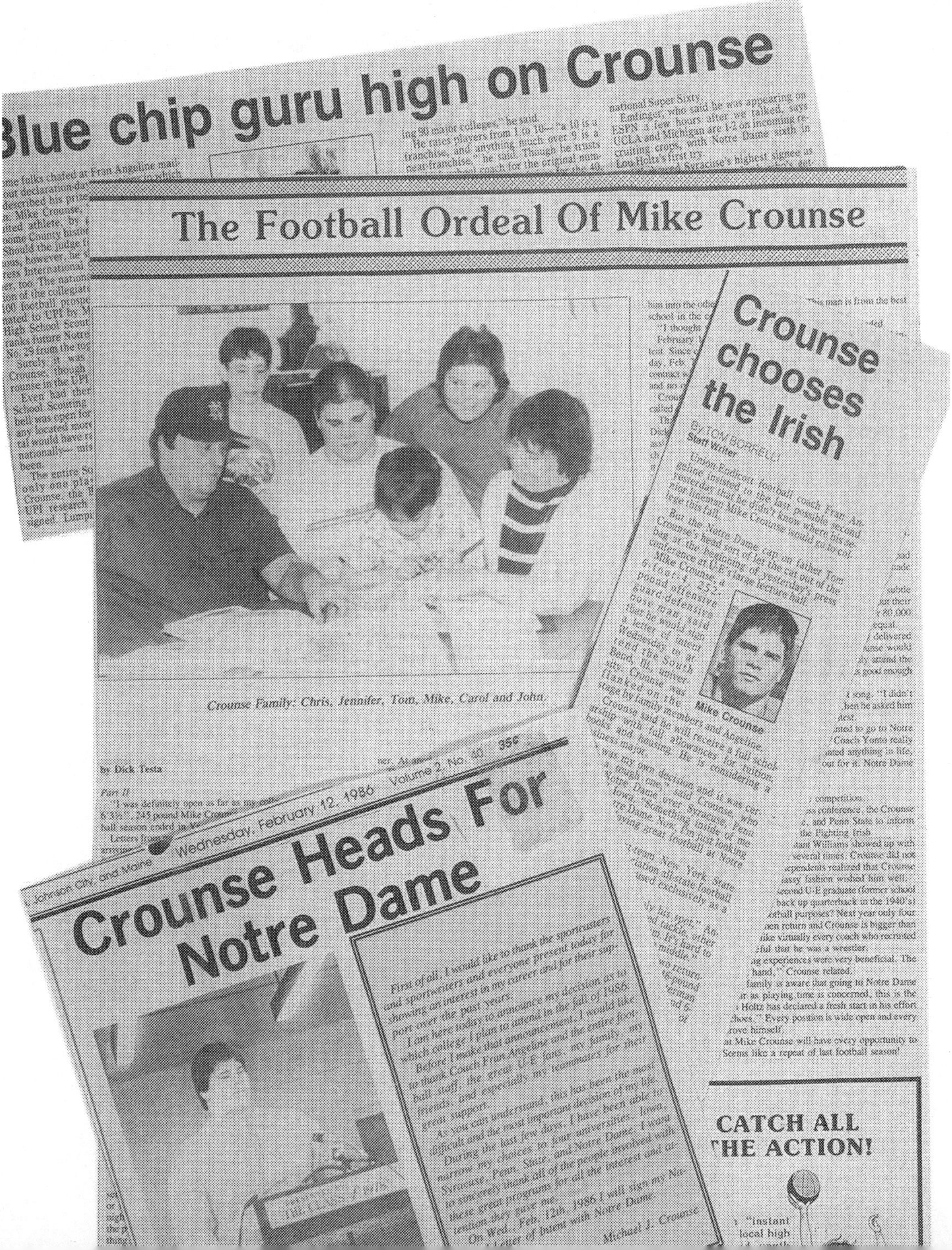

Blue chip guru high on Crounse

The Football Ordeal Of Mike Crounse

Crounse Family: Chris, Jennifer, Tom, Mike, Carol and John.

by Dick Testa

Crounse chooses the Irish

By TOM BORRELLI
Staff Writer

Union-Endicott football coach Fran Angeline insisted to the last possible second yesterday that he didn't know where his senior lineman Mike Crounse would go to college this fall.

But the Notre Dame cap on father Tom Crounse's head sort of let the cat out of the bag at the beginning of yesterday's press conference at U-E's large lecture hall.

Mike Crounse, a 6-foot-4, 252-pound offensive guard-defensive nose man, said that he would sign a letter of intent Wednesday to attend the South Bend, Ill., university. Crounse was flanked on the stage by family members and Angeline.

Crounse said he will receive a full scholarship with full allowances for tuition, books and housing. He is considering a business major.

"It was my own decision and it was certainly a tough one," said Crounse, who picked Notre Dame over Syracuse, Penn State and Iowa. "Something inside of me said Notre Dame. Now, I'm just looking forward to playing great football at Notre

Mike Crounse

Wednesday, February 12, 1986 Volume 2, No. 40 35¢

Crounse Heads For Notre Dame

First of all, I would like to thank the sportscasters and sportswriters and everyone present today for showing an interest in my career and for their support over the past years.

I am here today to announce my decision as to which college I plan to attend in the fall of 1986.

Before I make that announcement, I would like to thank Coach Fran Angeline and the entire football staff, the great U-E fans, my family, my friends, and especially my teammates for their great support.

As you can understand, this has been the most difficult and the most important decision of my life. During the last few days, I have been able to narrow my choices to four universities: Iowa, Syracuse, Penn. State, and Notre Dame. I want to sincerely thank all of the people involved with these great programs for all the interest and attention they gave me.

On Wed., Feb. 12th, 1986 I will sign my National Letter of Intent with Notre Dame.

Michael J. Crounse

CATCH ALL THE ACTION!

girls came to my classroom and asked with awe, "Is that Joe Paterno?" When I related this later to the man they call *"Jo-pa"* in *Happy Valley*, I changed my description of the girls' inquiry from one of "awe" to almost a "swoon." We both decided that I should pass that reaction on to his wife. These are really two unique coaches. Lou Holtz performed a few of his magic tricks, with coins, at the Crounse residence later that day.

In the summer it was not unusual to have a relaxing swim or tennis match interrupted by a recruiter's phone call or unannounced visit. All of this comes with the territory — at least my territory. We are very proud of the high percentage of our U-E football seniors who had an opportunity to continue their education...many with scholarships of varying amounts.

Some of these scholarships, in today's market, would be worth between $40,000 and $90,000 for a full, four-year education. *Not bad, huh?!*

Speaking engagements were also more time-consuming than one might think — both in preparation and presentation.

I could list many more "extras" which placed a burden on the time-factor, but I'm sure you get the idea. It is also true, that after a temporary setback and scare from a heart attack in January, 1977, I did some serious introspection during my recovery. One does have a lot of time to think. The major result of this was that I decided to delegate more responsibilities to my assistants. They responded beautifully, and this freed me up somewhat. I stopped putting in nearly 20-hour workdays, I can tell you that. (Maybe only 15-hour workdays.) I was fortunate to have received this "wake-up call" (and to have survived) at this juncture in my career.

Chapter Six

"Upon the fields of friendly strife are sown the seeds that, upon other fields, on other days, will bear the fruits of victory."

— General Douglas MacArthur

GO FOR THE RING!

— *THE MID 60'S, **1964-1966***

— 1964

"Vestal is going to win its third straight Southern Tier Conference championship and there's nothing anyone can do about it," trumpeted the pre-season headlines. And, with good reason. An abundance of championship experience was returning — plus Bobby Campbell. In fact, the Golden Bears were coming off back-to-back championships ever since Campbell had stepped on the field as a sophomore in '62. What a tremendous motivation this prediction was to the rest of the league, especially to Ithaca and U-E, neither of whom had a Campbell, but both returned some solid veterans. Don't try to tell those two teams that they were supposed to be bridesmaids again!

Through the indefatigable efforts of our U-E Booster Club, Athletic Department, and Administration, we realized a dream come true — *PERMANENT LIGHTS!* We anxiously awaited the arrival of the gigantic poles (on which the lights would be mounted) from California. They were erected while we were away at camp. The "Vestal" headlines, plus the sight of our permanent lights upon returning from camp, served as inspirations to our squad.

The opening weekend proved portentous as Ithaca stepped up and decided to "do something about these blatant predictions" by playing Vestal to a 6-6 tie.

Since '64 would eventually be U-E's first *STC* championship (the *STC* was formed in 1947, remember), we feel obligated to take you on our climb — our quest — by quoting the local media's capsule-summaries, game-by-game:

First the headline — then the summary:

'Tigers show EFA the Lights.'

"With Mickey Murtha pitching two touchdown passes and Union-Endicott defenders able to keep the ball away from Fred Greene sufficiently, the Tigers opened their football season with a smart 20-7 win last night at Ty Cobb Field and showed why some consider them Vestal's successor to the Southern Tier Conference throne."

'U-E Rips Elmira To Sit Atop Tier.'

"Senior quarterback Mickey Murtha engineered three touchdown drives and scored once on an interception, and his understudy Randy Zur threw a TD pass as Union-Endicott buried Elmira Southside, 34-0, last night in Elmira."

'Bring Back Vestal' - Kibler.

"A couple of years back the New Yorker ran a cartoon lampooning automobile advertising and the America media for battleship-sized cars.

In the cartoon the battered victim of a hit-run accident is telling a solicitous cop: 'I think it was a Lincoln. It had that big-car feel.' All of which is apropos of nothing except that last night there was the chance to interview another accident victim, Binghamton North's football coach Cardin Kibler, whose Indians had just been wiped out to a man, 49-0, by Union-Endicott."

'48-7 by U-E The Mostest.'

"When September crept up on summer this year and football began to encroach upon baseball, local sports fans were asking one another this question. Would this be Union-Endicott's year to replace Vestal as King of the Southern Tier Conference? This was pretty much resolved on Johnson Field's frozen wastes last night as the Tigers drubbed Johnson City, 48-7, for their fourth consecutive STC victory. It was the worst drubbing ever inflicted on a Johnson City team, at least since 1923 when The Press JC records begin."

I remember this game well. It was a bitter, brisk night at *Johnson Field,* but you'd never have known it by looking at our players standing there, as they listened to the announcer introduce JC's "unscored-upon Defense." I'll tell you our players' reaction: When we finally took the field, our captain, John *"The Plow"* Blishak, literally ran through one of the goal post supports. (It might still be quivering!) On our opening play from scrimmage, battering *"Blish"* carried on a *Trap* right up the gut and, behind some crisp blocking, didn't break stride until he had reached paydirt. It was the first of several more that night before the substitutes took over. Blish's comment to me, immediately after scoring: "I guess they are no longer 'unscored-upon'."

Ironically, Blish would join JC as a long-time assistant after his college days in Oklahoma.

Back to the summaries:

'U-E Uses Panzer Tactics.'

" They say that air travel is getting people from place to place a lot faster these days. Don't try to tell that to Union-Endicott coach Fran Angeline. Angeline's Tigers took the ground route last night at Ty Cobb Field and racked up 351 yards rushing as they clobbered outclassed Binghamton Central 55-0 in a Southern Tier Conference game."

'U-E Juggernaut Crushes Ithaca.'

"'They didn't show us anything we didn't expect,' said Ithaca coach Joe Moresco, 'For goodness sake, they didn't have to.' Unbeaten U-E didn't even require a change of pace as it stampeded the Ithacans last night, 33-7. Ithaca came in unscored upon since the opening minute of the season and left with a new kind of streak: scored-upon in four consecutive quarters, as Fran Angeline's Tigers continued their quest of the impossible, not one open frame all year."

Actually, it wasn't quite as easy as the media made it sound — is it ever against Ithaca? — especially with its *All-American* linebacker, Jerry Beach. This game would be our best effort of the entire season, including the two remaining games.

'U-E Beats Auburn, 14-6.'

"The undefeated Union- Endicott Tigers had to go all out last night to down a scrappy Auburn High, 14-6, at East high Stadium. A crowd of 3,000 including a large U-E delegation watched the game in ideal football weather."

As I recall, it was Halloween, and the trick or treat was almost pulled off by a fired-up and veteran Auburn *Maroon* team playing before its home crowd. We were lucky to *get out of there alive!* Little did any of us know at that time, that within two years we would be losing our valuable backfield coach, Bob Adams, and our athletic director, Hank Vetter (our sometime-chauffeur), to long and distinguished careers at Auburn, as head coach and athletic director, respectively.

And now the stage was set: Undefeated Vestal at 6-0-1 versus undefeated U-E at 7-0-0. I don't believe any single high school game in these parts has ever received so much of a build up. The *STC* coaches, and a few others, were polled for their predictions. The headline blared the results of this poll: ***'U-E 7, Vestal 0, Campbell 9.'*** It was billed as *"the game of the century."* Others called it *"World War III."*

A crowd, estimated at 16,000 - 17,000, got its money's worth...and then some. This game sent sixteen players to the two-platoon *All-STC* team — nine from U-E — a *STC* precedent. I really don't think anyone in the league would have argued if all of the Vestal and U-E starters had been selected. (However, that just isn't done.)

Several of these players would join the coaching ranks after college: from Vestal, besides Campbell, Barry Ilse would return to his alma mater; from U-E, besides Blishak, Mike Buchak and Tony Mastroianni would serve long tenures at Binghamton and JC, respectively. And we were happy to add Wayne Tidick to our staff for a long, dedicated career. (Incidentally, Bobby Campbell would also become my chief assistant, and sometime-tennis partner at *Golden Valley Football Camp* in Sidney.)

And now, the game:

'It's a Draw but U-E Bags a Flag.'

> "In a nutshell, there were two separate games: U-E completely dominating the first half and threatening to make it a rout with two first- quarter touchdowns. But the Tiger attack, behind awesome blocking, all but burned itself out in those first 12 minutes of play. The second half was just as dominating by the Bears, beating U-E at its own game, stopping the Tiger attack dead in its tracks and at the same time got its own, fumble cursed offensive going."

The second half was all Campbell. (Sound familiar?) The sub-headline read, *'U-E 13 Early, Then Bobby.'* But the main headline had captured the significance of the 13-13 tie: *We had won our first championship!*

We had dedicated ourselves through a trail of blood, sweat, and tears. Although the *Bears* had also finished undefeated, with a 6-0-2 record, and certainly played us evenly, we did not apologize for winning the crown outright, via a 7-0-1 record including a convincing 33-7 victory over Ithaca at 5-1-2.

Instead of classes on the following Monday morning, our new superintendent Richard *"Mac"* McLean, set a precedent by organizing an impromptu pep rally to honor the team. We were invited up on the stage. Mac, a former tackle-would-be-quarterback, displayed a potent arm while passing miniature footballs to a very receptive, enthusiastic, and appreciative student body. (Times have changed, and so have pep rallies — unfortunately — in this man's opinion.)

Yes, we had arrived — and we didn't hear any more *"Yabba, dabba, doo's,"* either.

— 1965

Our league mourned the sudden loss of our good friend, colleague and competitor, North's Cardin *"Kib"* Kibler, during the off-season.

Although '65 was somewhat anticlimactic for us, each season would present a new challenge, with new personnel — both our own and the other guy's. The role of defending champions was new to us. I am convinced that the climb to the top, no matter how far down one starts — filled with its share of trials and tribulations — is easier than remaining on top.

Two new coaches entered the league: Dick *"Conky"* Lalla, my predecessor as Colgate University's captain, came to Central with some impressive coaching credentials. Among them was the development of an exceptional quarterback in Schenectady — Pat Riley (yes, the *NBA* legend). Although relatively unknown at the time, it certainly didn't take long for Jim Weinman to make his mark at North. In fact, after our impressive opener over a strong Ithaca team, North upset us — and others — and just kept rolling. My only regret about Jim's brief, glittering, three-season stint, is that he wasn't really here long enough to "pay his dues." (*No fair, Jim!*)

However, we didn't exactly throw in the towel after being upset — nor did we sit around feeling sorry for ourselves. One cannot afford that luxury in this league.

We had several highlights in '65. Aside from beating Ithaca 20-0, we beat EFA, considered a contender, 27-6, and at mid season had another thriller at Vestal...in front of a packed house estimated at 12,000. It was a seesaw battle — with all kinds of excitement — ending in a 19-19 tie. (Both teams experienced frustration — for the second year in succession!)

As things turned out, the biggest game of the season came again at the end. But this time, it was JC at U-E. Both teams had the added pressure of the knowledge that North had already clinched at least a share of the title with a 13-12 victory over Vestal the previous night. So, both JC and U-E had a shot at a share of the title, depending on the outcome. Behind its leading rusher, Ron Lazo, JC pushed us to the brink. Junior safety, Randy Zur, made two key interceptions for us and Tony Mastroianni, our pint-sized dynamo, rushed for 140 yards in just 14 attempts. These were the two key statistics in this hard-fought 21-19 victory. Obviously, our 3 extra points — all runs by Tom Coonick or Ange Pasquale, loomed large as the margin of victory.

Our steady leader as captain in '65, was our center/linebacker, Dave Chernega. We also had a most unusual "weapon" in our arsenal — and he wasn't even a starter. Dick Seefried was like a "6th man" in basketball. He would enter games in obvious passing situations, automatically making him a marked man. At one stage of the season Dick had caught four bombs from our dynamite quarterback, Tony Pelino — and all four were for *touchdowns!* (How would Jerry Rice of the *49'ers* like that?!?) I've never seen nor heard of anything like this — at any level — since then.

So, we ended up sharing the championship with North, both of us with identical 6-1-1 records. North was led all season by several *All-Star* selections. Except for its senior quarterback, John Severance, they would all be returning in '66, promising to make life miserable for all of us next year.

What a season 1965 was, when you think about it. Someone pointed out that only a few points (in different games) prevented six out of the eight teams from being absolutely even. *It was that close!* Yes, '65 reflected parity, in every sense of the word.

— 1966

A couple of things happened around now:

The first one didn't affect anything — except the U-E uniform budget. We had a new athletic director, Bob Wurtenberg, who usually travelled by motorcycle (so there would not be any offers for rides to scouting forthcoming). Hoover and Moresco "ganged up" on me, and eventually forced a jersey change. For a few years, we had been wearing what we thought were exquisitely designed jerseys. One set featured an all-orange body with two-tone sleeves. The upper part was black with white "TV numbers," while the rest of the sleeve was orange. The other set was the exact opposite, with the orange and black reversed. Dick and Joe's complaint was that, because of the white striping on the ball, we were "gaining an unfair advantage of deception, especially under the lights". They both contended the color combinations on our sleeves blended in too much with the ball. (So, apparently, our *"three-yards-and-a-cloud-of-dust"* offense was developing some deception of its own.) Incidentally, much later (probably in the 70's) the league adopted our proposal to have teams wear their flashy, color jerseys at home, and use the white jerseys as visitors. To remain with the opposite format made no sense, and everyone agreed.

We, too, vigorously protested something annually — Vestal's *"Short Punt"* shift. Our argument dealt with the manner in which the *Bear* ends and backs shifted (especially its ends), throwing their arms up in a jerky, swinging motion, while resetting their feet and alignment. We felt strongly that this action simulated a snap, and therefore would often draw the defense offside. We felt that any action used with deliberate deception, for the purpose of drawing an opponent offside, was an infraction according to the rule book. Obviously, it became a matter of interpretation by the local officials. We even proposed that, if they weren't going to make it an infraction, they ought to at least outlaw it. Although many of them did agree that there was a "fine line" involved, nothing was ever done about it. We even approached the league about this. When I realized that we had lost our case, and that Hoover and Moresco had "won" their jersey protest, I accused the league of favoring seniority. To this day, Dick knows that I still feel that the shift was illegal.

The second development had a profound impact on the entire league. The Elmira schools, both charter members since the league's inception in 1947, suddenly withdrew from the league.

We'll never know the real reason why. All kinds of rumors were flying, of course. One was that EFA and ESS were having a tough time competing any longer. (I think someone was just "blowing smoke.") I feel that the other prevalent rumor had more credibility — that a few outspoken administrators from the Triple Cities had been hinting at the possibility of forming an "All Triple Cities League." Therefore, the Elmira schools felt that they had better hook up with the *Sullivan Trail League* already in existence in their neighborhood, before they were officially forced out. It is doubtful that any administrators who were actively involved back then would agree on the reason for the withdrawal.

In any event, most of the coaches were shocked — it took us by complete surprise. As one who not only coached against, but who had played against these great competitors from the west, I felt a personal, sentimental loss. (*"...and the sturdy sons of Elmira, to the Blue and White are true"* is a phrase that is an integral part of the lyrics of U-E's *"Alma Mater."*) A few of us felt that the departure of the Elmira schools marked the beginning of a slight deterioration in the quality of football in this area. Although it is certainly still a strong league today, we are convinced that it could never quite match the parity, competition, and fan appeal of that stretch of 1947-1965. Also, although noticeable to only a few perhaps, the exemplary camaraderie of the "brotherhood" of *STC* coaches began to erode to a certain degree. The new league would go through many growing pains (and "names") from then on.

Can you believe that, initially, Ithaca was not included in the plans for a new league by some Triple Cities administrators? This became evident at an early re-organizational meeting in 1966 held at Owego Free Academy. Although Dick Hoover and I had no formal vote (as mere coaches), we vehemently protested the obvious omission of Ithaca on some proposed, tentative schedules. (*A "railroad job?!"*) Our position was that it was unfair and unethical to ask such a highly respected and valued charter member of the old *STC* to leave — with no place to go — just for the sake of accommodating a few "new kids on the block" (new schools in the Triple Cities area). In retrospect, I hate to think of what might have been, had Dick and I not attended that particular meeting. Ithaca remained — and Ithaca's athletic director Joe Tatascore, Joe Moresco, Dick and I all breathed a collective sigh of relief.

The '66 championship was really a foregone conclusion, with very little argument from anyone. North not only had a wealth of experienced talent returning, as the defending champions, but also could boast of five returning bona fide *All-Stars*. The *Indians* dominated the league, and repeated as champions, but without sharing it with anyone this time. They beat both Vestal and U-E convincingly. The only blemish on their record of 7-0-1 (actually 4-0-1 within our temporary *STC* that was down to six teams now) was a tie at the hands of an undermanned, but inspired, 0-4-1 Ithaca team. Hey, this was still the *STC,* where on any given day, ANYBODY could knock off ANYBODY ELSE — *and often did!* A side note: The *Little Red* quarterback who engineered this upset was Joe Moresco, Jr., making for a mighty proud papa!

We had a lot of excitement in Endicott at the end of the season, too: A breakthrough over Vestal (finally — *whew!*), with yet another of its patented, speedy backs...Al Fenstemacher. *No tie this time!* U-E 20, Vestal 12. Even though we finished as runner-up with a 6-2-0 record (JC and North had beaten us), this felt just as gratifying as most championships — the monkey was off our backs. This Vestal versus U-E match-up eventually would be referred to as the *"Championship of the River,"* and the league would agree to schedule it as the annual final game.

This '66 season saw three future head coaches graduate. We're proud that two of them wore the *Orange and Black*. Our versatile, hard-nosed halfback/corner, Bart *"Goosh"* Guccia, would become my successor after several years of dedicated, loyal service as an assistant, and U-E's first lacrosse coach, as well. Our premier quarterback/safety and captain of the team, Randy Zur, after a brilliant career as the Syracuse *Orangemen's* quarterback, would eventually line up on the opposite side of the field as Central's coach. Garry Scutt was a thorn in our side as a dangerous halfback for the Oneonta *Yellowjackets*. He would go on to some great things, including a stint with the Green Bay *Packers* of the NFL, and eventually succeed Joe Moresco at Ithaca. Garry has also been the head baseball coach at a couple of schools in our league.

Our neighbors at Maine-Endwell also graduated three men during this era ('64-'66), who would eventually return to their alma mater as head coach at different times: John Furey, Jack Touhey, and Regan Beers. M-E also sent a tough little linebacker our way — Joe Lucia. Joe would join our football staff, and also take over the U-E swimming program before moving on to Cornell University as its head swimming coach. Johnson City graduated a tough competitor — its versatile athlete, Dave Skonieczki, who would have a brief fling coaching at Binghamton after college and before deciding to change careers. A scrappy, tough little linebacker from Central, Doug Stento, would return to Binghamton's sideline as a longtime, loyal assistant. EFA's rugged center, John Harrigan, would follow his dad, Marty's, footsteps in coaching by joining the Vestal football staff for a long, dedicated tenure.

ALL STARS — The mid 60's (1964-1966)

1964

School	*Position*	*Player*	*School*	*Position*	*Player*
JC	RB	CARL MCLAUGHLIN	EFA	GD	ROGER MALONEY
VHS	G	DICK SHIRLEY	IHS	E	RICH MILLER
VHS	RB	BOB CAMPBELL	IHS	T	JERRY BEACH
UE	E	FRAN PILARCEK	UE	C	PETE THEODORE
UE	E	MIKE BUCHAK	UE	QB	MICKEY MURTHA
UE	T	JOE McBRIDE	UE	RB	JOHN BLISHAK
UE	G	JOHN SIGNORELLI			

1965

UE	T	JOHN MATISI	IHS	RB	DICK BACKER
UE	C	DAVE CHERNEGA	BN	E	JIM HOWLAND
VHS	E	ART ALDEN	BN	G	GARY FARNETI
VHS	T	BILL PENDLEBURY	BN	QB	JOHN SEVERANCE
VHS	G	DICK SHIRLEY	BN	RB	TINY PAOLUCCI
VHS	RB	AL FENSTEMACHER			

1966*

* *Evening Press Triple Cities All Stars*

	OFFENSE			**DEFENSE**	
BC	T	TERRY McNAMARA	BC	LB	ROY SLEEPER
UE	QB	RANDY ZUR	UE	T	GEORGE BUCHLER
CC	E	EARL ROGERS	ME	T	GLENN McGREGOR
CC	RB	JOHN TILLAPAUGH	VHS	E	BRAD MAIN
JC	C	DON CARR	VHS	CB	DAN STARNER
JC	RB	JIM MACKO	VHS	HB	JOHN MOSS
VHS	G	WES PAWLOSKI	BN	E	BUCKY McGILL
VHS	RB	AL FENSTEMACHER	BN	MG	TINY PAOLUCCI
BN	E	JIM HOWLAND	BN	LB	GARY FARNETI
BN	G	HARRY HOOVER	BN	CB	JOHN TAYLOR
BN	T	NATE EUSTIS	BN	HB	RICHIE ALLMAN

The 1964 Union-Endicott* Tigers *brought their first* STC *Championship trophy to the school after 17 years of league participation.

The "teacher" of football "coaching" language students.

Chapter Seven

"Courage grows strong at the wound."

MUSINGS:

TEACHING / COUNSELING / LITTLE LEAGUE / SPECIALIZATION / OFFICIALS

Teaching

I never separated teaching in the classroom from coaching on the field. They were one in the same. The football field was my classroom, and if you were to ask one of my Latin or German students, they would probably tell you that my classroom was my field, as well.

Coaching is teaching.

The main difference is the built-in motivation. Many years ago, the chairperson of the *New York State Education Department of English* wrote an article entitled, *"Football Is the Best Taught Subject in High School."* What she was implying was that a student is in the classroom because his presence is mandatory, but an athlete is on the field because he chooses to be there. Therefore, she went on to say that the football coach has a distinct advantage over the academic teacher. There are many who would readily agree with this assessment.

One such person would be a former head coach of a very high-profile high school in the Chicago area (St. Rita's, as I recall). Early in my coaching/teaching career, I had an opportunity to hear this coach lecture at a football clinic held at *"Kutsher's"* in Monticello. He brought the house down with the following anecdote:

> The principal had summoned him to his office one day, because he was concerned about the classroom attendance of a certain player on the squad. "Your left tackle hasn't been attending Chemistry class regularly — in fact, he missed three out of five classes last week. And yet, he has never missed football practice. How do you feel about this?" asked the principal. The coach considered the charges against his ace tackle, and the principal's question. Here was his answer: "I've sold my program, Father — *now you sell yours!*"

I can assure you that I always attempted to find each student's "motivation button" in the classroom, as I attempted to find each athlete's on the field. Actually, I always felt that I had a distinct advantage by being in the classroom — just for the sheer visibility, if nothing else. But in reality, there was much more to it. By rubbing elbows with my teaching colleagues daily, we shared the same classroom problems and concerns, and often, the same students. The teachers knew that, when asked, I would gladly intercede for them in discussing with a student/athlete his lack of progress in a particular subject, or perhaps a disciplinary problem. A coach does have a certain amount of leverage along these lines if he chooses to exercise it. I was in a good position to 'sell" my product (football) to the Music teacher down the hall — to the Drama teacher next door — because we could develop a mutual interest.

I was also able to become acquainted with the entire student body, as well as the entire faculty, by mingling with all of them, all day long, every day. As a classroom teacher, I was not a separate "jock" whom most of them would see or recognize only down on the field.

I wonder how many language students have had their pictures in the newspapers and have been quoted in the *SPORTS* section? Mine have — on a couple of occasions over the years. They enjoyed this exposure immensely. They realized that they were a part of something "beyond the classroom." It didn't hurt their self-esteem, either.

Way back in the 60's, this coach had the distinct pleasure of a lengthy, private chat with the coaching legend, Vince Lombardi. He had come to the Triple Cities for a rare speaking engagement — a banquet sponsored by the area *Rotary* clubs. I was honored to be on the welcoming committee. You'd never guess the main thrust of our conversation. Here's your first clue: Unknown to most of his adoring fans, Coach Lombardi was a high school Latin teacher in New Jersey (St. Cecilia, I believe) when he was just getting started.

We spent almost an entire hour or so discussing the similarities between Latin and football. We agreed that there were several — especially discipline.

Counseling

There are many occasions in a coach's life when he becomes a counselor, an advisor, or an advocate for a young athlete who has turned to him for help. Often the coach is the only adult with whom an athlete feels comfortable in sharing his problems. At times a boy would bring his amorous problems to me. If it were serious enough, his girlfriend, and sometimes his parents, would join us. On these occasions, I had to draw upon my fatherly instincts *sans* formal training.

Sometimes a player might be in trouble with the law, in varying degrees. I have found that most law-enforcement officers are extremely cooperative — we are both "pulling for the kid."

Often a coach is the only advocate a youngster has. The increase in single-parent homes during the past two decades is mind-boggling — and problems have increased proportionately. A boy often finds himself in the middle of domestic crises, both large and small. Sometimes it is strictly a matter of economics and the ever-increasing constraints of the family budget. But more often it deals with tense relationships with other family members. Marital problems of the parents are usually reflected in an athlete's overall attitude and performance. Intervention is a very sensitive situation for a coach — again, *sans* formal training. This is because some parents feel threatened by "outside help" and interpret it as interference. Some feel that an offer to help is demeaning. In these circumstances, any effort by the coach to try to alleviate the situation can become counterproductive.

And guess who is caught in the middle of all this? — the athlete. I could rattle off the names of several of our young men who, remarkably, somehow rose above very difficult domestic situations. The deck was stacked against them, but with an abundance of intestinal fortitude, and perhaps a little help from "outside," they perservered — they gutted it out. I have always had great admiration for these men. Their presence now, as parents, makes our society and community richer.

Little League

Several questions keep bouncing around about the value of *Little League.* (Our discussion encompasses all leagues, all sports, for the little folks.) Some parents are concerned about it; others wonder about it; and some think it's the greatest invention since sliced bread. As a former *Little League* parent, a long-time resident in a *Little League* neighborhood, as well as a high school football and tennis coach, I have made several observations and have formed many opinions about *Little League* over the years. I have been involved in some rather heated discussions about the merits of some extremely talented little seventh grader (eleven, twelve, or thirteen years old) participating at the varsity level *IN ANY SPORT.*

This doesn't happen in football, but is commonplace in tennis, golf, and some other sports. How does this happen, anyway? It's because of the constant PUSH, PUSH, PUSH of some unknowing parent who is probably living vicariously through their child's athletic skills.

Before a seventh grader can participate at the varsity level in this state, the *NYSPHSAA* requires not only that a child pass certain special physical standards, but also that his parents submit a letter (an "application," in reality) stating that the child's emotional stability and maturity can handle varsity competition. I don't believe the dedicated people in our state department realized what a "can of worms" they were opening years ago, by passing this legislation allowing qualified, exceptional seventh graders to compete at the varsity level in certain sports. (No doubt, this was instigated through the efforts of some politician with a vested interest at the time.) I have never met a "pushy" parent or "personal club-coach" who didn't feel that his little darling, his protege, was ready, both physically and emotionally for the "big time."

My opinion as a parent-coach? Why do you suppose our governing body in Albany requires this special letter of application from the parents? No child of mine would ever be allowed to even "think about" varsity competition in any sport as a seventh grader, even if he had the potential of the next Emmitt Smith, or the next Andre Agassi. Why not? That's a fair question. Hey, I'm aware that there are always a few exceptionally gifted young athletes out there who can physically compete at the varsity level in some sports. However, I don't know any who are ready, emotionally, at such a tender age. Or even at the pro level. Just ask the former tennis-darling, Jennifer Capriati.

Let's just take one phase of the varsity experience to illustrate my concern: a bus trip. Sounds innocent enough, right? Considering the number of bus trips in some sports, some requiring a round trip of several hours, you'd better be advised about exactly what goes on. Do you honestly think that the 18 and 19 year old seniors are discussing athletic strategy or game plans on these trips? *C'mon, Mom and Dad!* We're talking about both male and female athletic teams here. Sooner or later there will be detailed discussions about boyfriends, girlfriends, parties, and all the "trimmings." I can assure you that your little one's auditory canals will be wide open.

Forgive me, but I am convinced that there is much, much more to it than some little seventh grader going out there and trying to whip some senior — there is *BEING A WHOLE CHILD*.

I know an intelligent boy fairly well, who just recently decided to give up a promising football career in his senior year. His reason? "I've been out there for all these years for all the wrong reasons — for my dad, mainly." How about that?

I have also observed some amateur volunteer coaches who give of their time and mean well, but who are sometimes misguided in their demands of little kids. I remember my shock at one particular *Pee-Wee* football practice long ago — under the "lights" — car headlights ringing the field. I was told that they were just concluding a three-hour practice in preparation for the "big game," scheduled for the next day. Please forgive my shock.

I have observed parents yelling like zoo animals at their young child's *Little League* games, as though there were something at stake. I remember my initial surprise (and disgust) when I first heard each ten, eleven and twelve-year old's batting average and other individual statistics blared out on the public address system as he stepped up to the plate. (This was my first experience as a *Little League* parent.) I saw more than one small set of legs quivering as each little guy would step up and listen to his own "stats." I also saw some parents puff-up, while others actually became embarrassed and hung their heads upon hearing their child's name and stats announced to the entire neighborhood (depending on the quality and condition of the amplifiers in the P.A. system).

Consider this: The *NYSPHSAA* has always discouraged any publicity of any athletic contests for modified or junior high school sports. (This includes 14-year olds, as well.)

In conclusion, I am not anti-*Little League*. I believe that it can serve as a valuable instructional tool — as long as it is conducted in MODERATION by all concerned. I endorse fully, and without reservation, our state department's suggested ban on publicity at the younger levels of athletic competition. Unfortunately, I seriously doubt that many *Little League* advisors, organizers, coaches, or administrators will ever buy it.

Specialization

The *NYSPHSAA* tells me that the following brief article I wrote a few years back, has now appeared in almost all of the states. A couple of coaches from different sections of the country contacted me after reading it. They concurred with my thoughts, so I'm convinced that this isn't just a regional concern. It may be even more appropriate today:

"The Great Robbery in High School Athletics"

by Fran Angeline

"Many of us have been acquainted with high school athletics at one time or another. Some of us have known, or known of that outstanding all-around athlete — the youngster who possesses a wealth of natural talent. We should be aware that these gifted, multi-sport athletes are a rapidly vanishing breed — at least in the larger high schools. Why is this happening? Should we be concerned? As a coach and parent who has observed this development for several years, I feel obligated to try to answer these questions. Let's address the first one: "Why?"

"In our society there has been an ever-increasing emphasis on organized sports at a much younger age. During the past couple of decades, youth leagues, clubs and the like have become ubiquitous. It is not uncommon today, especially in the suburban areas, to find some athletic programs geared for the pre-school child. Some of these programs function the year-round. A few of these children are encouraged to "specialize," even at that age.

"By the time athletes enroll in junior high school (or middle school), some are influenced to specialize. And as they enter high school, if they still enjoy several sports, many will feel the pressure to concentrate in one area. You see, somewhere along the line some adult — usually the coach — has sold the promising athlete the idea that the only road to excellence, including a scholarship, is to participate in "his" sport only — more often than not, all year-round. In fact, a few coaches demand this — at least in principle.

"Most experts would agree that some natural athletes would become more proficient in a given sport if they were to concentrate on strictly that sport for an entire year. Most experts would also agree that, due to physique and so forth, a few young athletes should concentrate on only one sport. But remember, we are discussing the "thoroughbred," the "blue-chipper," the one with "all the tools," the one who could "play them all" — and play them well.

"When the coach sells the athlete the idea of "putting all his eggs into one basket," is he really doing it for the athlete? ... Or for himself? Is college, perhaps, early enough to specialize? Rather, should not the talented athlete experience a variety of athletics during his most formative years and not be forced into an early choice?

"Do we, as educators and parents, owe it to him to encourage him to expand his horizons? Should we be concerned? Each of us must decide for himself."

I'm reminded of one boy in particular, who approached me prior to his junior year. He had never played football before, but asked for a shot at it. We welcomed him, of course. He had an exemplary work-ethic, became an *All-League* receiver/ kicker, and even continued playing football in college. He seemed to be having a lot of fun participating in his "new" sport. One day out of curiosity, I asked him why he had abandoned his other sport, at which he had been extremely adept. I found his response both interesting and revealing. Perhaps some well-meaning parents ought to listen to his answer: Basically, he responded that he had been participating in this other sport since he was about five years old — in different organized leagues and at all levels — and that he "had simply become sick of it."

I can't tell you how many young men who had been sold on specialization during their youth, approached me in later years as wiser adults, and in retrospect, told me "how much they wished that they had participated in as many sports as possible." Furthermore, many said that they realized too late, "that they had been victimized by some over-zealous, selfish coach."

Officials ("Zebras")

"You think that I was bad last night? — *Wait till you see me today!*" exclaimed the official.

A fellow *"zebra"*, Bill Starring, related that succinct rejoinder by Joseph *"Butch"* Burczak to JC's Coach Hank Diller before working a JC game one Saturday in the 60's. To complete the picture, it was related further that Butch, after his response, "leaned back on the bench where he was sitting and continued taking a few more drags on his cigar, completely at ease." Apparently Hank, while scouting a game at which Butch was working the previous night, felt that Butch's performance was sub-par. Hank was informing him of that fact during pre-game warm-ups at JC the next day, earning Butch's retort. (And Butch, I always felt, was one of our better officials.)

I would feel remiss if I omitted officials from this 36-year journey through Southern Tier football. They were an important part of the trip — unfortunately, sometimes more important than they should have been. Besides the reference above, a few other moments of levity occurred pertaining to officiating — mostly in the 60's.

One soggy, muddy night in '64 at *Ty Cobb Field*, one of our players, Mike Buchak, lost a contact lens during play. Conditions couldn't have been much worse for a search (and Mike didn't have a spare set). Players, coaches, and officials began scouring the muck for the missing lens. It was like looking for the proverbial *"needle in a haystack."* After a surprisingly brief search, Bill Starring, officiating the game that night, proudly held a tiny object on his finger and asked, "Is this it?" It was, and I'll bet you can guess what Bill said to me after I had thanked him profusely: "You're welcome, coach," he offered. And then added with a little mischievous twinkle and coy grin, "We aren't all blind, you know." I'll never know how he found the lens in that terrain, but I'm sure glad he did.

While we're on the subject of sight, or lack of, I must mention Don *"Cheetah"* Tomanek. We had been teammates at Colgate University and the rest of us used to watch him go through a daily locker room ritual of inserting his special contact lenses (a relatively new phenomenon for athletics in those days). Cheetah's eyesight was very poor then, and now he was an official. High school rules stipulated that an official should always be assigned to "inspect" any taping on all players before each game — to make sure that the taping was strictly protective and legal. Out of four officials (eventually a complete crew would consist of five), one would think that the guy with the poorest eyesight would be the last one assigned to "inspection duty." Can you guess who was usually given this assignment? Prior to his permanent move to Florida, it always seemed to be Cheetah. I used to pull him aside and ask Cheetah, kiddingly, how on earth he could even see the tape, let alone discern its legality?

Another rare occasion found four former college teammates together on Binghamton's field, just before yet another battle. But this time all four of us had different roles than in our playing days: Central was hosting U-E and Central's coach at the time was Dick Lalla (known as *"Conky"* in his Colgate days). Two of the officials assigned to the game were Cheetah Tomanek and Jack Spalik, a couple of Colgate's (and Johnson City's) finest. As the four of us stood around reminiscing and bringing each other up-to-date before the game, Conky, whose team was a decided underdog that night, suggested that we all go out someplace and enjoy ourselves "right now" — that the kids could play the game without us. I remember telling him that my "enjoyment" was going to take place on the field for the next couple of hours (we had a *powerhouse!*) — but that I'd be happy to meet with all of them after first "taking care of business"...as always.

I imagine that officials worry about inadvertently getting in the way during the course of a game. Of course, it comes with the territory, and everyone has seen it happen at times, at all levels. I can remember only two of these times ("casual" contact doesn't count) in all our games. This is a real tribute and testimony to the physical condition and agility of our officials. But, it still happens to the best of officials, and the following incidents occurred under similar circumstances:

Both Bob Harter and Steve Charsky, working separate games, were unable to avert the paths of powerful, raging U-E fullbacks. *Collision-time!* I'm happy to report neither man was injured that seriously. The rest of their respective officiating crews got a big bang out of these two collisions, as I recall — all part of their fellowship, and taken in stride, I'm sure. One, who was still "buzzing" at halftime didn't complete the game. The other, after sitting out a quarter, returned to the action and did finish the game.

Incidentally, it happened to a coach, too. M-E's Nick Ryder, a rugged, ex-University of Miami fullback, was struck down with a head-wound at Binghamton's stadium once. (I think the sideline first-down chains had caused the damage.) Nick, more embarrassed than anything, I'm sure, was taken by ambulance to the hospital. He received a few stitches and returned to the sideline before the game was over. (Can't keep a good man down for long!)

Not all officiating episodes were quite so "humorous." Why do a few officials forget that the spectators have paid good money to see youngsters compete against each other — not to see the "zebras?" Why do these same few not realize that these kids and their coaches have been busting their humps, with their share of trials and tribulations — every day for a long time — just for the opportunity to go out there and compete against each other fair and square? Here are a few officiating anecdotes that took place "on the road" in a few non-league games:

At Auburn (1964). Early in the game, our captain, John Blishak, had asked an official for clarification on a particular ruling. "Just get back to your huddle — we're all aware of your record down there," was the response. (How's that for "courtesy?")

At Norwich (mid-70's). We dominated the game, in spite of the officiating. The entire crew of officials, and one in particular, were inept. Toward the end of the game, one official (the weakest one, it so happens) came over to our sideline to apprise me (as was customary) about the time-out situation. "Sir, Norwich has used up two of its time-outs — you have all of yours left," he stated. Now you should understand that this official was standing only a few feet from me at the time. That was his mistake, his lack of judgement. I mean he had to know I had been building up steam as time went on. I simply said the first thing that came into my mind (not that a response from me was necessary). Gripping his shoulders (fairly gently — I think), I said, "Sir, you don't have any [time-outs] left...."

His eyes grew as big as saucers. As soon as that game was over, I had never seen a quicker exit by a group of officials in my life. Those guys were fast! They sprinted through the end zone, hopped into their cars, and were out of there — *pronto!*

At Rome (1980). Considering our depleted ranks due to previous injuries (missing three starters), and the quality of competition (highly ranked in the state), we were enjoying, arguably, our finest first half — ever. Holding a shockingly comfortable half-time lead already, the next play would have just padded it more. (I'll try to avoid getting too technical.) Rome's fine quarterback, Mark Blair, faded to pass from inside his own 15-yard line. A couple of U-E defenders reached him and spun him around. This spin caused him to become disoriented, and he weakly dumped the ball off to avoid a sack — but it was backwards toward his own goal line. The ball was bouncing around in Blair's end zone, and one of our guys alertly pounced on it.

Ruling: *"Incomplete Pass."*

I couldn't believe it! It was worth a time-out to me, as I summoned the referee who was on top of all of the action and had made the call. Then I proceeded to "walk" (talk) him through each step as I, and everyone in the stadium had seen it. He agreed totally with each step, including the last one of our recovering the ball in the end zone, and therefore, that it was a TD. "Then call it," I said — "Let me see your arms signal a TD."

His shaky words still ring in my ears: "Geez, coach, I can't do that now."

At Liverpool (in the Carrier Dome, *a year later — 1981).* A carbon copy of the Rome situation and mechanics happened to us once more. This time the ruling was *"In The Grasp."* I futilely argued that there was no such rule in high school — only in the *NFL* (to protect its million-dollar quarterback investments). Once again, the ruling stood unchanged.

At Ithaca ('86), our outstanding linebacker, Mike Guarnieri, was flagged for *"Unnecessary Roughness,"* carrying a 15-yard penalty with it. Upon further investigation, the accusing official showed me how Mike had used his forearm to ward off a block. I reminded this official that Mike was on defense, and that we teach the use of a "*Forearm Shiver*" to our defensive personnel — all perfectly legal (as long as it is not a blow to the head). I was "hot," and offered to demonstrate to this official (who I felt was big enough to handle it — he was bigger than I) what a legal "*Forearm Shiver*" looked (and felt) like. Only my assistants, who were holding me back, prevented me from an on-site demonstration of this popular defensive tactic. Perhaps it is irony that this official's son played some brilliant defense for us a few years later — and the "*Forearm Shiver*" became his best weapon.

Would you call these anecdotes examples of ineptitude, stubbornness, vanity, timidity — or "all of the above?" If all of this sounds like latent sour grapes, or whining, you should be advised that we won all five of the games just mentioned.

Here are a few "mystery calls" that still leap out at me. I won't even discuss the number of *"Inadvertent Whistles"* — NONE IN OUR BEHALF — that we have experienced. Why did they always seem to rear their ugly heads (piercing sounds of the shrill "inadvertent" whistle) in tight games and crucial situations? These probably happened to us more when we were on defense, and they seemed to come in bunches. We realize that these were not intentional, and always received an apology from the inadvertent whistler. But strangely enough, over a period of years a goodly number of "inadvertent whistles" seemed to be called by the same official. Coincidence? I would prefer to think so.

At Ithaca. I don't even remember the year, but I sure remember the circumstances: a tight game; a real defensive slug-fest. We had finally mounted a drive, and faced 4th-and-goal from just a few inches out. There's a *Quarterback Sneak* for the winning margin. We make it. Easily. A couple of officials made the TD signal. We win. *Elation!*

But wait, what's this "mystery flag" fluttering out of the pile like an obscene gesture? ...The infraction? *"Aiding and Abetting The Runner."* The detailed explanation was that our fullback had crashed into our quarterback, and therefore, "illegally helped" him across the goal line. *C'mon!* Down in the trenches, when 22 young men put their guts on the line in any goal line situation, on any level, there is usually a mass — a huge pile of 22 bodies twisted at all angles — as soon as the ball is snapped. (That's what this great game is all about!) We were penalized, and didn't make it from our new spot, much further away from the goal line.

What do you tell the kids? Maybe I should have listened more carefully to the following admonition from this same official earlier in that game (after I had questioned another call): "You're not gonna make a fool out of me on TV." (This was one of the pioneer-televised games in the league.) And lots of people always tried to argue with me that television had no bearing whatsoever on the performance of officials — no pressure. *Tell me about it!* You don't think an official can control the results of a game if that is his intent? Walk in my moccasins for a while.

At Vestal (1979). Arguably, the biggest game in U-E's proud football history up to that point — for all the marbles. At stake for us (aside from beating our arch-rival); closing out an undefeated season; winning the championship; retaining our unprecedented ranking of *Number One* in the state. Emotions on both sides were running high long before the game — if I could have, I would have put on a uniform myself. Here's how the game's referee greeted me just outside our locker room, a few minutes before taking the field. I have no trouble with this quote — *verbatim:* "I heard all about your play last week...."

The referee's reference was to our gigantic stepping stone to tonight — the previous week's game versus Ithaca. Most of the first half had been a defensive struggle. We finally reached inside the Ithaca 3-yard line just before halftime, but were out of time-outs. We had often practiced "time-management" — different ways of stopping the clock — when there are no more time-outs. The situation was perfect. Our outstanding quarterback, *"Fast Eddie"* Kobah, exemplified poise as he lined up our team with no huddle, took the snap, and intentionally over-threw our wide-receiver, versatile Gene Bucci. This stopped the clock. It was a perfectly legal and ethical play. We scored from there and broke the game open in the second-half.

Now, let's return to just outside the visitors' locker room at Vestal. The referee continued his greeting with this admonition (*verbatim*): "...You're not going to get away with that *in my game.*" Boy, did he bring me back to earth in a hurry. He really took the wind out of my sails. How's that for arrogance? I always thought it was their game...the players', the coaches', the schools', and the communities'. Well, in spite of this unsolicited pre-game warning, and an unprecedented 100 yards (approximately) in penalties walked off against the *Tigers* that night, they somehow maintained their poise (much better than their coach, I might add), and culminated a glorious season by achieving a low-scoring shutout.

Of all of these, you be the judge of which one you feel is the worst one — the toughest one to live with. But, you'd better wait until I share one more with you:

Rome at U-E (1982). Number One in the state versus *Number Two*. Both undefeated. Both proudly wearing their *Orange and Black*. A crowd estimated at 12,000 - 13,000, including Dick *"Mac"* MacPherson and several of his Syracuse University assistants filled *Ty Cobb Field*. After a scoreless first-half, our line finally sprang its premier tailback, Bobby Norris, off-tackle for a 53-yard TD. 7-0. Just before the fourth-quarter, Norris and our diminutive, gutsy quarterback, Al Pedley, collaborated on what looked like the same exact play. But their deception worked to perfection. Norris was tackled by a couple of Rome defenders while Pedley cleverly hid the ball, and took off around the end for a huge run — down inside of Rome's 20-yard line. The U-E bench and stands *erupted!*

But, what's this flag way back near the line of scrimmage? No sweat — it must be some defensive infraction on Rome when they were tackling Norris. I should have known better. The call was a *"Holding"* penalty — *but it was on Norris!* Have you ever seen a back get tackled because of his excellent fake, and then try to get up and get to the huddle for the next play? So this long, crucial run was brought all the way back, and then some. I couldn't believe it, and apparently I had lots of company, because the yardage walk-off for this "infraction" was accompanied by the loudest booing that had ever rushed forth from that stadium (and still holds the "record").

This singular, controversial call absolutely deflated us. Naturally, it had the opposite effect on Rome. In the waning minutes of the game, Rome's speedy, all-purpose man, Paul Pelton, returned a punt to our 16-yard line. They went on to beat us, 8-7, mainly on the arm of their nifty quarterback, Chris Destito. Indeed, it has to rank as one of the classic high school games anywhere.

What might have happened had Pedley's long run not been called back? The facts are: we were ahead, 7-0, and would have had a first down and 10, on their 20-yard line, with lots of momentum. The rest is pure conjecture. If I could, I'd gladly accept and trade all of the other calls combined, which have been discussed here, for that one against Norris. That call can never be erased, not even in the sands of time.

In my entire life as a player, coach, scout, and spectator — at hundreds of games at all levels — I have never seen nor heard of *"holding"* called on a faking back who is getting tackled. Nor have I ever seen or heard of enforcing the *"aiding and abetting the runner"* infraction called at Ithaca.

Of course, there are always a few of the well-meaning faithful around who try to placate the offended team, school, community, players, or coach with these words: "Don't worry, these calls will balance out in the long run."

I have news: *THEY NEVER DO...NOT EVER*.

I have never taken these flags or incidents personally, however, and therefore, harbor no grudges against any of the offending parties. How could I? If I did, I would be saying that they did this to a bunch of hard-working kids. With intent. I may be naive, but I don't think any adult would, or could, knowingly be that malicious in what is really just a game — certainly not a life or death issue. (We did have to rescue an official from one of our players who was trying to break down the thick, wooden door of the officials' room — this was in frustration following a controversial field goal attempt versus Central in 1975.)

These few men are accountable to themselves, *"The Man In the Glass"*, not to me. For the record, I have found that most high school football officials have a genuine affinity for kids and football. Most of them are very conscientious about their responsibility to these kids and to the game. Most of them are not in it for the money (which isn't that great). After all, it is an avocation to them, and perhaps for some it is an extension of their playing days. I sincerely believe that most officials realize that they have done their job if they are as inconspicuous as possible on the field. That is the coaches' measuring stick when evaluating them. Think about it. Win or lose, how often have you left a stadium, and have not even been aware of the presence of officials? If so, they must have worked a solid game.

Who is the best? That question is like asking who is the best football player you ever faced. I won't duck the question. Having played all over the state against the best competition possible, it is my opinion that the referee from Waverly, Jack Terwilliger, would be tough to surpass for consistency and overall game-management.

There is more camaraderie among officials and coaches than one might realize — some lasting friendships. Pat and I have been guests at a couple of banquets, held annually by both the Triple Cities Chapter and the Elmira Chapter of Football Officials, and enjoyed ourselves very much. As a matter of fact, upon my retirement, the Elmira Chapter honored me at their banquet. Pat has found a prominent place for an exquisite plaque, representing my association with the Elmira Chapter, on the wall of my "Championship Room" (which she calls, *"Fran's Shrine"*) at home. Elmira's gift will always conjure up some pleasant memories of the mutual respect we shared with each other.

Snow was always a potential foe for field and fans at Ty Cobb Stadium...
or at any late season football game in New York's Southern Tier.

Chapter Eight

"The spirit, the will to win, and the will to excel are the things that endure. These qualities are so much more important than the events that occur."

— Vince Lombardi

THE BITTER and THE SWEET

— THE LATE 60'S, 1967-1969

The late 60's produced several players who would make their mark as coaches in the area. Johnson City's Mark Decker would eventually become Owego's main man, while Bob Griffiths would return to his alma mater as an assistant. Vestal's Tony Policare would become the *Golden Bear's* head coach, and Ted Oliver would become an assistant in the area. Ithaca contributed Dan Gottfried (whose dad, Chuck, would become JC's coach). The Bryant brothers from Owego would join the ranks — Tom as an assistant, and Bill as the personable athletic director at Ithaca.

Little did I realize then that two of our young *Tigers* — Ed *"Fols"* Folli, an *All-League* safety, and Dan Consol, an outstanding offensive tackle, would make so many contributions to our football program after college. Fols would become our defensive secondary and special teams coach, as well as our very successful baseball coach. Dan would develop offensive linemen and double-up as our staff comedian, especially with his impersonation of celebrities and advertisers. (His specialty: The voice of local retail barker, Tommy Van Scoy.)

North graduated two of these future coaches in succession. We were elated that one of them, Tony Romeo, decided to move west and become our defensive coordinator — the man mainly responsible for the swarming U-E defenses for many years. Hank Nanni would return to the Binghamton sidelines as its offensive coordinator and eventually, as basketball coach. Across town, Central also sent an outstanding player west, as Tony Rose would join our staff (and become our "Handy Andy," too).

Television was making inroads in high school football during this span, and began televising a game each week. Most fans, players, coaches, officials and administrators loved the exposure — that's human nature. This coach always felt that each school should be compensated, monetarily, for allowing TV and its advertisers to use/exploit the players and coaches. However, I was a lone voice.

Moreover, I felt that there were some serious drawbacks to this phenomenon. Television placed even more time-constraints on an already-loaded daily schedule for the coach because TV required all kinds of advance information including detailed line-ups. A few of us (very few, obviously) will always wonder how much extra pressure this placed on the players (just teenagers, remember — some as young as 15), and officials as well. (Do you remember the official in the last chapter who told me once, "You're not going to make a fool out of me on television?")

The physical set-up of television at a stadium usually eliminated an entire section for fans — usually at the best vantage point in the stadium. In some stadiums this could translate into a sizeable loss in revenue, as well as in cheering. Lastly, some teams had the honor(?) of being televised often — much more than others. In those early days, we always felt that this provided the scouts with yet another opportunity to study these teams in action, at their leisure, in their living rooms — thus, gaining an unfair advantage. One has to wonder if all of this exposure was actually worth it or not.

The league went through some anxieties during these years. There were many relatively new schools springing up in the area. All had been playing against a few of the *STC* schools, and in some cases, with great success. At a meeting held at the U-E Board of Education Office on Lincoln Avenue during the early stages, a few of these "new" schools — feeling their oats — stated emphatically, "We'll play anybody, anytime." Obviously, they had experienced some success against one or two *STC* schools, and wanted a piece of the big pie.

Dick Hoover reacted strongly to this statement and I jumped right in to echo his concern. As nearly as I remember, he said,"You may have had some success against a couple of us, and may have even beaten up on one from time to time — but, playing us weekend after weekend would be a different story, and I don't think you would like the results." Unfortunately, for the most part, Dick's realistic words of advice fell on deaf ears.

Finally, the league decided to have two divisions (the precursor to eight divisions): The *"Western Division"* would be comprised of the old six *STC* schools; the *"Eastern Division"* would consist of the "new kids on the block" — Catholic Central (which would become Seton Catholic Central), Chenango Valley, Maine-Endwell, Owego Free Academy, and Susquehanna Valley. This new league was called the *"Southern Tier Athletic Conference" (STAC)*, and would exist for fourteen years, adding more teams, and therefore, multiple divisions.

In our annual post-season meeting after the '67 season, held at Central, an early adjustment took place, even before the new league had tried its wings. In retrospect, this adjustment, although seemingly insignificant at the time, would set an irrevocable precedent forever (and its tenor still exists today). Coach Diller of JC approached the old *STC* schools and pleaded his case of JC being the smallest school in the *Western Division*. (This was my first knowledge of that fact — it had never entered my mind while coaching there in the previous decade — nor would I have cared if I had known that JC was the smallest of all eight schools in the old *STC*.) For this reason, he asked if we would have any objection to JC's moving to the *Eastern Division*, with the understanding that the *Wildcats* would still maintain the old rivalries, as often as the schedule would permit?

I don't remember one objection. What *naivete* on our part! It quickly became a done deal.

Before we leave this subject, it should be noted that the gap between JC's enrollment and the largest schools (Ithaca, U-E, and Vestal at the time, I believe) had widened since the inception of the old *STC* in 1947 — but I'm not sure how significantly. A new catch phrase, *"EQUALITY OF COMPETITION"* (*i.e.*, enrollment rather than quality-of-program becoming the only criterion for competition), was born and has been growing in stature ever since. It is well documented that this has always been a bone of contention for some of us — allowing a few schools to be a *"big fish in a small pond,"* strictly on the basis of enrollment.

As we were to learn in time, much of it depended on who decided the make-up of each pond.

Talk about some type of state playoff system, or at least post-season play, began to surface at this time. Also, the *NYSSWA* began to rank teams around the state.

The *Two-Point Conversion* after a touchdown became an option in 1969. Personally, I have never liked this choice. I have always felt that, rather than improve the high school game, it has detracted from the kicking game and the decision also puts undue pressure on a high school coach. I have always felt that the *Two-Point Conversion* works better in college and more so, in the *NFL,* where the single point-after is so automatic with their specialists...all well-paid kickers.

During this three-year span, Vestal's record was 22-2-0, while Ithaca's was 21-3-0. Although U-E was a factor in '69, with a 6-2-0 record, no one else actually threatened these two powerhouses at all.

Vestal and Ithaca had several standout players during this span. Two Vestal backs would compete in the *NFL* after impressive college careers:

John Moss was pro-size as a schoolboy. (We haven't lined up opposite too many fullbacks with frames approximating 6 feet 5 inches and 225 pounds.) Big John was just as valuable on the other side of the ball, and would eventually be tapped by the University of Pittsburgh and then, by the Detroit *Lions*.

John Schultz, although a more normal-sized back, was equally devastating. He would take his speed and slashing running style to the University of Maryland and then to the Denver *Broncos* where he became one of their tri-captains. A few years ago John and I bumped into each other at breakfast one morning. At my request, he showed me his *Super Bowl* ring. I remember that I was so impressed with this runner-up ring that I couldn't imagine what the champion's ring would look like. As we reminisced that morning, John confessed to me that in all of his football days, he had never been hit as hard — "with black and blue marks lasting days afterwards," — as he had when playing against U-E. Whether that's true or not, it was very kind of him to say. But then, that's typical of this unassuming young man.

The last of Dick Hoover's sons, Kirk, was a dangerous quarterback during this era. As the 60's neared their close, I remember musing what a thrill it must have been to coach one's own sons. Vestal's year-by-year records during this span were: 1967, champions, 8-0-0; 1968, champions, 8-0-0; 1969, 6-2-0.

Ithaca was no less impressive and was just gearing up for the early 70's. Its records during this same span were: 1967, 6-2-0; 1968, 7-1-0, (ranked as *Number One* in the state by the *NYSSWA;* the first team from around here to achieve this honor); 1969, 8-0-0, champion and ranked *Number Two* in the state.

Three names that will conjure up some pleasant memories for the *Little Red* faithful during this era are these skill-position, super athletes:

"All-Everything" Steve Webster started for Ithaca as a freshman (unheard of in this league!). He became an *All-American*-caliber running back/linebacker/punter/kicker/kick returner. (What's left?) He was a big, bruising freight train with exceptional speed and deceptive moves.

Walt Snickenberger has to be one of the most talented, versatile wide receivers ever seen in this area, while Tom Parr, Ithaca's gifted quarterback/safety, would go on to a record-setting career at Colgate University as co-captain and quarterback.

During the late 60's, Owego Free Academy was the dominant team in the *Eastern Division* with an impressive, aggregate record of 17-5-1. Coach Dick Wheaton's *Indians* captured the crown in '67 and '69, and were runners-up in '68.

Our '67 and '68 seasons were mediocre by our standards. We had a hard-nosed, small running back by the name of Joe Roberto. Years later, whenever Joe discussed his tour of duty with our military forces in Vietnam, he related how he often would draw upon his high school football experiences to help pull him through some precarious situations. Our captains were, respectively, Gary Iacovazzi and John Pinto.

We had a unique quarterback-alumni procession worth mentioning at this time. Kirk *"Corky"* Barton, our '67 quarterback, would take his golden arm to the University of Buffalo, following in the footsteps of U-E's Mickey Murtha there. Murtha broke all of the passing records at the University of Buffalo, formerly held by Johnny Stofa (Miami *Dolphins* of the *NFL*), before his career was over. Then along came Barton who proceeded to break Murtha's records.

Ironically, two of Murtha's and Barton's favorite targets during these record-breaking seasons were Chuck Drankoski, a '65 M-E graduate (who would eventually serve brief stints as a U-E assistant and head coach at Norwich High School), and Ithaca's Joe Moresco, Jr. Barton's successor at U-E was Kenny Nigh, who not only did some nice things with the football for us, but served as our resident-poet, as well. Some of his productions are still in my file of memorabilia.

There were three unusual occurrences in the late 60's:

The first, we'll call *"the hidden ball trick."* During one of the first televised games around here, Ithaca was playing the big one of the season at Vestal. I don't know all the details, nor the circumstances surrounding this, but at a certain juncture in the game, the referee (Tom Carey, I believe) was trying to get the game ball (rubber, I believe) from Joe Moresco. Joe was holding the ball behind his back, out of sight, and only Joe can tell you why he was not about to relinquish it. This went on for what seemed like an eternity to the spectators — and this "game" of keep-away was *captured in its entirety on TV!*

The second occurrence was during the last week of the season after *Ty Cobb Field* had been inundated with the first huge snowfall of the year. It is documented that a few hundred people from the community showed up with their snow shovels and worked through the night to remove the snow. (The ground was too soft to use the big plows.) One of this number of volunteers was our superintendent of schools, Dick McLean. Do you know many superintendents today who would sacrifice a night's sleep and roll up their sleeves for the love of the game? (Thanks, Mac!)

A third rarity took place in '67: JC at U-E. It was a very cold, muddy night. After just a few minutes of action, it was difficult to distinguish any players or numbers out there — just twenty-two muddy teenagers getting it on. JC took a halftime lead, 6-0. Since we were conveniently at our home field, we switched to our other set of game jerseys (clean, dry and *visible!*) at halftime.

When we came out for the second half, the weather had not improved. Coach Diller immediately recognized the jersey change and protested to the officials that there was not enough contrast between their muddy jerseys and our "new" ones. The officials, almost apologetically as I recall (that didn't happen to me too often) — in going by the book and upholding this protest — asked us to switch back to the sad-looking, "steaming" pile of mud (jerseys) on the middle of our locker room floor...whimpering plaintively to be laundered. Try to imagine how it felt to put these on again. So, when we returned for the second half...once again...there were two muddy teams...once again...only distinguishable by their helmets...once again.

Were our players happy about this development? Final score: U-E 19, JC 6. You be the judge.

One of these '67 *'Cats,* Jim Truillo, would eventually join our staff. Of course, we have never allowed him to forget about the night of "the jersey switch."

We had some solid players in the '69 season, and were definitely in the overall picture. We were led by our captain, Monte Cole, a rough, tough defensive end and our versatile quarterback/safety, Tom Mason. I've never seen a quarterback hit opponents any harder.

Near the midpoint of that '69 season, marking about the first third of my coaching career, I experienced the absolute nadir of my career — and what would have to rank as one of the genuine heights of it — both within a span of a few weeks. It is said that one remembers a loss more so than a victory. That may be true. I'll bet you didn't think I was going to mention any bitter along with the sweet.

Well, at mid-season, the Chenango Valley *Warriors* and U-E *Tigers* clashed for the first time. This was an average CV team by anyone's standards — one that had been struggling within its own division throughout the season. However, it had a superb athlete at the controls, Dick Barvinchak. It also had a lot of heart. Despite these attributes, U-E was a heavy favorite, at least on paper. (However, games are not played on paper.) Barvinchak scored on a long, perfectly executed option-keeper in the opening minutes of the game, and the CV defense truly lived up to its nickname, *"Warriors,"* by a gutsy goal-line stand at the end. In between, the post-game write-up describes what happened best: "U-E absorbed 105 yards worth of penalties to kill at least four scoring opportunities." The final score: CV 6, U-E 0.

A new sound erupted from the U-E "faithful" that night — a resonating boo. It reminded me of *New York Giants' Stadium*, except that these were not professionals who were being booed so loudly. Had we spoiled our fans? The adage, *"What have you done for me lately?"* came to mind.

But, the effect of the results of this game didn't end there at the field. After a lousy night's sleep, the Angeline household discovered that we had had some "visitors" at our house overnight. Apparently, some disgruntled fans had entered our garage during the night and had completely covered our station wagon with a mixture of flour, eggs, ketchup, and karo syrup. (Naturally, we called the police, but the perpetrators were never caught.) Believe me, it took a long time — time that I just did not have — to remove this mysterious mix of ingredients from the car. I'm sure that other coaches have similar stories. Anyone in this profession had better be thick-skinned or he won't last long.

I was soon to learn, however, that the worst was yet to come: Upon my arrival home on Monday night, Pat informed me that all three of our children had come home from elementary school quite upset. Our middle child, Larry (who would be named to an *All-American* squad one day), was especially distraught. It seems that some of their classmates were chastising their dad — calling him a bum, uttering several other epithets, and saying that he ought to quit or be fired. These youngsters were really only repeating what they had been hearing from their parents all weekend long. The problem was, how did one explain this to three little folks, aged six, seven, and eight, who loved their daddy? The loss itself, the booing, and the car-prank bothered me, but did not endure for very long. The hurt I felt for my children, however, ran very deeply. One had to wonder if the pittance received in a coach's paycheck was really worth that kind of pain. This memory can never be erased.

A few weeks later, we all picked ourselves up off the ground and climbed the mountain. We travelled across the Susquehanna to meet the highly regarded *Golden Bears* who were 6-1-0 at that time. There was much, much more at stake than the *"Championship of the River,"* or even the *STC* championship — and our guys must have sensed this. Considering all of the factors, that night had to be one of the most perfect, inspirational performances by any of our squads. Ever.

The *Tigers* were not to be denied. U-E 32, Vestal 14. It's called *P-R-I-D-E!*

Coming off the field, several "glad-handers" emerged from the shadows to shower us with hugs, phony handshakes, and congratulations — the same ones who had booed us previously. The same ones who had called me a bum were now calling me a genius. I was neither a bum nor a genius — just a hard-working guy who was trying to do his best with what he had.

There were also many sincere, loyal fans who were quite overcome with emotion. There were copious tears of joy — but no one shed any more than this coach, his wife, and his children.

The U-E football rollercoaster of the late '60's had both its steepest decline and highest peak in 1969.

U-E Saves Its Best for Vest

Not Just CV's Barv Marvelous at U-E

By SOREN NIELSEN

The upstarts in bleachers, across the field, from a stunned Union-Endicott crowd began the countdown at 16 seconds. When they reached zero, the unlikely miracle was officially in the books.

Chenango Valley, a 60-40 loser last weekend to Owego, had beaten U-E three-TD conqueror of Owego. ... Warrior defense had ... the strong-running ... for 46 minutes foll... only score in the 6...

U-E had more th... cion that Dick ... might pass the bal... ceiving the kickoff... cion paid off whe... defenders rushed ... er the quarterbac... thrown 52 times f... last week. The fa... py.

The next play ... be the whole ha... vinchak rolled l... tion play, looked ... ing Jim Ken... again as Kendri... outside, took o... without any ... Jim, then cut l... and went 84 ya...

Barvinchak's ... longest scorin...

since Don Link's 86-yard kickoff return against what was then Eastwood High of Syracuse in a 1961 loss.

TD Tale

CV	U-E	SCORING PLAY	TIME
		First Quarter	
6	0	Barvinchak, 84 run. Levers kick short	1:38

Statistics

	CV	U-E
First Downs	6	16
Rushing plays, yds.	23-93	53-146
	2-6-1	8-19-3
	22	104

Mason Hurls 3 In 32-14 Win

...on had thrown only one ...own pass all year until ...ght, but twice he found ...ar catcher Mike ...ky all alone in the end ... the other time he ze... ...n David DeAngelo.

...ile Mason was loo... ...the Vestal defens...

235-pound fullback Jo... Crooks was running like a p... in picking up 134 yards on ... carries after never showi... 60 for any previous game. T... converted tackle's 34-y... blast with 5:55 left was ... lockup play for coach F... Angeline's Tigers.

...owing the se... ...last Vestal ...rst, by C... ...ame five ...estal had ... down fro... ...tly made ... fumble ...score, a ... Toth.

CV stuns U-E, 6-0; North, Ithaca winners

THE SUN-BULLETIN—Binghamton, N.Y., Monday, Oct. 13, 1969

34

STAC football continued along its wild and exciting way Saturday with Chenango Valley's 6-0 upset of Union-Endicott providing the biggest surprise.

In other action North High trounced previously unbeaten Maine-Endwell, 30-6, and Ithaca protected its unblemished record by downing Owego 15-6.

Dick Barvinchak, CV's quarterback, scampered 84 yards on a option play early in the 1st quarter for the only scoring in the CV-U-E game. CV's record is 1-3 for the 1969 season while U-E stands at 2-2.

U-E gained 146 yards on the ground and picked another 100 yards in the air, but several timely interceptions by CV defenders and some devastating penalties stifled all the U-E drives.

Tom Moffit picked off a Tom Mason pass in the 2nd quarter to stop one U-E march, and Barvinchak grabbed another Mason aerial on his own 21 to deny the Tigers once again.

After passing for a phenomenal 456 yards in CV's 60-40 loss to Owego last week, Barvinchak was limited to a 22 yard passing game on Saturday, partially due to a hand injury he suffered in the first quarter.

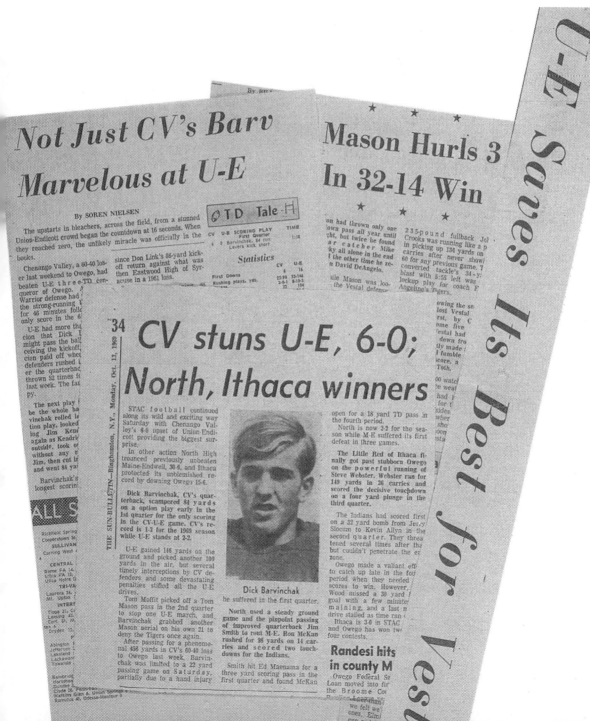

Dick Barvinchak

North used a steady ground game and the pinpoint passing of improved quarterback Jim Smith to rout M-E. Ron McKan rushed for 98 yards on 14 carries and scored two touchdowns for the Indians.

Smith hit Ed Maenama for a three yard scoring pass in the first quarter and found McKan open for a 18 yard TD pass in the fourth period.

North is now 2-2 for the season while M-E suffered its first defeat in three games.

The Little Red of Ithaca finally got past stubborn Owego on the powerful running of Steve Webster. Webster ran for 149 yards in 26 carries and scored the decisive touchdown on a four yard plunge in the third quarter.

The Indians had scored first on a 32 yard bomb from Jerry Slocum to Kevin Allyn in the second quarter. They threatened several times after th... but couldn't penetrate the e... zone.

Owego made a valiant eff... to catch up late in the fou... period when they needed ... scores to win. However, ... Wood missed a 30 yard ... goal with a few minute... maining, and a last m... drive stalled as time ran ...

Ithaca is 3-0 in STAC and Owego has won tw... four contests.

Randesi hits in county M...

Owego Federal Sa... Loan moved into fi... the Broome Co...

...we felt we... ...ones. Elm... ...ego and C...

ALL S...

Richfield Spring... Cooperstown 36... SULLIVAN... Corning West ... CENTRAL ... Rome FA 14... Utica FA 13... Utica Notre D... TRI-VA... Laurens 24... Mt. Upton ... INTERS... Tioga 21, C... Lansing 42... Cort. St. M... Dryden 11... Abington ... Lawton ... Lakeland ... Lackawan... Towanda ... Bainbridg... Horsehea... Dundee ... Clyde 36, Penn Yan ... Watkins Glen 6, Union Springs ... Romulus 40, Odessa-Montour 0

ALL STARS — THE LATE 60's (1967-1969)

1967

OFFENSE School	Position	Player	DEFENSE School	Position	Player
OFA	T	GARY KLOSSNER	ME	L	STEVE JOSLIN
OFA	RB	TOM BRYANT	JC	LB	JIM MACKO
UE	E	TRACY GALLOWAY	UE	L	JOHN SCHAFFER
IHS	E	WALT SNICKENBERGER	UE	S	KIRK BARTON
IHS	C	JIM ELMO	IHS	L	DAN GOTTFRIED
BC	T	STEVE KOST	BC	L	JERRY GAMBELL
BC	G	JERRY GAMBELL	BC	HB	DAN ZEMBEK
CC	G	GARY MARTIN	CC	LB	DOUG KOZEL
CC	QB	STEVE STILLEY	VHS	L	JOHN MOSS
CC	RB	DOUG KOZEL	VHS	LB	CHUCK PARR
VHS	RB	JOHN MOSS	VHS	HB	BILL TILLOTSON

1968

BN	T	JAKE ZUMBACH	ME	T	LEO HAUPTFLEISCH
VHS	G	WARREN PLYMALE	OFA	LB	BRAD BIDDLE
VHS	G	BOB VANDERBURG	UE	T	MONTE COLE
VHS	HB	JOHN SCHULTZ	UE	DB	ED FOLLI
VHS	FB	DAVE DREW	IHS	DB	TOM PARR
IHS	E	WALT SNICKENBERGER	IHS	S	WALT SNICKENBERGER
IHS	E	JIM HIPOLIT	VHS	E	MATT OLENSKI
IHS	T	STEVEN STANTON	VHS	E	MIKE KACHER
IHS	C	BEAVER VanOss	VHS	MG	BOB VANDERBURG
IHS	QB	TOM PARR	VHS	LB	DAVE DREW
IHS	HB	KEVIN FILLEY	VHS	LB	TED OLIVER

1969

VHS	C	TOM LLOYD	BN	LB	DENNY POWELL
SV	HB	JIM WILLIAMS	ME	L	STEVE FENSON
CV	E	CHUCK SLAGLE	CC	L	BILL KOZEL
CV	QB	DICK BARVINCHAK	CV	DB	DICK BARVINCHAK
BC	FB	ROMAN KAZMIERSKI	BC	T	TED DAVIS
BC	T	TED DAVIS	IHS	L	GARY HUNTER
UE	E	MIKE PRISLUPSKY	IHS	LB	GARRY WILHELM
UE	T	JOE MARINO	IHS	LB	STEVE WEBSTER
UE	G	BOB GRANT	IHS	DB	DOUG McELROY
IHS	G	GARY SHIPPOS	UE	L	JOE MARINO
IHS	HB	STEVE WEBSTER	UE	S	TOM MASON

The Athletic "Competition"

"It is not the critic who counts, not the man who
points out how the strong man stumbled,
or whether doer could have done better.
The credit belongs to the man who is actually in the arena,
whose face is marred by dust and sweat and blood,
who strives valiantly, who errs and comes short again and again,
who knows the Great enthusiasms, the Great devotions
and spends himself in a worthy cause,
who at best knows in the end triumph of high achievement,
and who at worst if he fails, at least fails while Daring Greatly.
So that his place shall never be with those cold and timid souls
who knew neither victory or defeat."

— T. Roosevelt

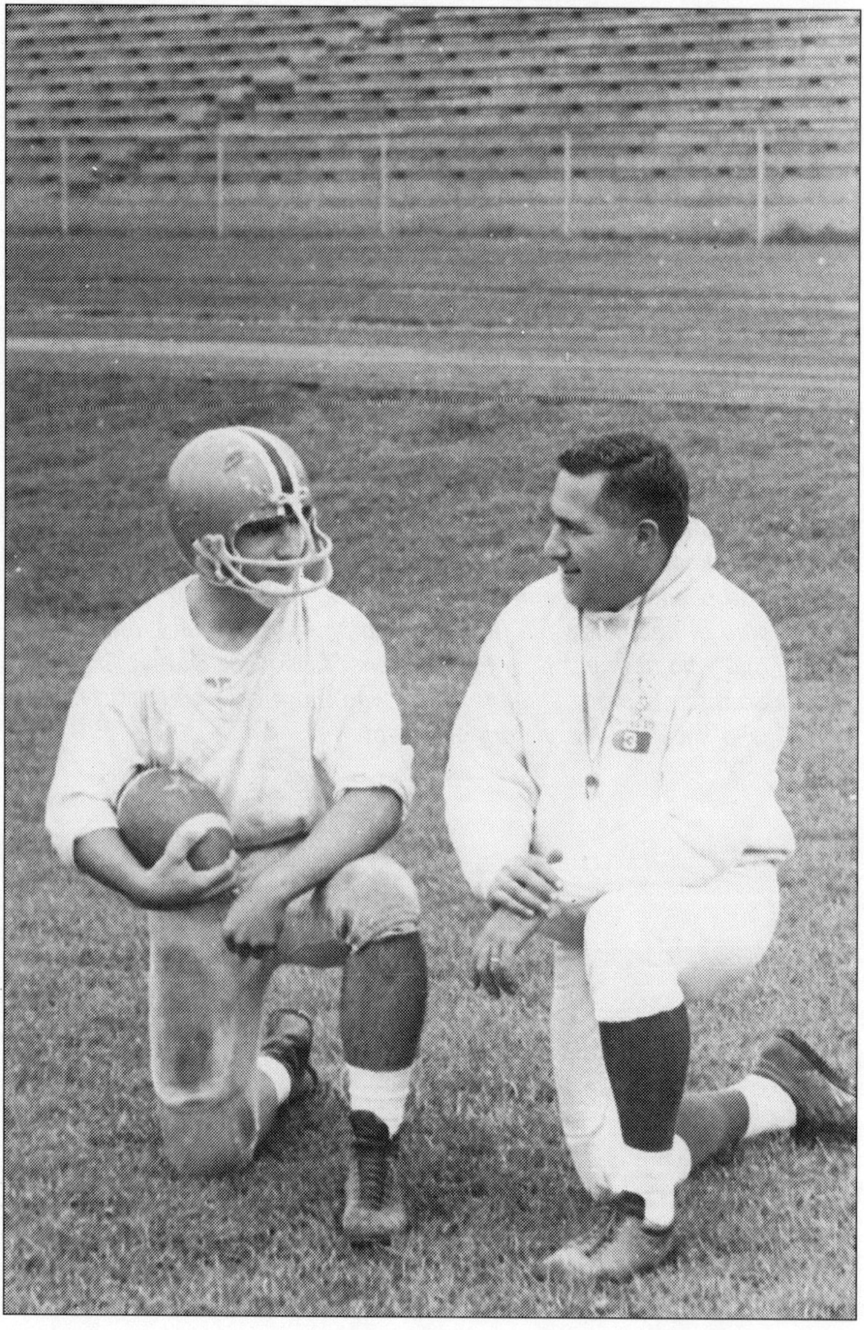

The coach with 1970 All Star *team captain, Jerry Hanley, who, like so many Southern Tier athlete/scholars, used his abilities wisely to advance his education and his enjoyment of life.*

Chapter Nine

"Fight on my merry men all, I am a little hurt, but I am not slain;
I will lay me down for to bleed a while,
Then I'll rise and fight with you again."

— Anonymous: *"The Ballad of Johnnie Armstrong"*

HANGING ON

— THE EARLY 70'S, 1970-1973

More changes took place in the early 70's. Apparently, our league decision-makers believed in the philosophy of "more means better." Therefore, they readily accepted two more schools to the league — both Homer and Cortland were added to the *Eastern Division*. A few years later, two more schools were welcomed aboard — Oneonta and Norwich, resulting in a total of fifteen teams now. *One happy family!* (I apologize for any sarcasm.)

While all of this was going on, in 1971 the *NYSPHSAA* finally consented to allow what many of us had been proposing for a decade or more: A nine-game schedule. This was a real breakthrough.

To make the league balanced again (numerically?), three divisions were established — five teams per division. This would last only four years. (Does anyone notice a trend developing here?)

Ithaca continued its total domination of the league in '70, '71, and '72, with Vestal nipping at its heels consistently, and U-E, a factor in '71. Including their '69 team, The *Little Red* rattled off an unprecedented four undefeated seasons in a row, rolling up a remarkable 33-0-1 record during this stretch, while also adding another mythical *New York State Champion* trophy in 1970 to their ever-bulging trophy case.

And why not? Steve Webster was named the *"New York State Player-of-the Year"* in '70. Ithaca also had two exciting trigger-men at the controls: Tom Snickenberger, a rangy, 6 feet 4 inch quarterback, eventually exchanging a football for a scalpel as a highly respected Orthopedic surgeon in the Triple Cities today. And the '72 quarterback/safety was the last of the Moresco sons, Tim — pound-for-pound as tough as they come — who would continue his sparkling career in the defensive secondary with Syracuse University, the Green Bay *Packers,* and the New York *Jets*.

Vestal also had some impressive manpower to keep pressing them during this span, with the likes of the Moss brothers, Chuck and Kevin — *twin terrors!* The great John

Schultz was winding up his high school career. Another *Golden Bear* standout, lineman Doug Kerr, would become a prominent Orthopedic surgeon in the Triple Cities and eventually perform arthroscopic surgery on one of this coach's deteriorating knees. (So, he and Ithaca's Tom Snickenberger are both still "operating" on their opponents years later...in a different "arena"...with different "tools"...and with much higher stakes.)

Coach Jud Blanchard of North and I unleashed a relatively new weapon around here during this span: The use of the field goal as a complement to the offense. The conference soon sat up and took notice of two, very talented "golden toes": North's Dennis Chavez and U-E's Jim Bennett. In fact, Chavez' field goal in our '70 game provided North with its margin of victory: North 16, U-E 14. (He was only a freshman then!) Unfortunately for us, he would repeat the same process and provide North with the winning margin again in his senior year ('73): North 17, U-E 14. In between, the 1971 score was: U-E 27, North 14, but no field goals were kicked; However, I'd be surprised if this unusual occurrence from '72 doesn't still hold some kind of record:

Both of these rival kickers were at their peak. In a real defensive struggle, nine points were scored — *all by field goals!* Fortunately for us, Bennett kicked two while Chavez kicked one. U-E 6, North 3.

I knew that I would miss my old coach and close friend, Ty Cobb, when he passed away in the spring of '72. I hold so many pleasant memories of this warm, affectionate, gentle man — a man with the highest scruples. He and his lovely wife, Helen, helped plot our honeymoon at their favorite beach in Ocean Park, Maine, and we vacationed there together thereafter. Ty taught us all, including our children eventually, how to "ride the waves" body-surfing. As a native of Maine, he gave us a highly qualified education in the "propah" way to eat a steamed "lobstah" — getting the meat out of every nook and cranny. I wouldn't eat the tomalley ("green goo"), and he'd chide me with that unique Maine twang, "Whah, Frannie," — he always called me Frannie — "yaw not eating the best paht."

Ty was joined by another old pal in that "special place for coaches" — Binghamton North's Gordie O'Reilly. Gordie had become like a father to me at camp. We had developed a special relationship. He used to tell my parents how he envied the ease with which I could fall asleep.

A couple of veteran football officials also passed on. Bill Starring was snatched from us suddenly. Bill was a true sports fan, and even popped up at a few tennis tournaments in the summer. And it never seemed the same going up to Ithaca, whether playing or scouting, without seeing Augie McCali. He was a big presence on the field. I remember how he loved good, clean, hard-nosed line play. He would often comment (in praise) that some lineman was really "doing a number" on his counterpart.

Our 1970 team at 5-3-0 was led by our rugged *All-Star* (both ways: fullback and corner), and captain-elect, Jerry Hanley (my brother-in-law). We experienced two setbacks that year. First, we were "snake-bitten" by losing our premier, three-year starting quarterback/safety — the multi-talented Tom Mason. He suffered a pre-season injury from which he never fully recovered, although he gave it his best shot on virtually a leg and a half. The other setback happened at the hands of Vestal, on a night when The *Bears* thoroughly out-manned, out-gunned, and buried us, 68-27. John Schultz set a rushing record that night of 302 yards on just 24 carries.

The finale in '70 was a classic in every sense. The two undefeated heavyweights, Ithaca and Vestal, met for all the marbles. The game contained all the elements of one of the most exciting championships ever played — including an extremely crucial, and controversial, play which I'll try to reconstruct as best I can.

Vestal punted to Webster (who finished his high school career by amassing 3,481 yards on 542 carries, incidentally!). The ball hit the ground and was lazily rocking around. Vestal's coverage personnel, thinking the ball was dead, let up (some accounts say that a few players from both teams had even begun to enter the field for the change of possession). Apparently, no whistle had blown, however, so Webster (probably deserving an *"Oscar"* for feigning nonchalance and disinterest in the ball) alertly picked up the ball and raced 92 yards — *untouched!* The *Bear* defense was superb all night long, but Webster also took a kickoff back 80 yards for another TD. The final score: Ithaca 22, Vestal 20.

Another nail-biter during this era found the *Tigers* travelling to the *Bears'* den to challenge Vestal. It was the middle of the '71 season and the *Golden Bears* were enjoying their top ranking in the state. U-E exploited the use of the field goal to the fullest degree — and it almost resulted in a major upset. Combined with a relentless, swarming *Tiger* defense (Dave *"Ukie"* Bayer, playing on the nose, stepped up very big for us, as I recall — and he had lots of company), Jim Bennett's field goals of 19-, 33-, and 46-yards (no "gimmie's" there!) kept Vestal off-balance for most of the night. With a few minutes remaining, U-E led, 9-7. Vestal's prize halfback, Bill Cooksley (Endicott bloodlines), made one of the most spectacular runs by an opponent ever witnessed by this coach. With time at a premium, and the game on the line, Bill seemed to be swallowed up by a horde of *Orange and Black* defenders after a short gain. However, his legs kept churning. Uncannily, Bill spun out of that pile and took it in for the winning points, 13-9.

Perhaps we should have realized earlier in the season that Bennett's toe was portentous, as his 39-yard field goal was the only score in a defensive struggle versus a JC team that was always well-prepared under Coach Paul Munley.

This '71 U-E team, a prime contender, had its share of fine players, led by Captain Dom Pisani, a *"Blue-Chip"* tackle/linebacker, and a slick quarterback, Rod Zur (called *"The Glider,"* for his fluid motion and hurdling ability). Every man on that squad also exemplified pride, all season long. They more than earned the right to remove their inherited moniker (compliments of one sports writer in reference to the previous season's Vestal debacle) — *"Pumpkins."*

We then experienced a couple of tough years in a row. Our'72 captain-elect was Dennis Belardinelli. We finished this season with a very disappointing 4-4-0 record. We felt that we had better talent, experience, and size than the record reflected (definitely one of our biggest teams). We must have done a poor job of coaching. Unfortunately, the '73 season was also a struggle for us. But realistically, with only our captain-elect, Curt Parvin, returning as a bona fide starter (and he was a really good one), and one tackle and one quarterback with some experience, our expectations were not too high.

The 1973 season belonged to Vestal all the way. The *NYSSWA* agreed, by presenting the *Golden Bears* with the trophy that depicted the *Number One* team in the state. They posted a 9-0-0 record with a very talented group that worked well together.

In the *Eastern Division*, Bob Costello's Chenango Valley *Warriors* made plenty of noise in both '70 and '71, as champions (co-champions with OFA in '70, each with a 5-3 record) with an aggregate record of twelve wins, five losses, no ties.

After three-division competition began in '72, it didn't take long for Jack Radzavicz's Cortland *Purple Tigers* and Mike Norris' Homer *Trojans* to make their marks as they were co-champions of their respective divisions in '73 — Cortland, with M-E: 8-1-0 in the *"Central" Division*; Homer, with SV: 6-2-0 in the *"Suburban" Division*.

Two schools emerged as powerhouses in both '72 and '73: Coach Nick Ryder's 17-1-0 Maine-Endwell *Spartans* in the *Central Division*, and Coach Cal Rucker's 14-3-0 Susquehanna Valley *Sabers* in the *Suburban Division*. They not only had a couple of classic games with each other, but beat up on a few of the larger, more-established area schools, as well. (Ourselves included....)

Two future head coaches emerged during this span:

Steve Deinhardt of North was a unanimous choice as a lineman on U-E's *All-Opponent* team in 1970. Shortly after Binghamton's merger of North and Central in the early 80's, Steve would make an indelible mark by building the Binghamton *Patriots* into a consistent power. He eventually added the role of athletic director to his duties.

Dave Williams was one of Vestal's men in the trenches. He would return to his alma mater as a long-time assistant, and just recently, was elevated to head coach.

Two men, Joe Holly and Larry Rowe, who have made their marks as outstanding administrators, first paid their dues with brief stints as head coach at Central. Our Jerry Hanley had a brief stint of coaching at the prep-school and college levels before entering the business field and becoming a very successful banker in the Philadelphia area.

ALL STARS* — THE EARLY 70's (1970-1973)

** Remember, only the names from the more prominent teams discussed in each chapter will be listed from now on:*

1970

OFFENSE			DEFENSE		
School	*Position*	*Player*	*School*	*Position*	*Player*
WESTERN					
VHS	E	MARK HALLER	UE	DE	JERRY HANLEY
VHS	HB	JOHN SCHULTZ	VHS	L	DAVE CAMPBELL
UE	T	RICK THOMAS	VHS	DB	MARK NELSON
UE	E	MIKE PRISLUPSKY	IHS	L	REX STARK
IHS	T	GEORGE DENTES	IHS	E	JOE BACKER
IHS	QB	TOM SNICKENBERGER	IHS	DB	STEVE WEBSTER
IHS	HB	STEVE WEBSTER			
EASTERN					
CV	HB	JIM KENDRICK	CV	L	MIKE HUGHES
OFA	E	AL HOPKINS	CV	LB	MIKE GEENTY
OFA	T	STEVE BURRELL	CV	DB	KEN DEMOSKI
OFA	HB	BRUCE LAYMAN	OFA	E	BERNIE BAILEY
			OFA	DB	LARRY SCHWEITZER

1971

WESTERN					
VHS	G	DOUG HINK	VHS	E	KEVIN MOSS
VHS	C	LEO COOK	VHS	G	CHUCK MOSS
VHS	HB	BILL COOKSLEY	VHS	DB	BOB GLEASON
IHS	E	NICK MARSELLA	UE	T	DAVE BAYER
IHS	T	GEORGE DENTES	UE	LB	DOM PISANI
IHS	HB	CHARLEY HUGHES	UE	S	TOM BALENO
UE	E	JIM BENNETT	IHS	E	NICK MARSELLA
UE	T	DOM PISANI	IHS	T	STU DEAN
UE	G	FRANK SKIERSKI	IHS	LB	GEORGE DENTES
UE	QB	ROD ZUR	IHS	DB	LEE TUNON
UE	FB	DAVE BANGO	IHS	S	JACK WARNER
EASTERN					
CV	E	JIM BENKO	CV	E	PERRY KENDRICK
CV	G	STEVE TAYLOR			
CV	HB	JIM KENDRICK			

1972*

* *Three divisions now:* Metropolitan; Central; Suburban

METROPOLITAN					
VHS	E	MARTY OLENSKI	VHS	T	JIM AIKENS
VHS	G	PAT O'BRIEN	VHS	G	JOHN MERRITT

The 1970 Ithaca Little Red *were undisputed kings of the league and earned their ranking of* Number One *in New York State high school football.*

VHS	C	DAVE FERRIS	VHS	LB	WAYNE PELLOW
VHS	RB	LEN KAMINSKY	IHS	E	STU DEAN
IHS	E	STU DEAN	IHS	T	ROB AINSLIE
IHS	T	CHARLEY WELLS	IHS	DB	TIM MORESCO
IHS	RB	DAVE PITZER			
IHS	Q	TIM MORESCO			

CENTRAL

ME	T	STAN KUHLHELM	ME	E	KEN ZUNIC
ME	T	WALLY YELVERTON	ME	MG	CHUCK FENSON
ME	QB	MARK FRENCH	ME	LB	JOE McKEE
ME	HB	DAVE CARD			
ME	HB	DAVE HASEGAWA			

SUBURBAN

SV	T	AL ROBINSON	SV	E	CURT ROBY
SV	T	DAN GORMAN	SV	L	TOM STEBBINS
SV	G	MIKE SMITH	SV	L	DAVE MUSKA
SV	C	BOB MILLER	SV	LB	RAY CARLSON
SV	QB	DAN SMITH	SV	DB	DAN FARRELL
SV	HB	JIM GARRIS			
SV	FB	PAUL ANDERSON			

1973

METROPOLITAN

VHS	E	TOM ROLOSON	VHS	E	VINCE BOUSA
VHS	T	GAVIN KERR	VHS	E	JOHN MATTIMORE
VHS	G	CARL RATHJE	VHS	G	FRED GOODALL
VHS	QB	JIM GYLES	VHS	T	DUNCAN McCORMICK
VHS	HB	BILL BROWN	VHS	LB	DAVE WALTER
VHS	FB	BILL SELSMEYER	VHS	S	PAT GILLARD
VHS	T	DUNCAN McCORMICK			

CENTRAL

ME	E	KEVIN LOVELAND	ME	E	KEN ZUNIC
ME	T	KEN ZUNIC	ME	LB	JOE McKEE
ME	G	MIKE KORUTZ	ME	HB	KEVIN LOVELAND
ME	C	PETE BURNETT	CORT	E	JIM CASEY
ME	QB	MARK FRENCH	CORT	MG	SAM CUTIA
ME	RB	STEVE BIZILIA	CORT	LB	DAVE ALOI
ME	FB	RICH ABRAMS	CORT	HB	TONY OPERA
CORT	G	SAM CUTIA			
CORT	RB	DOTY WILLIS			

SUBURBAN

SV	T	DAN GORMAN	SV	E	DAVE MUSKA
SV	G	TERRY DIX	SV	LB	DAN FARRELL
SV	C	KEITH DODD	SV	HB	BOB FANCHER
SV	QB	DAN SMITH	HOM	E	ED JONES
SV	HB	TED STORTI	HOM	T	LOUIE MORGAN
HOM	E	BENNETT BEAUDRY	HOM	LB	BERT DAVENPORT
HOM	G	DON WRIGHT	HOM	HB	BRIAN WILCOX
HOM	HB	BOB AVERY			

Commitment to Excellence

"I owe most everything to football, in which I have spent the greater part of my life. I have never lost my respect, my admiration or my love for what I consider a great game. And each Sunday, after the battle, one group savors victory, another group lives in the bitterness of defeat. The many hurts seem a small price to have paid for having won, and there is no reason at all that is adequate for having lost. To the winner there is one hundred percent elation, one hundred percent laughter, one hundred percent fun; and to the loser the only thing left for him is a one hundred percent resolution, one hundred percent determination. And it's a game, I think, a great deal like life in that it demands that a man's personal commitment be toward excellence and be toward victory, even though you know that ultimate victory can never be completely won. Yet it must be pursued with all of one's might. And each week there's a new encounter, each year a new challenge. But all of the rings and all of the money and all of the color and all of the display, they linger only in the memory. The spirit, the will to win and the will to excel, these are the things that endure and these are the qualities that are so much more important than any of the events that occasion them. And I'd like to say that the quality of any man's life has got to be a full measure of that man's personal commitment to excellence and to victory, regardless of what field he may be in."

— Vince Lombardi

Chapter Ten

"A man's reach should exceed his grasp."

— Robert Browning

A CORNERED TIGER

— THE MID 70'S, 1974-1976

"Yeah ... But Who's On First?"

More juggling and jockeying within the three divisions took place in the mid 70's. Had the enrollments of the schools involved really changed that drastically? Or had some schools simply improved their programs? Perhaps some programs had fallen on hard times? You be the judge. We hated to see Binghamton North, the second charter member of the old *STC* (JC was the first), switch to another division, but we basically had no voice whatsoever in these matters.

In one of the annual winter meetings, one athletic director proposed that *"the Big Three"* (that was the label given to Ithaca, Vestal, and U-E from then on — not necessarily referring strictly to enrollment) each field two teams, an "A" team, and a "B" team. I remember our exact reaction to this ridiculous proposal: We asked, "And who will decide exactly who plays on these "A" and "B" teams? Only we coaches can decide — and therefore, who, do you think, will gain from this?"

Apparently all of the voting members in the room realized the ramifications of this strategy: We would not only field our usual "first team" — undiluted — but we would have fewer substitutes on our "A" team to insert, in the event of any runaway games. It also became crystal-clear that by also fielding a "B" team, although not as strong as the "A" team, we would be gaining a wealth of experience for these future "A" players. It didn't take long to determine the farcical nature of that proposal, and it was shot down unanimously.

Eventually the league was reduced to eleven teams. Susquehanna Valley, one of the smallest of all eleven teams, volunteered to move into the division with *"the Big Three."*

This move was spurred on by its marvelous coach, Cal Rucker. It says here that Cal Rucker is, arguably, the most unassuming and most under-rated coach this area has ever had. The "new look" was designed as a two-year set-up. This ongoing team-shuffle reminds one of a version of "musical chairs," or of the famous Abbott and Costello quip, *"Yeah ... but who's on first?"*

These constant changes caused a few of us some serious scheduling problems in trying to fill a schedule with non-league games. ("League" games is a misnomer — these should be called "non-division" games — since the six schools in the "other" division weren't exactly rushing forth to schedule us.) So, we had to search far and wide for opponents — all over the state, and beyond. Believe me, our search became extremely frustrating year after year. (I often wonder what our phone bill was in those hectic days?)

Some of us began pushing for dissolving the two-division concept and forming one big league — patterned after *"the Big Ten,"* consistently one of the most prestigious college conferences in the nation. Personally, I would still like to see this concept here. Think about it. The strongest *Big Ten* schools always play each other. The weakest ones almost never play the strongest. Those in the middle (*"on the bubble"*) play in both directions. All these years, they have lived compatibly in spite of ALL LEAGUE GAMES COUNTING toward their coveted championship. (Inter-divisional games have NEVER counted in our "league.") *Big Ten* schools are still free to fill the remainder of their schedules with non-league foes from anywhere they choose. Those who are interested in national exposure, usually fill their schedules with a few nationally-ranked teams each year. By doing this, they can firm-up their schedules as far as a decade in advance, and not be forced into an annual hassle of a search for competition.

Back to *STAC*: Since Ithaca was experiencing the same scheduling problems, we decided to double-up and agreed to play an unprecedented home-and-home series for the next two years. (Only the pre-designated game would count as the league game; the other would be a non-league game.) Is it any wonder that these four games over a two-year period were referred to as a real "black and blue" block of games on our schedules? Everyone else in the league, fully aware that the *Little Red* and the *Tigers* really "get it on" whenever they clash, was extremely content to let the two of us knock the stuffing out of each other — which we did. These were four great games in '76 and '77. Several bumps and bruises later, we felt fortunate to have emerged on the right side of the scoreboard on three of these occasions.

Johnson City began to make headlines when the '75 season rolled around. Chuck Gottfried had brought his crew-cut and solid coaching experience to the high school ranks after a long, successful tenure at both the collegiate and pro levels. Chuck took over the JC reins in '73. The *Wildcats* established themselves as a powerhouse, beginning in the mid-70's. They captured three divisional championships in a row — '75,'76, '77 — accumulating an impressive record of 23-4-0 during this stretch, and achieving the rank of 12th in the state in '77.

Area fans began asking this frequently-heard question: "How come you [U-E] don't play JC every year?" On the contrary, please remember that, beginning in '69, JC had requested, and was granted, a move away from the *Big Three*. That move and resolve have become permanent and have never wavered. We always said that we could easily be found in the yellow pages if anyone wanted to play us. Even after our sub-par, early 70's stretch, the phone has never exactly jingled off the hook with a welcome challenge. (Only exception in all those years: Bellport, Long Island, in 1990. Coach Joe Cipp called, wanted to play in Endicott, said that he was loaded — and he was.)

I was always sorry that JC and U-E didn't meet every year. It was a natural, ancient rivalry. And when we did meet over the years, it was usually a very competitive game. We had always maintained a positive relationship with Paul Munley, and I do believe it was mainly through his efforts that we did meet as often as we did. (Thanks, Paul.)

— 1974-1975

Besides JC's prominence in the other divisions, Owego won the *Central Division* in '74 with an impressive 7-1-0 record, Coach Brian Smith's Catholic Central *Crusaders,* and Cal Rucker's Susquehanna Valley *Sabers* shared the *Suburban Division* title in '74 with identical 6-2-0 records. SV won it outright in '75 with a 5-3-0 record. Jud Blanchard's North *Indians* threatened the *Central Division* in '75, but fell short with a solid 6-3-0 record. Coach Joe Bramante's M-E *Spartans* were ranked third among the state's "large schools" in the middle of the '76 season. They ended up with a fine 7-2-0 record overall, but couldn't match-up with JC's undefeated divisional-record.

The *Golden Bears* kept rolling along in '74 and '75. Including '73, they had three undefeated teams in a row, posting an accumulative record during that span of an amazing 26-0-1. They were co-champions in '74, and outright champions in '75, as well as picking up another designation as the *"Best in the state — Number One."* These three Vestal teams had everything — size, speed, and experience. If it wasn't Tim Throup finessing you, it was burly Rusty Bronson pounding you from his fullback spot. That '75 club was *really something!* (Just ask Brockton, Massachusetts about that Vestal team and about a guy named Bronson.) Coach Hoover was once quoted that year as saying he felt the *Golden Bears* could beat anybody in the country — and he *may have been correct!*

Most folks had forgotten the old *Tigers* midst the recent Ithaca and Vestal twin-team show of the early 70's. We spent some quality-time during the winter, spring and summer of '74 studying the *"Wishbone"* offense. We visited some college coaches who had been using it successfully. Since we had always been option-oriented, we became excited with its multi-possibilities, influenced to some degree by our returning personnel and our inconsistent offensive production in recent years. We installed the pure, triple-option *"Bone"* that season featuring an unbalanced line to our left — taking advantage of our left-handed quarterback, Tom Fiori.

We continued to use the *'Bone*, or portions of it, as our basic attack (depending on personnel) for the remainder of my coaching career.

During the pre-season we informed the boys that we had read somewhere that a cornered tiger was the meanest of all the animals. We were positive of our direction, and had already forgotten some negative comments by a few self-proclaimed "experts" — every community has them — some, more than others — who had been surfacing in '72 and '73. Under the solid leadership and slashing running of our captain-elect, Bob Veruto, the *Tigers* began snarling again — *with a vengeance!* I suppose the fact that so many had written us off, will always make 1974 a very special and very gratifying season. Our players had never lost faith in their coaches, nor had their coaches ever wavered in their commitment to the players.

The *Tigers* went on a real tear, cutting a wide swath of an unprecedented 319 points in an abbreviated eight-game schedule, thus becoming the highest-scoring U-E team in history at that point. They finished the season undefeated at 7-0-1, and shared the championship with Vestal. Considering the past couple of seasons, as well as their average size and speed, these '74 *Tigers* truly "reached beyond their grasp."

Who were these gladiators who possessed such desire and such a chemistry that clicked? Twelve of a possible 22 were named to the *All-Star* team, including Tony Roach, my skinny, gutsy, little neighbor (one of the *Mersereau Park* gang) who made it in three different positions: Wide receiver, punter, and kicker.

Another one was Cliff Young — legally blind — who exemplified the courage of this team. His teammates had to read him the scouting notes posted on the board. Obviously, he saw "enough" on the field by himself — especially if "it" wore a different-colored jersey. To this day, I marvel at his feats!

Tom Mills, who did a great version of Saint Peter during a skit at pre-season camp, opened big offensive holes from his guard spot.

We had quite an offensive backfield tandem — *"The Big V,"* Bob Veruto of course, and Gary Crooks. The movie, *The Sting,* was receiving rave reviews at that time. We renamed Bob and Gary after the two scheming, lovable characters in that *Oscar*-winning film: Bob became *"Johnny Hooker"* (Robert Redford), and Crooksie became *"Henry Gondorff"* (Paul Newman). They provided us with a very potent one-two punch, rushing through, over, and around the defenses for the entire season. Crooksie would line up on the opposite side of the field one day as JC's coach.

A couple of other guys who didn't make the *All-Star* team were instrumental in this scoring machine: Tom Fiori, the *"Ice Man"* with his cool, blue eyes, was the quarterback who really triggered this potent *'Bone* offense with aplomb. Lee Spadine was the "other" back (left halfback). His main role was as a blocker — a precursor of a *"Moose"* Johnston-type, the Dallas *Cowboys' All-Pro* fullback — only much smaller. Lee typified the unselfish attitude of this team. His stats-per-game might read one or two carries and maybe a reception. His many crunching "lead" blocks would only "show up" where they count....On the scoreboard. Lee was the quintessential *"Unsung Hero."*

Following are the media's capsule-summaries of our '74 season, in sequence — first the headline, then the summary:

'Late U-E Burst Buries Ithaca, 27-7.'

"Union-Endicott did all of its scoring in the second-half, the last three touchdowns in a 6-plus minute portion of the final quarter last night, that stamps the Tigers as one of the few teams challenging the Vestal juggernaut."

'U-E intimidates JC, 47-22.'

"'We'll take what we're given,' was Union-Endicott coach Fran Angeline's assessment of his club's offensive strategy yesterday in a surprisingly easy 47-22 rout of Johnson City at Green Field; U-E ran and passed to its left all day and numerous moves by Johnson City coach Chuck Gottfried seemed to do little to stem the onslaught."

'U-E rallies, defeats Central.'

"Union-Endicott turned two Binghamton Central first-half fumbles into scores and utilized power running by Gary Crooks and Bob Veruto in a pair of fourth-quarter touchdown drives for a 29-19 Southern Tier Athletic Conference football victory last night."

'U-E, Veruto Nifty ... All Way to 50.'

"Bob Veruto, twisting away from what few Homer tacklers were left in front of him, gained 214 yards and scored three touchdowns as undefeated Union-Endicott crushed Homer, 50-6, last night, and firmly established itself as a threat to Vestal supremacy."

Sometimes it seems as if everything bounces your way...although a coach would like to spread these "good bounces" over an entire season. Against Homer, Ronnie Rejda, *"The Bionic Man,"* our premier kicker, executed three perfect on-side kickoffs — and we recovered *all three!*

The second-half of the season follows:

'U-E Warms to Task, Burns M-E.'

"Maine-Endwell acted the part of a rude guest, and got just the treatment you'd expect from an angered Union-Endicott team last night ... A football in its ear, 47-6."

'58 U-E High In 22 years.'

"Touchdown-wild Union-Endicott puts together its biggest offensive thrust in 22 years and defensively muzzled the shotgun in thrashing winless Oneonta, 58-21, yesterday."

A sidelight: The *Yellowjackets* had a mountain of a man in the trenches, Mark May — just a growing underclassman then — maybe 6 feet 4 inches and 265 pounds. Does his name ring a bell? It should. After a brilliant career at The University of Pittsburgh, he became an *All-Pro* with the *Super-Bowl Champion* Washington *Redskins,* as one of the original, renowned *"Hogs."*

While our players were filing off the bus at Oneonta, long before game time, a young (perhaps a little wide-eyed then) Mark May asked Hovie, one of our assistants, "Which one is Longo?" Hovie did some quick thinking, for he knew that our equipment man, heavily-bearded Mike Fabrizio, himself a 6 feet 1 inch and 275 pound bull (former U-E lineman), was in the back of the equipment truck. He was out of sight, but about ready to open the rear doors.

Hovie replied to Mark, "Oh, we don't dare allow Longo to ride with the rest of the team — he's too wild — we keep him locked up in there (pointing at the rear doors of the equipment truck)." Perfect timing — what a *psych-job!* The rear doors of the truck creaked open almost on cue. Fabrizio (nicknamed *"Magilla-Gorilla"*) appeared in the doorway with his bulging, black leather motorcycle jacket and boots, and leaped down. I can tell you that Mark's eyes dilated to the size of saucers before realizing the sham. He was a great kid, and we avoided his side of the field when his *Yellowjackets* came to U-E the next year.

Another rarity occurred in that '74 season — our scheduled seventh game versus Bishop Grimes of Syracuse was cancelled. I couldn't *believe* this was happening to us! Grimes just plain reneged on its commitment to play in Endicott. I even brought our local pastor, Monsignor John Carey from St. Ambrose, into it. I wondered aloud whether the "northern Catholics" played by a different set of ethic-rules? As I recall, we even voiced our disapproval to the Bishop in the diocese of Syracuse, as well as to our governing body, the *NYSPHSAA.* They obviously didn't intervene, or were ineffective, because the game never came off.

I have heard of this type of thing happening to a few teams before — but these isolated cases had taken place long before the season had begun, not at virtually "the eleventh hour." From a financial viewpoint, all of our game-programs had already been printed (and could not be re-used) at considerable cost and effort. *What a waste!* Initially, I was shocked — then extremely teed off. I refused to return several phone calls from the apologetic coach.

Finally, after cooling off, I became worried...especially about our momentum. After all, the *Tigers* had an undefeated season going, and were becoming a scoring machine. It felt as if our world was collapsing around us. This is how we adjusted:

First, we staged an inter-squad game — officials, uniforms, the works — under the lights that Friday. Our frosh and junior varsity teams played a preliminary game. We felt that this would be a good opportunity to showcase our entire football program for our parents and fans, while keeping the momentum of "game conditions" going. Quite a crowd showed up. Then on Saturday, we also took the entire squad to Geneva, New York as guests of Hobart University and its captain/wishbone-fullback — our Jerry Hanley. Their game was versus their rival, the University of Rochester. In summary, we tried to make the most out of an extremely lousy situation.

Apparently it worked, as we entered the eighth weekend:

> ***'Undeflated' U-E Corks CV, 53-7.'***
>
> "About 1,900 balloons petered out of their helium supply at Chenango Valley High's football field yesterday afternoon, but the mighty Union-Endicott football bubble was not among them. Far from it. U-E scored 32 points in a five-minute span of the first quarter and — the Legion of Decency will be happy to hear — tapered off a bit from there before winding up a 53-7 victor."

And now, the stage was set. The media must have sniffed out this match-up early in the season, since the drumbeat began, in ink, as soon as the first weekend's results were in. This countdown continued throughout the season with an increasing crescendo each weekend.

I wonder if anyone in the media, although well-meaning, realizes how difficult he makes a coach's job by doing this? Every coach is trying to keep his charges in focus for the job at hand — playing each game, one-at-a time, and not looking ahead. Furthermore, when an anticipated, highly-charged contest is publicized two months in advance, it is degrading (and often inspiring) to the other opponents on the schedule. This focus-business is tough enough at the pro-level, let alone with our youngsters. Especially with a good team, keeping it focused on the next opponent — no matter what lies beyond — is probably the most challenging intangible for a high school coach.

Anyway, the media's "dream" match-up had finally arrived: Undefeated Vestal with 8-0-0, the defending champion, would lay it on the line at undefeated U-E with 7-0-0 (no thanks to Bishop Grimes). For the first time in a decade these two would meet unscathed. The report said that a crowd in excess of 14,000 was there in eager anticipation. As we exchanged pleasantries during the pre-game warm-ups, I remember remarking to Dick, "With a crowd like this, we ought to get a split of the gate, take Mary (Dick's wife) and Pat out, and have a good time." We both agreed that it ought to be a great game to watch — and it was.

Two different post-game newspaper headlines announced:

'STAC Powerhouses Battle to 8-8 Standoff Before 14,000.'

'U-E — Vestal; 8-8 Doesn't Leave No. 1.'

This report followed the second headline:

> "It was the standoff on the Susquehanna. Vestal and Union-Endicott — fighting for Southern Tier Athletic Conference prowess and for the pride of their 24-year-old rivalry — flogged each other to a disappointing 8-all tie last night."

Sorry, but I disagreed with this assessment then, and still do. I was accurately quoted afterwards in print: "There are two *Number Ones*, and I don't mean 1-2." A third newspaper gave this account:

> "A well-behaved crowd of over 14,000 packed U-E's stadium, the standing fans ringing the field a dozen deep before fences were opened allowing hundreds to sit on the banked end zone area."

Gee, did these last two reporters see the same game? One account with negative undertones, and one with positive. This is something that I'll never understand. After all, these are just teenagers out there — amateurs in the truest sense. I'm happy to say that 99 percent of the reporters I've known have been very positive, very up-beat in their accounts.

I was happy to see someone finally recognize the exemplary behavior of such a huge crowd. To the best of my knowledge, we never had any problems with any of the enormous Vestal versus U-E crowds in '62, '64, or '74 — a tribute to the mutual respect among Vestal and U-E fans, a reflection of the diligence of Bob Wurtenberg and his auxiliaries, and a measure of the officials' exemplary work at these games.

Vestal's money-man all season, Tim Throup, scored in the second-quarter, and also ran in for the two-point conversion. His counterpart, Bob Veruto, scored all of U-E's 8 points on runs in the third-quarter. The rest of the game featured stout defense, and several booming punts by both teams.

The final statistics reflect the parity of the two teams: Number of plays and yards

— Vestal, 51-202; U-E, 59-230. First Downs — twelve for both teams. When Dick and I met afterwards and shook hands, we both held our heads high — after all, we both had much to be proud of. We agreed that everyone was a winner and that the fans had gotten their money's worth.

Although we were a 6-2-0 factor again in '75, the *Tigers* lost our three-year starter and the heart of our defense, captain Mike *"Moose"* Longo. His leg injury came at the halfway mark of the season and we never seriously threatened Vestal (nor did anyone else). To show you the kind of respect Longo demanded, he was chosen on the *All-Star* squad although only playing for half of the season.

Along with Longo's injury, we had another mental adjustment to make at mid-season. Everyone understands that injuries come with the territory. However, no teenager should ever have to experience this other crisis: The negotiation process between the U-E teachers and board of education had broken down. A teachers' strike was imminent. Classes, the remainder of the football schedule, and all other extra-curricular activities were in jeopardy. It became ugly. All kinds of grievances, demands, and threats by both sides were aired in all of the area media for days. (It seemed like an eternity at the time.) And guess who was caught in the middle?...The children, the players, and their coach. It was finally resolved after much brouhaha — but at what cost? One can only surmise. This much is fact, though:

A gutty, well-coached Central team came to Endicott as underdog, for an unprecedented Tuesday-night game that had already been postponed by heavy flooding a couple of times.

Seeing Central coach Randy Zur, always with that unique "Zur" smile, was a new experience for me... a new emotion. This was my first experience at facing "one of my own" as an adversary. The very next year, I would repeat that experience with another of "my boys" — Bill Baker of SV. In later years I would face Dave Sammon of Vestal, and Gary Crooks of JC, not to mention the many others who would populate the area coaching staffs as assistants.

I thought back to what I had felt my first year of coaching in '57, when this role was reversed, and I faced Ty Cobb. I remembered that I had so much respect for the man that I wanted to show him how much I had learned and wanted to beat him to prove my respect for him.

However, now the shoe was on the other foot. I don't know what thoughts were swirling through "my boys'" minds as they squared off against me. I'm sure that they wanted to "get the old man." From my perspective, however, I can tell you exactly what I felt: a deep pride...the satisfaction of following their progress and achievements...love. This may come as a shock to many of you, but I can honestly say that winning or losing took a distant back seat to these other emotions — at least for each of our initial engagements.

The "Zur-cumstances" surrounding Randy's stint as Central's head man were quite unique in this — and in future Central versus U-E battles — not only because of our close "teacher-pupil" relationship, but also because his dad, Charlie, was an esteemed member of the U-E Board of Education, his sister, Marsha, was a U-E cheerleader, his mom, Louise, and his brothers, Rick and Rod, were staunch *Tiger* supporters — and because Randy still called Endicott "home." Furthermore, our good friend and former boss, Dick McLean, was now drawing his paycheck from Binghamton as its superintendent of schools. There must have been some mixed emotions whenever we met.

In our first encounter that Tuesday-night, Central played inspired ball. Behind the relentless running of Dickie Farrell, who had been better known for his prowess on a tennis court prior to this night (he'd become Binghamton's very successful tennis coach eventually), the *Bulldogs* upset us, 12-10 (although I'd love to have an instant-replay — and subsequent re-evaluated ruling — on Rejda's attempted field goal in the closing seconds).

This loss knocked U-E from the ranks of the undefeated and lord knows what else.

— 1976

We began a long-standing pre-season scrimmage with Shenendehowa, consistently ranked at, or near the top in the state, and coached by the highly-respected Brent Steuerwald. Our staffs have become quite close over the years — an abundance of camaraderie — and this traditional rivalry continues today. Central shared the championship with us in '76, each team with an identical 3-1-0 divisional record. (Remember: *"Only divisional games count"* — *STAC* rule.)

Actually, Central finished 7-1-0 overall so perhaps the previous year's game wasn't quite the "upset" that it was cranked up to be. U-E finished 8-1-0. Central ended up with its first state-ranking ever, I believe — 23rd. U-E ended up ranked 5th. Central had an exceptional athlete as its quarterback/safety, Dave Pessagno. The "teacher" is happy to say that the *Tigers* avenged 1975's loss by breaking a 7-7 halftime tie, exploding for three third-period touchdowns, and beating the "student's" team, 36-15, for the only blur on Central's perfect record.

Afterwards, we knocked off a highly-touted Newburgh club on our only visit downstate that year. It warmed this coach's heart to see those U-E spectator and marching-band buses roll into the stadium through the distant gate. The dust created by our fleet of buses — there must have been at least eight big *Greyhounds* — was awesome. The spectator buses were organized by Nino Samiani, the dynamic student-government president at the time. Nino would become the U-E basketball coach, an expert in computers, and my singing partner in later years.

This fleet of buses must have had quite a psychological effect on the Newburgh fans and players. It certainly lifted the U-E *Tigers*. It is a sight which can never be erased from my memory.

I can also remember the care-free, casual faces of our opponents as we lined up for a field goal attempt from our side of the 50-yard line on that beautiful, balmy Saturday afternoon. Their expressions quickly turned to shock as our *"Bionic Man,"* Ron Rejda, set a record that still stands today. *A — 51 — plus — yard — rocket — shot!* It not only split the uprights, but almost reached a small stream, at least 20 yards behind the end zone. This game prompted the *NYSSWA* to elevate us to a lofty *Number Two* spot in the state-rankings.

But someone forgot to tell Ithaca.

Earlier in the season, we had to come from behind to edge the *Little Red,* 13-10, at home. Although this had been designated as the non-league game of the two, our troops should have anticipated what was in store for them in the rematch. (Especially with our elevated stature in the state.) The eighth weekend of the season found Ithaca itching for another shot at us on the shores of Cayuga Lake. (Always beware of an ill-wind off Cayuga's waters!)

Behind the relentless pounding by its vastly under-rated fullback, Jeff Backer, with 28 carries for 128 yards, a determined, aggressive offensive line unveiled an unbalanced formation for the first time. Along with pin-point, 13 for 181 yards, passing by steady quarterback, Mike Biondi, and a stubborn defense, the *Little Red* took a commanding and shocking 25-0 score into the locker room at halftime.

Wow! Can you imagine what it felt like to have "the world" within your reach — the championship, an undefeated season, the top ranking in the state for the first time — and to be down by 23 points against a team you had already beaten once? But this '76 U-E team was an unusual group. Pride, poise, and determination come to mind immediately.

Our many fans (possibly more there than Ithaca had) also must have sensed this. Fans the world over ought to take note. (It's too bad the '69 U-E "faithful" versus CV, or the '78 U-E "faithful" versus M-E, yet to come, couldn't have had the ATTITUDE and LOYALTY of this shivering, stunned U-E crowd.) Instead of folding up shop and grumbling, throwing in the towel and booing, inventing excuses, or perhaps heading home, they did a most unusual, unheard of thing. These U-E fans formed a gauntlet on the field near the goal posts at our end. As we re-entered the field for the second half — and began to jog through their long columns — the cheers, the boisterous support, and the pats-on-the-back were something to behold. It definitely had a positive effect on all of us.

Considering the circumstances, I have never witnessed an out-pouring of support such as that night — it is indelibly engraved in my memory bank. Nor have I ever witnessed a come-back such as the *Tigers* staged that night — mostly on the ground, at that. The scoreboard lit up in the second half, too — but now on the visitors' side. It finally read, "Ithaca 32; Visitors 28."

Afterwards, a sports reporter captured the moment: "In the eerie silence inside the U-E locker room, the players knelt in a circle weeping as coach Angeline told them, 'That was the greatest second half performance any team ever had — you just ran out of time, baby.'"

Who were these young, gutty, come-back men? I should (but could not) list every one of them, since each had contributed something. Our captain, Bill *"Doctor Mind"* Hughes, was always the quiet, inspirational leader. We also had a couple of explosive backs — versatile Ron Rejda was named to the *All-Star* team in three different categories: halfback, defensive back, and kicker. Tom *"Burnin' Ben"* Bennett led the entire league in rushing with 155 carries for 1107 yards, and in scoring with 90 points. Tom joined the U-E staff after breaking several records at C.W. Post College.

I can't explain the excitement and thrill, for both Pat and myself, of having our oldest child, Chris, on the varsity as a sophomore quarterback. He played behind *"The Chairman,"* Terry Hogan. Terry was the youngest of the four *"Hogan's Heroes"* brothers (Don, Dan, Rich) — all fine football players for us over the past two decades.

But, our '76 season was far from over (although it might have seemed that way in Ithaca that night). We still had one game to go — VESTAL! There was even more emotion than usual in this rivalry, since Coach Hoover had announced earlier in the season that this would be his last. It was a bitter, blustery night — our field was frozen — there were small patches of ice in certain areas. Taking a page out of the *NFL* book, we had our guys bring sneakers for traction — and were sure happy we did.

We conducted a special pre-game ceremony to honor our respected guest. Wurt, Bill Hughes, Pat and I met with the Hoovers at mid-field. We presented Dick with an engraved plaque, and Mary, a bouquet. The inscription on the plaque read simply but succinctly:

"An outstanding coach...A fierce competitor...
A great guy...From all your friends across the river.
— Ty Cobb Stadium, Nov. 13, 1976."

Both squads and both sides of spectators gave the Hoovers a well-deserved standing ovation.

A few minutes before kickoff, I became quite concerned. How would our squad react after the Ithaca loss? How would they react to the special emotion of the evening? Might they be hanging their heads and feeling sorry for themselves?...*Not this outfit!* There was electricity in the air as the *Tigers* pounded out a 43-0 rout. They had never been better.

After the game — I'll be honest — I had mixed emotions. As thrilled as I was for our young men, our school, and our community, I knew that we were losing a great competitor and friend. After shaking hands, I embraced him. As Coach Hoover walked off the field for the last time, and into the night...a piece of me left with him.

The 1975 Vestal* Golden Bears *were 9-0-0 and ranked* Number One *in the state. Many still believe this was Vestal's best squad ever.

ALL STARS — THE MID 70's (1974-1976)

1974

OFFENSE			DEFENSE		
School	Position	Player	School	Position	Player
METROPOLITAN					
VHS	E	TOM ROLOSON	VHS	E	DAVE ENGLE
VHS	QB	PAT GILLARD	VHS	T	JERRY HARMON
VHS	HB	TIM THROUP	VHS	LB	DAVE WALTER
VHS	K	TOM ROLOSON	VHS	CB	JEFF COOK
UE	E	TONY ROACH	VHS	S	PAT GILLARD
UE	T	BOB NEDBALSKI	UE	E	KRAIG DUNHAM
UE	G	TOM MILLS	UE	T	MIKE LONGO
UE	G	CLIFF YOUNG	UE	MG	STEVE KAZMARK
UE	C	MIKE WESKO	UE	CB	PAUL KOCUR
UE	HB	BOB VERUTO	UE	S	MIKE O'NEIL
UE	FB	GARY CROOKS	UE	P	TONY ROACH
UE	K	TONY ROACH			
CENTRAL					
JC	K	PAUL RAMEY	JC	E	GABE POMPETTI
OFA	E	JOE MARZO	JC	T	MIKE CROMPTON
OFA	RB	STEVE KERSAT	OFA	T	MIKE KNAPP
OFA	QB	JOHN MARZO	OFA	LB	GARY SMITH
OFA	T	BRIAN DERENTHAL			
SUBURBAN					
CC	E	MARK FARRELL	CC	E	JOE BRADY
CC	T	JIM MAYER	CC	DB	MARTY GALLAGHER
CC	G	JOHN ROACH	CC	DB	JOHN KOZEL
CC	RB	DAVE GOETZ	SV	L	AL KROCKENBERGER
CC	K	DAVE MELINSKY	SV	L	LARRY LITTLE
SV	E	JIM WAITKAVICZ	SV	LB	BILL MILLER
SV	T	MARK RUSTINE	SV	LB	MIKE WHALEN
SV	C	MIKE PFLANZ	SV	DB	TIM O'NEIL
SV	RB	KEVIN WHITTEMORE			
SV	QB	BUTCH KENYON			

1975

METROPOLITAN					
UE	E	BEAVER SHIRLEY	UE	T	MIKE LONGO
UE	T	CRAIG GRANT	UE	G	STEVE KAZMARK
UE	HB	JOHN VERUTO	UE	LB	MIKE LOGAN
UE	K	RON REJDA	UE	HB	PAUL KOCUR
VHS	E	MARK PINEIRO	UE	P	BEAVER SHIRLEY
VHS	T	MARK SELSMEYER	VHS	E	KELL PURDY
VHS	G	DAVE LaBONTE	VHS	E	WYATT ROZBORIL

VHS	C	KELL PURDY	VHS	T	JERRY HARMON
VHS	QB	BILL KRIVYANIK	VHS	G	DOUG McCROSSEN
VHS	FB	RUSTY BRONSON	VHS	LB	TOM KNAPP

CENTRAL

JC	G	JOHN TUPY	JC	E	JIM RILEY
JC	C	TOM ARNOLD	JC	E	DALE COOK
JC	HB	RICK BALLES	JC	T	PAUL HIEBICA
BN	E	JIM MULLINS	JC	G	MARK CZEKALA
BN	T	BOB GITCHELL	BN	LB	MARK RAGARD
BN	G	BRIAN WHALEN			
BN	QB	RICK BARKER			

SUBURBAN

SV	G	MARK BAILEY	SV	LB	BILL MILLER
SV	QB	GARY BURDASH	SV	CB	JIM TALLO
SV	FB	KEVIN WHITTEMORE			

1976

METROPOLITAN

BC	E	MARC FEEKO	BC	E	MARC FEEKO
BC	G	RAY HANDY	BC	T	FRAN GENNARELLI
BC	QB	DAVE PESSAGNO	BC	DB	DAVE PESSAGNO
UE	T	DAVE BENNETT	BC	P	TIM FAUGHNAN
UE	G	CRAIG GRANT	UE	E	BILL HUGHES
UE	C	BILL MILLS	UE	T	JOHN VILLANTI
UE	HB	TOM BENNETT	UE	LB	DAVE KINSELLA
UE	HB	RON REJDA	UE	DB	RON REJDA
UE	K	RON REJDA			

SUBURBAN*

** only two divisions now*

ME	G	JOHN MILLS	ME	E	CHUCK BERTONI
ME	HB	JACK VIVONA	ME	T	BRIAN NALEPA
ME	K	SMOKEY GREEN	ME	DB	KEN YACOVONI
JC	G	JOHN McDONALD	JC	T	PAUL HIEBICA
JC	T	BERT WRIGHT	JC	LB	RICK BALLES
			JC	DB	LOUIS MILLER

Chapter Eleven

"When the blast of war blows in our ears
Then imitate the action of the tiger:
Stiffen the sinews, summon up the blood.
Disguise fair nature with hard-favor'd rage,
Then lend the eye a terrible aspect."

— Shakespeare

"THE BEST TEAM EVER?"

— *THE LATE 70'S, 1977-1979*

"They are the best team ever," remarked a retired Coach Hoover in reference to the '79 U-E team...and he had lots of company agreeing with him.

The occasion was a banquet at the *Vestal Elk's Club*, with all of the area *Elk's Clubs* in attendance. My staff and I were being honored there that evening, following our unparalleled '79 season. Dick was there as the guest-speaker. In assessing this U-E team, he made comparisons with a few of the other great teams in this area that had achieved everything a high school team could achieve — and believe me, both Vestal and Ithaca had produced some exceptional ones. He said that, while one of his Vestal teams, or Ithaca's, might have been better offensively, or perhaps another better defensively, and possibly yet another better in the kicking game, this U-E team was the best ever, overall, with such balance in all phases of the game. Can you imagine how we felt with a legend deferring to us? It is certainly something that we'll never forget. (Incidentally, we must have put quite a dent in the *Elk's* delicious, unique, "venison-only" banquet that night, because we were never invited back....)

What are the events that led up to this statement?

As the late 70's rolled around, it just never seemed the same without Dick Hoover patrolling the sideline. However, Bill McGuire, a long-time assistant of Dick and newly appointed head man, saw to it that there was no drop-off in the quality of *Golden Bear* football. He fielded some outstanding teams. The late 70's still featured a three-horse race in *Division I* with Vestal posting a record of 21-4-2 and U-E almost identical with a 21-4-1 record. Ithaca was close behind, winning 18, losing 8, and tying 1.

In *Division II,* Johnson City continued to post impressive numbers with a 20-6-1 record and began receiving some pressure to switch to *Division I,* especially since it began receiving "large school" ranking at the state level. As I recall, JC's usual reaction to this annual pressure/proposal was, "We have to build up our program first." Also, the following statement is well-documented: "We'll play two of the three *(i.e., 'The Big*

Three' of Ithaca, U-E and Vestal), but not all three...." And so, JC was allowed to stay in the division with the smaller schools.

I know that I, personally, was looking forward to the late 70's with eager anticipation. Perhaps it was the knowledge that I'd finally have both of my sons with me at the same time. However, I think it was even more the fact that I really knew most of these players (and their parents) well. I had watched them grow up with my sons...all the way up from kindergarten, through *Pee-Wees, Little League,* modified, and JVs. Some had been guests at our home several times, and vice-versa. For this reason, during the late 70's the *Tigers* were probably a more closely knit "family" on the field than during any other period of my career.

— 1977

The year '77 was a season of great parity, not only within the two divisions, but inter-divisional as well. There were seven bona fide contenders. They proved this not only by their divisional records, but by their inter-divisional records as well. Each one was capable of knocking the other one off (or tying) — and often did. This season might have produced the most teams of equal ability from both divisions ever in *STAC* — comparable to '65 in the old *STC*.

The *Division I* contenders and overall records were: *"The Big Three"* — Vestal (6-2-1), U-E (6-2-1), Ithaca (5-4-0), and a fourth — SV (5-3-0). *Division II* had three as good as any: JC (8-1-0), M-E (5-2-2), and Owego (4-3-2).

When the dust had cleared, U-E and JC were the champions of their respective divisions — but by different routes. JC's championship was assured long before its finale. Coach Gottfried had proclaimed in print that his JC team was the best team in the area. Obviously, he was considering a well-earned 18-16 victory over U-E as the major contributing factor in this claim. And Chuck could very well have been correct. Since JC had beaten us, we certainly had no argument. However, everyone knows that the other three *Division I* contenders would have welcomed a shot at JC, but were not on its schedule. So, there was some argument there. OFA, meantime, had a claim of its own to make as it nixed JC's bid for an undefeated season with a shocking upset in their finale. This turn of events, however, was meaningless in the overall picture.

From our perspective, it is one of the few times I can remember, that we "backed into" a championship. Although we had stumbled in our divisional finale against Vestal, we received some mathematical help from the rest of the division, and finished with the best divisional record, 3-1-0. Actually, we struggled through an injury-riddled season — including injuries to both of my sons and our captain, Bill Mills (the last of the magnificent Mills brothers to leave his indelible mark on Southern Tier football, just as his older brothers, Rusty and Tom, had done). Considering our situation, we have no complaints whatsoever about the results of the '77 season.

— 1978

There was a distinct mathematical imbalance between the two divisions (5-8). *Division I* had only five schools, meaning only four games that counted, and had the unenviable task of trying to fill our schedules with five more games. U-E came up one short in '78, as did other *Division I* schools at other times. (However, I doubt that the rest of the league lost much sleep over our scheduling problems.)

Everyone in *Division I* was sorry to lose such a valiant competitor as SV. How could anyone not feel admiration for its voluntary two-year stint in *Division I*, even though it was one of the smallest schools in either division? The *Sabers* always performed courageously and were extremely formidable opponents. Their performance, spearheaded by the Kimmel brothers, Jon and Jamie, reflected the fierce competitiveness and intensity of their fine coach, Bill Baker. (We feel very fortunate to have won our last meeting ever: 7-6, in 1977.)

Vestal ran roughshod over everybody in '78. The *Bears* were easily the top team in the area, if not the state. (They got my vote.) They had several legitimate big weapons in their arsenal — the most prominent of which was their burly, strong, halfback/linebacker, Mike Gates. After the final statistics for the season had been compiled, Mike just missed the coveted 1,000-yard rushing mark — but 160 points on the scoreboard *ain't bad!* He was equally valuable on the other side of the ball and became the second player from the Southern Tier selected as the *"Player-of-the-Year"* in the entire state. (The first one had been Ithaca's Steve Webster in 1970.)

The *Bears* finished undefeated, 9-0-0. They were never seriously threatened all season, except for a few quarters in U-E's backyard. Our gang performed heroically, especially after our recent pratfall at the hands of M-E. With a throng estimated at about 13,000, U-E took leads of 7-0 and 14-8, before being outgunned in the 4th-quarter, 23-14. After the game Coach *"Mac"* McGuire stated for the record, "If we're not *Number One* in the state after that performance, I want to be told why." (No argument here!) "And U-E deserves *Number Two* in my book." That was a very kind remark, and one which I have never forgotten.

Mac and I often reminisce during golf outings these days. Invariably the conversation comes around to that exciting battle in '78 — a classic in every sense. But unfortunately, not even a decent drive, putt, or round of golf can change the outcome of that brisk November night. Vestal contributed a couple more assistant coaches to the area from its ranks of outstanding athletes — Tim Flick and Mike Rotondi, Jr.

We finished up as runner-up with a 6-2-0 record (3-1-0 in the division). Our captain was our hard-working, fire-plug fullback, Mario Ciotoli. I also enjoyed having two healthy (*finally!*) Angelines in the starting lineup. Although we had beaten Norwich handily the past two years, one particular thorn in our side was Lee Supensky (a dead-ringer for Jack Nicholson, incidentally), the *Purple Tornado's* hard-running back. He would become a teammate of U-E's Armie George, Larry Angeline, and Vestal's Mike Cappellett at Mansfield University before returning to his alma mater as a member of its football staff.

Ithaca was right behind us with a 2-2-0 divisional record (7-2-0 overall).

Other than our Vestal game, our game at JC had probably been our best effort of the season. On a gorgeous 70-degree afternoon at mid-season, led by our premier linebacker, Dave Wolf (who would become a *Division I-AA All-American* at Colgate University), we had our way — to the tune of 42-6. Dave, *"The Wolf Man"*, set an individual, single-game defensive record for us that day with 35 tackles.

JC won its division again, with a 5-1-0 divisional record, and 6-3-0 overall. The

Seton Catholic Central *Saints* (formerly known as the Catholic Central *Crusaders* before their merger with Seton in '76) were nipping at its heels all season long, and finished as runner-up with a 4-1-1 divisional record, and 6-2-1 overall.

We lost our popular, indefatigable athletic director, *"Big Wurt,"* a couple of months after the season — after a recurring bout with cancer. Wurt had been a tireless worker for the good of all. He was never too busy for anybody or anything, no matter how small or large. Wurt also left a huge void in the league as a key administrator within it. Personally, I had lost a close friend. It was a rough fall for the Angeline family. My dad, Frank, had passed away, unexpectedly, during the pre-season. The entire squad walked over to his wake. Our family was deeply touched. Pat's dad, Loftus, died after a lengthy illness, shortly after the season. I only wish that they had been able to see their grandsons in action — during their respective senior seasons. I know that they would have been very proud. These three men had all been champions to us.

— 1979

Many veteran fans from the Southern Tier, even those with other loyalties, still call the '79 U-E team not only "the greatest team in U-E history," but also "the greatest team this league has ever seen." From an analytical, technical view, Dick Hoover basically had said the same thing at the *Elk's* Banquet, and attributed his assessment of this team to its outstanding balance in all phases of the game — namely: offense, defense, and kicking. I prefer to leave comparisons to other people. However, I feel compelled to share these facts about this '79 U-E team with you. The *Tigers* broke records by the sheaths, both individual, as well as team records — not only U-E records, but also some Broome County and Southern Tier records, as well. And perhaps beyond. Most of these records are still intact today.

These are documented:

INDIVIDUAL RECORDS broken in 1979:

CATEGORY	INDIVIDUAL	TOTAL
PASSING — ONE GAME	*ED KOBAN*	*284 YDS (vs. JC)*
RECEIVING — CAREER	*GARY BEDDOE*	*982 YDS*
TD RECEPTIONS — CAREER	*GARY BEDDOE*	*12*
POINTS SCORED — CAREER	*TIM MARSH*	*207*
POINTS SCORED — SEASON	*TIM MARSH*	*112*
FUMBLES RECOVERED —ONE GAME	*ARMIE GEORGE*	*3 (vs. Central)*

TEAM RECORDS broken in 1979:

DEFENSE:

OPPONENTS' POINTS	*ONE SEASON*	*26*
OPPONENTS' RUSHING YDS	*ONE SEASON*	*661*
OPPONENTS' PASSING YDS	*ONE SEASON*	*447*
OPPONENTS' TOTAL YDS	*ONE SEASON*	*1108*

OFFENSE:

PASSING YDS	*ONE GAME*	*284 (vs. JC)*
TOTAL POINTS	*ONE HALF*	*51 (vs. M-E)*
TOTAL POINTS	*SEASON*	*413*
TOTAL PT. DIFFERENCE	*ONE GAME*	*78-0 (vs. Central)*
TOTAL FIRST DOWNS	*SEASON*	*163*
TOTAL YDS	*SEASON*	*3,294*

Another interesting fact about this team was the quality of its schedule. Of the five non-league opponents, three were perennially highly respected, state-ranked teams: JC, Sweet Home (Buffalo), and Susan B. Wagner (Staten Island, NYC). This U-E team had the rare distinction of starting the season ranked *Number One* in the state, and more importantly, ending it the same way (first time in U-E history). It also finished ranked 18th nationally. Moeller High School of Cincinnati, Ohio (coached by Gerry Faust who would soon be given the reins at Notre Dame), achieved the top ranking in the nation with a 12-0-0 record.

Most of the top twenty schools boasted records of 15-0-0. Just Moeller and a few others had fewer, but none had fewer than 12...except for U-E. Can you imagine how we felt with only 9 games? New York State was still "considering" post-season play — as it had been doing for a long, long time — but it was finally on the brink of the initial stages of a playoff system the very next year.

The composition of this team was rather unique. To begin with, we had a nucleus of nine seniors who had been with us for three years. We had never brought up anywhere near that many sophomores for varsity exposure as we did in '77. They provided us with the most experience and leadership we ever had. Aside from this invaluable experience, we had more legitimate speed (some *"burners"*) at the skill positions — more quickness, athleticism, and versatility than ever. We also had excellent size. More guys than usual had worked on becoming bigger and stronger during the off-season with diligent weight-training.

Unfortunately, we had a few huge egos on this team who needed to be kept in check periodically — or they would have outgrown their helmets as the season progressed. Their teammates did a great job of controlling these few individuals. We coaches only had to step in once in a while by ordering a few hill-runs (quite a few, actually). Our philosophy on the hill: "A chain is only as strong as its weakest link." It was strictly a reminder to all that no single individual was more important than the team, and that football was still a team game.

On the field, the chemistry was right — these guys clicked together — a "dream team." They were all business "down in the arena" and especially opportunistic most of the time.

Since an unprecedented 19 out of 22 starters were named to the *All-Stars*, nine received *All-State* honors, and one even received national recognition, perhaps we should take a look at Dick Testa's (Sports Editor of *The Valley News*) brief profiles of the component parts of this awesome machine:

OFFENSE (alphabetically):

"JOE AMORESE (*'AMMO'*): SR, 6' 1"-196' — TACKLE

Three-year varsity player / All-Star / excellent blocking techniques have earned several best blocking awards.

"GARY BEDDOE (*'HERMAN'*): SR, 6' 2"-176' — WINGBACK

Three-year varsity player / All-Star last two / All-State / extremely versatile / led STAC receivers with 32 catches in each of last two years / caught 12 career TD tosses / carried the ball 17 times for 200 yards / good blocker / member of Section IV mile relay champion track team.

"GENE BUCCI (*'BOOCH'*): SR, 5' 11"-167' — SPLIT END

Three-year varsity player / only two-way starter on squad / extremely versatile athlete / exceptional speed (which spread the defenses) / Empire Games 440 champion.

"SCOTT DENMON: SR, 6' 1"-179' — TIGHT END

Came on strong as a senior / scored first Tiger TD of year on 35 yard pass versus Sweet Home / caught 8 passes for 166 yards (20.7 average) and also nabbed a pair of two-point PAT tosses / plays basketball and baseball.

"BILL DOOLITTLE (*'DOC'*): SR, 6' 1"-201' — GUARD

Three-year varsity player / All-Star/steady performer / caught fumble in mid air to keep TD drive alive against Wagner / punishing trap blocker.

"DAVE HESS (*'I.M.'*): SR, 6' 5"-188' — TACKLE

Grew and gained strength during the off-season / All-Star / All- State / exceptional speed / led sweeps / saved two touchdowns by catching a Wagner defensive back from behind after 65 yard run with interception and likewise Vestal's Mike McDonough's kickoff return / throws discus in spring.

"ED KOBAN (*'FAST EDDIE'*): SR, 6' 1"-167' — QUARTERBACK

Team catalyst and co-MVP / All-Star / All-State / virtually impossible to defense because of ability to run and throw / exceptional ability to read defenses / ran for 380 yards (5.1 average) and threw for 770 and 8 TD's on 48-for- 93 / scored 54 points / key man on basketball team and STAC hurdle champion.

"TIM MARSH (*'ZUKE'*): SR, 6'-176' — HALFBACK and KICKER

Three-year varsity player / All-Star last two / All-State / one of the most versatile and talented athletes in U-E history / gained 682 yards in 105 carries (6.5 average) / threw two long TD passes on halfback option / scored 112 points on 14 TD's, 6 PAT runs, 19 PAT kicks, and a field goal / scored 207 career points / high percentage of kickoffs went into end zone / team co-MVP / plays basketball and baseball.

"CARL NORRIS: JR, 5' 9"-163' — HALFBACK

First-year starter / All-Star / gained 630 yards on 109 carries (5.8 average) / scored 12 touchdowns and 6 PAT points for 78 total / runs 10.1 for 100 yard dash and led off Section IV 880 relay champions / plays basketball / only offensive starter returning next year.

"ERIC PEDLEY (*'PEDS'*): SR, 5' 9"-201' — GUARD

Three-year varsity player / team captain / All-Star / All- State / fastest offensive lineman / devastating on traps and sweeps / very quiet / very steady / plays baseball.

"CHUCK WESKO: SR, 6' 2"-211' — CENTER

Three-year varsity player / All-Star / very accomplished snaps with perfect spirals on kicks / handles several types of blocking assignments exceptionally well / very quiet."

DEFENSE (alphabetically):

"LARRY ANGELINE: SR, 5' 10"-205' — NOSE MAN

Three-year varsity player / All-Star last two / All-State / All- American / in on 138 tackles all over the field, 5 QB sacks, recovered a fumble / very strong and quick / frequently double teamed by opponents / discus thrower in track.

"GENE BUCCI (*'BOOCH'*): SR, 5' 11"-167' — SAFETY

Three-year varsity player / All-Star for last two / All- State / only player capable of running step for step with split end Bucci / led team with 6 interceptions / in on 61 tackles / dangerous kick-return man.

"SCOTT DePOFI (*'POFFER'*): SR, 5' 10"-183' — LINEBACKER

Two-year starter / All-Star / intercepted 2 passes / leading tackler with 153 / has nose for the ball and hits with authority / also plays hockey.

"ARMIE GEORGE: SR, 6'-187' — END

Two-year starter / All-Star / led team with 4 fumble recoveries, 4 fumbles caused, and tied Villanti with 6 QB sacks / involved in 99 tackles / made a pair of interceptions / recovered 3 fumbles, blocked a punt, and intercepted pass all in first half against Central.

"JIM NEWFROCK (*'FROG'*): SR, 5' 10"-176' — HALFBACK

Two-year starter / All-Star / in on 134 tackles / intercepted two passes, caused 2 fumbles, recovered 2 / sprinter on Section IV 880 relay champs / also triple jumps and plays basketball.

"RICK OWEN: JR, 6'-174' — END

First-year starter / had four sacks / forced two turnovers, and intercepted a pass / made 87 tackles / plays baseball / very quiet person.

"VINCE PANICCIA: JR, 6'-179' — LINEBACKER

Leader of the few starting underclassmen / All-Star / involved in 118 tackles, caused three fumbles and intercepted a pass / very strong for size.

"NICK PICCIANO: SOPH, 5' 8"-167' — LINEBACKER

Only sophomore in the starting lineup / intercepted 2 passes / one of the harder hitters on team / hit like a linebacker, but covered receivers like a halfback / involved in several tackles all over the field.

"RANDY STRAIN: SR, 5' 11"-182' — LINEBACKER

Came on strong as a senior / All-Star / intercepted two passes, caused two fumbles, recovered one / involved in 119 tackles / excellent wrestler.

"KEN TATKO: SR, 6' 5"-235' — TACKLE

Two-year starter (last year on the other side of ball as tight end) / All-Star / All-State / involved in 133 tackles, four sacks / recovered three fumbles and intercepted a pass / throws the shot put and discus in track.

"STEVE VILLANTI (*'HUEY'*): SR, 6' 4"-243' — TACKLE

Three-year varsity player / All-Star / All-State / tied team honors with 6 QB sacks / in on 137 tackles / deceptive agility for size / wrestles and throws the shot put."

Here's a "side-statistic" that doesn't show up in any book, but might be of interest: Upon closer inspection of the 17 senior starters listed above, one would discover that 16 of them had the opportunity to continue their education and football. (The 17th chose to continue his education through another sport.) Nine of these 16 basically received full football scholarships, while most of the others received partial financial aid. Even a few senior reserves were recruited and continued with football in college. These "side-statistics" were overshadowed, perhaps, but they were surely without precedent then, and may stand forever. We are just as proud of these placement "side-stats" as any of the on-field achievements, records, and accolades.

It's time to "walk" you through this amazing season by quoting the media's capsule-summaries, game-by-game. First the headline, then the summary:

'U-E Sours Sweet Home with 47-0 Drubbing.'

"They were surly and swaggering when they arrived, but shocked and staggering upon departure. The Panthers of Buffalo's Sweet Home High School, generally regarded as one of New York State's annual gridiron giants, were more like Christians thrown to starving Tigers in Saturday evening's 1979 football opener at Ty Cobb Stadium. Union-Endicott's 47-0 rout could have been much worse as the visitors were pushed all over the bright green grassy field. Both the Tiger offensive and defensive units shared the honors in handing startled Sweet Home the worst loss in the proud school's history."

'Tigers Nail Norwich with Second Half Offense.'

"For most of a sunny Saturday afternoon a small, stubborn, scrappy Norwich football team, predicted as a pushover for the Union-Endicott scoring machine, clung to the edge of the cliff. It seemed inevitable that the bigger, quicker Tigers (even with "Fast Eddie" Koban nursing a sore ankle and not in uniform — author's note) would eventually shove the determined home team over the edge. However, it took much longer than anyone anticipated for the Tigers to amass the 34-0 final score."

'Tigers Put Central in the Doghouse, 78-0!'

"Unveiling a twentieth century point-a-year offense which missed by an extra point of matching the final two digits of the current date, Union-Endicott's unbeaten football team rolled it up on Central 78-0 Saturday evening at home."

As I recall, the reserves took over for most of the second half, played very well, and accounted for the last 24 points. One irate Central alumnus whom I know personally, sent me a blistering note accusing me of *"running it up"* (*i.e.*, leaving the first team in too long). However, I believe he eventually apologized (or semi-apologized, anyway) after he watched us continue to post some big numbers. I hope he realized that we never tried to embarrass anybody. He observed us continue to empty the bench each week, as soon as possible, as a philosophy. I'm sure he finally came to the conclusion that his reaction had been more of frustration — and loyalty to his alma mater — than of fact. As the season progressed (along with the numbers), a few letters-to-the-editor about the same subject (*i.e., "rolling it up"*) began to surface — obviously written by a few disgruntled fans from the area who felt they should vent their frustration with a pen.

'U-E meatgrinder 63, North numb.'

"Well, Binghamton North footballers 'crossed the Rubicon' by penetrating mighty Union-Endicott's previously unsoiled 35-yardline last night, and the Indians even had the audacity to score twice. But, after 48 minutes the Red and Blue were just as black and blue as U-E's three previous 1979 victims, getting caught in a 63-14 avalanche."

I remember we came away from that game with a lot of respect for the entire North team — especially its center, Dick Alston. I've never understood why, but the position of center is often overlooked at all levels of football. If Alston isn't the best we ever faced, he is surely one of the very best.

These mid-season state rankings may be of interest:

Number 18 — Shenendehowa. We had scrimmaged *The Plainsmen* in pre-season, and I'm sure Coach Steuerwald would be the first to tell you that it was the only time, in all of our many super, closely-contested scrimmages, we were completely dominant.

Number Seven — Johnson City (would be our guest in two weeks).

Number One — remained U-E.

Now, back to the game-by-game capsule-summaries:

'Top-ranked U-E's 34-6 is no comedown.'

"Perhaps when it was scheduled 2 years ago, it was expected to be a close battle of intersectional powers. What Union-Endicott's game with Staten Island's Susan B. Wagner High last night actually was, however, was the fifth in a series of U-E Laughers of the week, as the state's top-ranked team breezed to a 34-6 victory."

(Incidentally, Wagner became the state's *Number One*-ranked team not too many years later.)

'Tigers Maul Surprised Wildcats.'

"Johnson City football coach, Chuck Gottfried, remarked earlier in the year after scouting the Union-Endicott gridiron juggernaut, 'They have so much speed it should be illegal.' Saturday evening before almost 8,000, a crowd usually reserved for U-E — Vestal wars, Gottfried was a helpless spectator as U-E struck from all over Ty Cobb Stadium to humble the proud Wildcats 55-6. The U-E defense, which gave up just one run for as much as eight yards, certainly shared the spotlight with the point-a-minute offense. Johnson City is a fine football team, one which will probably win another Division II title. However, it was no contest."

Another account:

'U-E Charitable, 55-6.'

"'Explosive' is the word people keep using to describe Union-Endicott's football team. Johnson City found out just how explosive last night as the undefeated Tigers rolled to their sixth straight victory, 55-6." The word, "charitable," in this headline must have referred to this printed post-game quote by Coach Gottfried: "First of all I would like to thank U-E for not running it up. Fran Angeline and his team have been getting some bad press lately and I just want it known that we appreciate them pulling their first string after they got 48 (points). I'm not being sarcastic, either. If he had left his No. 1 offense in, they could easily have put 60 or 70 on the board."

I have never forgotten that quote. Other coaches had expressed similar feelings to me, privately. However, for a coach to say this on record showed me a lot. Is it any wonder that Chuck Gottfried was as successful as he was?

'U-E Gridders Grind M-E, 51-0.'

"Several spectators at Maine-Endwell on a sunny but chilly Saturday afternoon were anticipating Ambush II. What they witnessed was Blowout VII. The Union-Endicott football machine, apparently having some recollection of last year's 24-12 M-E surprise party, immediately crushed any notion of a rerun. U-E's explosive first offense did a whole game's work in half the time, hitting its average of 51 points by intermission, then retiring to the sideline after just one second half play."

I can remember vividly the booing when we sent in the reserves — and it was coming from our own fans who were sitting almost on top of us in the small, close visitors' stands behind us. Obviously, our *Tiger* fans were hungry — they wanted more — a lot more — *they wanted 100!*

And why? What would that prove? What possible good could come of it — for anyone? Does one try to humiliate a never-say-die *Spartan* squad and its first-year coach? (This must be what it was like in the Roman arenas in ancient times.) Besides, don't the reserves who have been working so diligently day after day to help prepare the first team for the opposition deserve a chance to go out there to reap the benefit of their daily hustle and sweat?

Well, we continued to raise our fans' blood-thirsty ire by playing every single boy for the remainder of the game. To M-E's credit, the score didn't change. They had every reason to throw in the towel, but did not. Perhaps our players AND FANS learned something about humility and compassion that day. After the game, M-E's coach, John Furey, was the second coach in as many weeks to go on record in coming to our defense, by stating, "U-E has been getting heat from people about running up scores, but I'd like to say that Fran [Angeline], his other coaches, and his kids are class all the way." Thank you, John.

'Tigers Pound Little Red, 35-0.'

"Ithaca's proud defense had not allowed a touchdown in six consecutive contests. That enviable streak lasted exactly three minutes and 43 seconds into Saturday's clash with Union-Endicott at Ty Cobb Stadium. Furthermore, the Little Red had surrendered just 24 total points while rolling up a 5-1-1 record. However, 24 Tiger seniors gave a memorable final home field performance in what will be a very memorable football season as U-E recorded its fourth shutout 35-0 in an 8-0 campaign."

Incidentally, at about this time, several letters-to-the-editor (not all from Endicott, either) began to appear, in rebuttal to the earlier grousing over *"rolling it up."*

'U-E Shuts out Vestal, 16-0.'

"For more than a half, the highest scoring football machine in Southern Tier history was held to one unsatisfying field goal, but then Union-Endicott found its sea-legs. And once it finally broke the touchdown barrier against its begrudging Vestal hosts, the state's No.1-ranked high-school team was in complete command of a 16 - 0 season-closing victory last night."

Another account:

'Tigers Blank Vestal, 16-0, in Mud.'

> "'Our offensive game plan was to control the ball and to run low-risk plays to avoid turnovers which U-E's defense has forced to blow open several games this year,' offered Vestal offensive coordinator, Dave Sammon. 'Because of the difference in size up front, we used an unbalanced line to double team Larry Angeline, who killed us last year. Still we couldn't budge them!' Thus surfaces, from the rice paddy which Vestal dares call a football field, the story of Friday's 16-0 U-E triumph over the Bears. While the high-powered U-E offense received much notoriety during a highly productive fall, the Tiger defense often remained in the shadows. However, they cast huge shadows as the first unit surrendered just three touchdowns all fall. The awesome U-E defenders opened the season with three straight shutouts and closed it the same way. The Bear offense never saw U-E's 35-yard line."

My recollection of that game? A staunch Vestal defense, an abundance of slick mud, AND LOTS OF FLAGS — as a matter of fact, ten of them, costing us a total of 96 yards, and who knows what else? I sometimes wonder how our troops maintained their poise out there at times — but they did, much to their credit.

Liverpool High School and Henninger High School of Syracuse finished their season ranked close to the top in the state. The Syracuse press held a post-season interview about state rankings with a few of the prominent *Section III* coaches: George O'Leary of Liverpool, Tom Acee of Henninger, and Bobby Campbell (remember him?) of Christian Brothers Academy. O'Leary was quoted as saying, "I didn't see U-E, but I understand they're a great football team." Apparently both Acee and Campbell had watched the *Tigers* a couple of times. "I was taken aback by their tremendous speed, when I've always heard of U-E teams as power teams," said Acee. Bobby stated, matter-of-factly (as Bobby has been known to do on occasion), "U-E versus Liverpool? — Neither Liverpool nor Henninger belongs on the same field with U-E." John Furey's (M-E) post-game assessment of U-E: "They're an incredible football team — *Awesome!* — They're quick, they're big, they love to hit — Everything you could want in a team, they have — and more."

As the season was winding down, one reporter's summary still rings today: "This U-E team, unquestionably Fran Angeline's finest and potentially one of, if not the best, in U-E's successful history, is an awesome collection of talented, versatile, all-around athletes. It does not defeat opponents, it destroys, demolishes, demoralizes, disassembles, and disintegrates them."

Ithaca and Vestal finished as runners-up with identical 6-2-1 records, including identical divisional records of 2-1-1.

In the *Division II* race, coach John Paske's (there's a guy who always seemed to get a lot of mileage out of the material at hand) Chenango Valley *Warriors* came out of nowhere to break JC's long stranglehold on that division, by shocking the *Wildcats* 22-20 in the finale. CV ended up with an impressive 7-2-0 record, while JC wound up just a hair back, recording 6 wins, 2 losses, and 1 tie.

As Shakespeare said: *"...then lend the eye a terrible aspect."*

ALL STARS — THE LATE 70's (1977-1979)

1977

OFFENSE			DEFENSE		
School	Position	Player	School	Position	Player
DIVISION I					
IHS	E	DAVE HARDY	IHS	DB	DAVE HARDY
IHS	G	DENNIS GALLAGHER	VHS	T	STEVE GARLOCK
IHS	RB	GREG JORDAN	VHS	LB	MIKE GATES
IHS	RB	MIKE LOGAN	VHS	DB	DAVE WHALEN
IHS	K	TIM MARCHELL	VHS	P	DAVE WHALEN
VHS	QB	GREG STENTO	SV	E	JON KIMMEL
SV	E	JON KIMMEL	SV	T	BILL RANSOM
SV	T	ROD THORN	SV	LB	ROB MUSKA
SV	G	ROB MUSKA	UE	E	BILL MILLS
SV	C	BILL RANSOM	UE	T	MIKE MOTT
UE	T	DAVE HAINES	UE	LB	DAVE KINSELLA
			UE	DB	LARRY STARCHOCK
DIVISION II					
ME	G	TIM MEADE	OFA	L	GARY OKSUTCIK
ME	RB	GARY BRECKNER	OFA	LB	STEVE ZENDARSKI
ME	E	BOB McDONALD	OFA	DB	RANCE BRODE
JC	T	TONY CAPRARI	JC	L	RANDY BUTTMAN
JC	G	DAVE KRECKZKA	JC	LB	GREGG KLEINSMITH
JC	RB	MARK SEAMAN	JC	DB	LOU MILLER
JC	K	TED JUNKO	JC	P	MARK SEAMAN
			ME	L	BOB RHODES
			ME	L	CHUCK BERTONI

1978

DIVISION I					
IHS	G	TOM OLIVER	IHS	L	BOB HICKEY
IHS	C	BOB ARMSTRONG	IHS	DB	DAVE HARDY
IHS	FB	GEORGE STILES	VHS	L	GEORGE PUZAKULICS
VHS	E	JIM OPIE	VHS	LB	MIKE GATES
VHS	T	JOHN BRIGGS	VHS	DB	JIM OPIE
VHS	G	MIKE PARTRIDGE	VHS	P	MIKE McDONOUGH
VHS	QB	CAL HARRIS	UE	L	LARRY ANGELINE
VHS	HB	MIKE GATES	UE	L	DAN DeHAAS
UE	E	GARY BEDDOE	UE	LB	DAVE WOLF
UE	T	JEFF BENNETT	UE	DB	GENE BUCCI
UE	QB	CHRIS ANGELINE			
UE	HB	TIM MARSH			
UE	K	TIM MARSH			
DIVISION II					
SCC	E	MIKE FARRELL	SCC	LB	VINCE MICHALAK
SCC	QB	BILL MUSCATELLO	SCC	DB	ANDY HOVANCIK
JC	L	MIKE DORKO	SCC	P	DENNIS CRAVER
JC	L	DAVE KRECZKO	JC	L	JIM McDONALD
JC	RB	JOHN SMEY			

1979

DIVISION I

VHS	RB	MIKE McDONOUGH	IHS	L	DAVE CUTIA
UE	E	GARY BEDDOE	IHS	L	GARY GIORDANO
UE	E	GENE BUCCI	IHS	DB	MIKE WEST
UE	T	DAVE HESS	VHS	L	RICK MYERS
UE	T	JOE AMORESE	UE	L	LARRY ANGELINE
UE	G	ERIC PEDLEY	UE	L	STEVE VILLANTI
UE	G	BILL DOOLITTLE	UE	L	ARMIE GEORGE
UE	C	CHUCK WESKO	UE	LB	SCOTT DePOFI
UE	QB	ED KOBAN	UE	LB	VINCE PANICCIA
UE	RB	TIM MARSH	UE	LB	RANDY STRAIN
UE	RB	CARL NORRIS	UE	DB	GENE BUCCI
UE	K	TIM MARSH	UE	DB	JIM NEWFROCK

DIVISION II

JC	E	MARSHALL PALMER	JC	LB	MIKE DORKO
JC	QB	BRIAN MATUSZAK	CV	L	DANTE VINCI
CV	T	ED KEPHART	CV	LB	RICK BOTTING
CV	QB	MIKE KING	CV	DB	TOM KRNA
CV	RB	PAUL GARRUTO			

The undefeated 1979 Union-Endicott **Tigers** ***earned the*** **NYSSWA Number One** ***ranking in New York State, the*** **STAC Division I Championship,** ***and the the pronouncement of "best team ever," from Vestal's Dick Hoover.***

Captain Paul Norris and the* "First Team" *after completing U-E's first 11-0 season in the 1989* Regionals *at Cornell University.

Chapter Twelve

"The greatest part of a man's life consists of his friendships."

— Abe Lincoln

"THE FIRST TEAM"

Just who are these guys who dubbed themselves, *"The First Team?"* Rick Marsi, a staff writer and columnist with the *Press and Sun-Bulletin* and author, once spent almost an entire week with us gathering background material for a special article he was putting together for the *"Living"* section (not the *"Sports"* section!) of an upcoming Sunday issue.

He attended a few of my Latin classes and conversed with some of the students. He spent most of his time on the practice field with us and, in doing so, braved some pretty inclement weather, along with his photographer, as I recall. (These two hardy souls won the admiration of our coaches and players alike, by their dedication to their work, with little regard for the elements.) He also became a resident-guest in our locker room, our football office, and on our sideline. He wanted to experience the "total picture." Why don't I let Rick retell you about my assistants — *"The First Team"* — and their relationship with me? Here are a few excerpts from his 1992 article, *'Top Tiger'*:

> "Benevolent authoritarians on the field, they bark orders, corrections and praise in a steady stream. Their whistles serve as sonic cattle prods, beeping constantly. 'Start! Stop! Keep moving! Let's hear the pop! Drive! Drive! Pick it up! Blow through there! Snap the wrist! Pump! Pump! Pump!' Like an attack troop, the students bash dummies, run pass patterns, practice defenses. Tuesday is the week's most physical practice. The contact is nearly nonstop.
>
> "Practice is over, a boom box is blaring and steam is coming out of the shower. In their changing area next to the players' locker room, Angeline and his coaches are peeling off layers of sweat gear. Surrounding them, cinder block walls festooned with menus from Italian restaurants they have conquered all over the state. 'We're undefeated at the table,' says Tony Romeo, matter-of-factly. Ed Folli sits on a bench in front of his locker icing an injured knee. Bart Guccia munches popcorn.
>
> "These men are Angeline's immediate family every day of the week from August through November. That includes weekends, when they are either coaching their own team or scouting others from Utica to Westchester County. Every Sunday morning they meet for three or four hours to watch tapes of their previous game and prepare for the next one. Every day after school they practice. In family terms, Angeline's

coaches act more like his brothers than sons. That includes all the ribbing they give him.

"Asked what Angeline was like when he coached against Romeo's North High School team in the 1960's, Romeo thinks briefly, then answers, 'Thinner.' 'The only man who can sleep and eat popcorn at the same time,' adds Folli. Talk of the coach's long-standing fondness for food soon meanders toward talk of his sweater. 'Remember your old brown sweater, your lucky sweater?' Guccia asks. 'There were a lot of wins in that sweater,' says Angeline.

"Although Angeline won't speculate about how he wins so much, he has no problem crediting his staff. 'I'm lucky to have them and to have kept them so long,' he says. 'Not only do they know football, but they know these kids. They're in school with them every day. If you broke up with your girlfriend, they know. If you failed a test, they know.'"

More than one rival coach has expressed to me upon a couple of occasions how they envied the stability in our football staff. Their reference was mainly to the three men mentioned above, having served as varsity assistants for close to twenty years. Why such a lengthy tenure ... a rarity? I can only try to explore a few possibilities for the answer.

For one thing, I began delegating more responsibilities during the 1970's and have been ever since. Prior to that, I tried to do everything. That, in hindsight, was both impossible and foolish. The above trio of Folli, Guccia and Romeo always said that "I let them work." So, perhaps, that was a contributing factor.

Our policy has always been to promote from within — whenever possible — anytime an opening would occur. That, too, may have been a factor.

Our greatest asset, arguably, was that we all got along with each other so well. It was a happy staff — and a happy staff is a productive one. It's a good thing, because I demanded a lot from them. They willingly accepted any assignment — no job was too great for this crew. I can't say enough about their loyalty, promise, dependability, dedication, and work ethic.

All three were assigned specific "special teams," but their main areas of responsibility were:

Ed Folli — offensive and defensive backs.

Bart Guccia — offensive coordinator (offensive line).

Tony Romeo — defensive coordinator (defensive line).

Two other men would have to be included in *"The First Team"* — Dick Hover and Russ Nicosia. As varsity assistants, both were a major part of the early building process, and served faithfully for many years. (Nick was with me the longest of any assistant — almost thirty years.)

I would feel remiss if I didn't include the following men, who gave unselfishly of themselves for many years, mostly in the solid development of future *Tigers* at the crucial freshmen, modified, and junior varsity levels. They also did a great job of scouting the opposition and of spotting at our varsity games. They were with our football staff from nearly ten to over twenty years:

Bob "Beef" Adams — varsity.

Tom "Burnin' Ben" Bennett — modified.

Gerry Bravi — freshmen.

Tom Breese — freshmen / JV / varsity.

Dan "Cott" Consol — modified / JV.

Ed "Duke" Decker — freshmen (head coach)

Maurice "Hammy" Hamilton — trainer.

Frank "The Duke" Hoyt — modified (head coach).

Frank "Huggie" Huggins — JV (head coach).

Mike Miller — freshmen / JV (head coach).

Tom "Mully" Mullins — modified

Tony Rose — modified/trainer

Frank "Sarge" Sorochinsky — varsity

Wayne "T" Tidick — JV (head coach)

Jim Truillo — modified

There were approximately a dozen other assistants who also did a fine job for us at all levels — but for a much briefer period. Some of them moved; a few of them became head football coaches elsewhere; a few changed careers; a few were let go. I was at Johnson City for only three years, but couldn't have accomplished much without my loyal right-hand man for all three years — Joe Ciesielski.

I formulated a *"Coaching Staff Policy"* in 1957, and was still using the same basic policy, with minor adjustments, in 1992. Whenever hiring a new assistant, my first order of business was to make sure that he understood the policy and that he would become very familiar with it. Here are its major components:

I. *"Coaching Relationships:*

1. Loyalty is a must.
2. Give your maximum effort toward providing an educational experience for each boy and toward developing character by instilling: sportsmanship, loyalty, integrity, scholarship, pride, appearance, conduct, etc.

II. *"Squad Relationships:*

1. Be realistic and consistent in disciplining players.
2. Treat players as men, not boys.

III. *"Community Relationships:*

1. If you believe in what you are doing and are proud of your profession, it will reflect in the community.

IV. *"Faculty Relationships:*

1. Try to develop a good relationship with other members of the faculty; take a sincere interest in their programs and they will, in turn, take an interest in yours; we need their support.

V. *"College Recruiter Relationships:*

1. Do everything you can to help these players further their education.

VI. *"Parental Relationships:*

1. Be tactful — we want them as friends of our program.

VII. *"Administrator Relationships:*

2. Make sure any administrator works through the head coach — never through the assistants up."

Each assistant was evaluated annually on the basis of meeting his duties and responsibilities, and adhering to this policy in its entirety. Seldom did I have to review these expectations with anyone. Over the years, I did feel obligated to let three assistants go, however — each man had his own agenda. There was no easy way to do this, but it had to get done — loyalty and the team must always come first.

I can't say enough about *"The First Team,"* and all the others whom I have mentioned. They coached because they not only loved the sport — they loved the child. There could not possibly be another reason on earth for their choice of profession. They were not in it for the pittance, for sure.

Most of the time it was not unusual for most of them to do over and above what was expected of them. The taxpayers of our school district got their money's worth — I'll tell you that.

An exemplary family? Our personal hurts and setbacks were shared by all, as were our personal joys. We experienced the peaks and valleys, the trials and tribulations, the blood, sweat and tears together. We laughed, cried, and sang together. We did not always agree with each other on everything (not an unhealthy situation, I might add) — but, those few disagreements took place strictly "in-house" (*i.e.*, in the office) at staff meetings. When we walked out that door to coach the team, we were a team, too. I'm reminded of a gem attributed to the legendary college football coach, Johnny Majors. After his team had just administered a resounding upset in one of the prestigious college post-season bowl games, Coach Majors said:

"It's amazing what a team can accomplish
when nobody cares who gets the credit."

Six of my coaches (and five players) have become head football coaches — I'm very proud of that fact. Actually, I am proud of all of my men. Together, we had, and will always have, a very special bond. Yes... I'm a very lucky guy. These men will always be *"The First Team"* to me.

Coach Angeline's other "Family" —
the staff for 1992 — his last season of football at U-E.

GOOD LUCK, FRAN
HE'S CUTE!
WATCH IT LADY, HIS TIGERS ARE MEAN!
TO A GREAT YEAR IN '82
Johnny & Jack

Chapter Thirteen

"Accept the challenges, so that you may feel the exhilaration of victory."

— General George S. Patton

DRASTIC CHANGES

— *THE EARLY 80'S, 1980-1983*

— 1980: Is the Tail Wagging the Dog?

"It was a lousy setup," Frank Roessner, currently the Editorial Page Editor of the *Press and Sun-Bulletin*, stated in a column at the end of the '80 season. This was in reference to the new-look *STAC* alignment. Let's examine this one-year *"package"* — a *"railroad job"* if ever there was one — the deepest abyss into which our league ever plunged, it says here.

The major elements and ramifications of this newest *STAC* experiment? Basically, *STAC* kicked us (the *Big Three*) out of the league. We were given our own "league," still named, appropriately, *Division I*. It consisted of only the three of us — *period!!* (Thank you, *STAC*.)

It would mark the first time in 62 years that the oldest rivals in the books (Central and U-E) would not meet. Can you believe it? — from the once prestigious, annual, traditional *Thanksgiving Day* clash — to no clash at all. *Amazing, indeed!*

Division II was sitting pretty — bursting at the seams with ten teams. How nice and comfy — they certainly wouldn't have to travel far! They wouldn't have to worry about a schedule. The better ones could continue to enjoy lofty rankings at the state level (*"large school division"*) by choosing to, and being allowed to, remain in the *"small school division"* here on the home front. Apparently the public's silence gave tacit approval to this fiasco. But even more remarkable is the fact that 99 percent of the media followed suit.

Roessner was the only media-maverick on this issue, as I recall. Frank certainly summed up the situation in a nutshell with this excerpt from his column:

> "The Southern Tier Athletic Conference looked silly this fall when it split its football teams into two ridiculous divisions — Vestal, Ithaca and Union-Endicott in one camp and everyone else in the other. It was a lousy setup, but nobody in Division II wanted to change it. The 'Big Three' in Division I had to go looking elsewhere for opponents."

Does anyone realize what we had to go through to try to fill a schedule? — The man-hours spent during the entire off-season and pre-season in this endeavor? The telephone expense for this search must have been astronomical. We were lucky to find three willing teams, all with high profiles on the state-level (which is fine) — but all located in the far flung reaches of the state: Buffalo (Sweet Home), Rochester (Aquinas), and Kingston.

Did anyone in *STAC* consider (or care about) a common concern of all school districts: the cost of these ventures? It involved not only the cost of traveling to these schools (It's a good thing there was no oil embargo then!), but also the cost of overnight accommodations in some instances. The travel expenses involved in scouting these teams was another cost-factor, easily overlooked.

Did anyone in *STAC* consider (or care about) the physical drain on these young student/athletes whom they (*i.e., STAC*) forced to take a 3-4 hour bus trip, play, and then spend another 3-4 hours returning home? These were not professional athletes — just high school kids.

Ithaca was very fortunate to fill its slate of 9 games. Vestal and U-E had to settle for only 8 games. (Was this fair?) My recollection tells me that, during our plight, no one (except Roessner) stepped forward to be heard in our behalf. No one said, "Hey! — This is wrong!"

Many fans have probably forgotten the above facts — perhaps because it lasted only one year — with better days ahead. One is supposed to mellow with age, but let me assure you that it still rankles me when I think of this travesty of justice in the world of high school athletics. The tail, indeed, was wagging the dog.

The Challenge: Playing Against the Best — a Way Of Life

Several years ago, a school from another division in our "league" was scheduled to play us the following year. During the off-season, officials from this school requested a meeting with us to discuss this. Represented by its coach and a couple of administrators, this school was welcomed to our Board of Education room by our superintendent, our director of athletics, and myself. The crux of their concern centered around that now well-worn, all-encompassing catch phrase — *"equality of competition."*

I want you to know that these guys were thoroughly prepared for their presentation/plea. Making reference to some kind of large notebook, they quoted detailed information about records, reputations (??), sizes of players, *etc., ad infinitum*. They expounded on all of the reasons why they should not be playing us, but that some other teams in the league should be. We agreed. However, the league set the rules and the schedules. We did not.

Would you believe that we spent two mornings on this subject? (Incidentally, the breakfast pastries, provided by our school district, were outstanding both days — nothing but the best in *Tigertown,* you know!) Our district also had to absorb the cost of a substitute teacher for me for both days. The only reason that I mention this trivia is that, you'll have to admit, we were most gracious hosts considering the circumstances.

Naturally, our only reluctance to go along with this unusual plea was because of our difficulty in filling our schedule.

However, as I told you already, this crew *was organized!* Out of the blue they offered us a carrot. One spokesman said, "If, by the grace of God..." ("Leave Him out of it!," I interrupted.) He restated, "If, by chance, we could somehow find a highly touted team from around the state that was willing to come here, would you let us off the hook?" When he received our immediate, positive reaction to this proposal (naturally), this same party said that he'd try to contact such a team "right now" if he could use our phone. My recollection is that he returned within minutes with a verbal commitment from an excellent team. We mailed out the necessary contracts to this school and everyone was happy. A very successful negotiation.

Even earlier than this, and prior to our long-established annual scrimmage with Shenendehowa, we had been scrimmaging against a school that was a little closer to home. This was a larger school than U-E (as is Shenendehowa), but a disadvantage in enrollment has never deterred us from a match. We had been having a very competitive scrimmage with this school for quite a few years, and had what I felt was a good, solid relationship. Then they had a coaching change (and subsequent philosophy), and the "rules" changed: The new coach, who was familiar with our program, called us (at least he extended us the courtesy of contacting us months before the season) to inform us that he wished to terminate the scrimmage. This was his first order of business as the new coach. Upon further discussion, he finally admitted, "The bottom line is that we want to establish a winning program." (That statement would have a familiar ring in later years.)

We spent years trying to get the biggest and highest state-ranked Long Island schools on our schedule. Only Bellport accepted the challenge — and that didn't happen until this decade. I remember the exact words from an athletic director from one of these high-profile football schools: "I'm sorry, but we have a full schedule this fall; however, we doubt that we would ever schedule you because frankly, *your reputation precedes you.*" Naturally, we accepted the decisions of these schools in good faith — but we have never understood why they would want to duck us.

No doubt you have probably figured out our philosophy about competition by now: What better way is there to improve than to compete against someone better than, or at least equal to, oneself? We have always tried to compete against the best teams available — come what may. Whether home or away was never a consideration. Personal records and rankings be damned — BRING ON THE BEST! The quality of competition was always the first and foremost priority. I guess I was raised that way — to beat or do well against someone of better or equal ability was honorable, and contained a feeling of accomplishment and self-esteem. To beat someone of inferior ability was a shallow, hollow victory, one with no particular feeling of achievement attached to it. We felt that we owed this philosophy to our players, community, school — and especially, to *"The Man in the Glass"* (*i.e.,* ourselves). Anything less than this would be cheating *"the man"* — he would know — so the others around him would know.

Can you guess who captured the *Division I* championship in 1980? How about all three teams — yes, tri-champions — a "first," I believe? This shouldn't have surprised anyone who had been following the three of us for the previous twenty-some years. We knocked each other off, in our usual closely contested battles, and ended up with identical 1-1-0 divisional records. Mark this, however: *fewer teams* does not necessarily equate with *lesser quality*.

These were three very good football teams. The Binghamton North *Indians* made their last season in history (they would merge with the Binghamton Central *Bulldogs* next year) especially memorable by winning *Division II* with a 7-1-0 record (7-2-0 overall). JC was runner-up with a 6-1-0 record (8-1-0 overall), and Owego Free Academy was in the hunt at 6-2-0 (6-3-0 overall).

More teams does not necessarily equate with *better quality* either. However, North, JC, and Owego all had good, solid teams. U-E just edged North in a rare (for us), high-scoring shootout, 33-30, and JC beat Ithaca. I still don't know how the two of us (Ithaca and U-E) got JC and North, respectively, on our schedules, but I'm sure glad we did. (Incidentally, several years would pass by before JC would appear on U-E's regular-season schedule.)

I was especially happy for Jud Blanchard, since this culminated an extremely emotional season for his school. It must have been a very gratifying season for this hard-working coach (Jud), and the last proud *Indian* squad. One North player who had contributed plenty in almost whipping us on that memorable night was Tom Mullins. We're happy that *"Mully"* would eventually venture west by bringing his short red hair and Irish grin to our staff, where he has continued to perform admirably.

The Invasion of Rome

In spite of this farcical alignment, a couple of dream match-ups emerged for U-E. We picked up a highly touted team from the west — Coach Nick Teta's Rochester Aquinas team, featuring its big, rangy, *All-State* tailback, Don Be'Ans. We were fortunate to get out of that one on the "right" side of a 7-6 score. We had also been negotiating with Rome Free Academy for at least a decade. Coach Tom Hoke's *Black Knights*, with the familiar orange and black colors, were considered among the state's elite annually — and with good reason, as we were about to find out.

The game became a reality. The '80 Rome team was undefeated and had a couple of legitimate *All-State* weapons in its arsenal. We were hurting with injuries at the time. We were warned emphatically by a few of the Syracuse-area coaches, "You're crazy to go up there — nobody can beat Rome at home, no matter how good you are." *What a challenge!* We told our boys that they were going to be participants in *"the Invasion of Rome."* Considering the circumstances, it has to rank as one of the best efforts by any team of ours over the years. Some teams cannot handle adversity, while others thrive on it.

The *Rome Daily Sentinel* had this to say after the game:

> "U-E won the battle of state-ranked gridders at RFA Stadium, 21-15. The defending state poll champions did it in impressive fashion, gaining the victory without a starting tackle, quarterback and halfback. 'Our kids showed a lot of character and plain old guts in winning this one,' U-E Coach Fran Angeline said. 'We faced a lot of adversity and responded well. What can you say about Gilroy and Norris?' This marks six straight wins for U-E since losing to Buffalo Sweet Home in its opener."

The reference to Dan Gilroy, our regular safety, was about the job he did, filling in for our regular quarterback, Bobby Koban. The reference to Bobby Norris, a reserve tailback, was about his stepping up to replace his injured brother, Carl — a rushing performance to the tune of 133 yards on 26 carries and a TD. Mark *"The Vulture"* Kohler, a sophomore reserve lineman, came off the bench very early to replace another injured starter, Dino Dutcher, a tackle. Mark did an admirable job of blocking Rome's rangy, *All-State* tackle, Eric Decker.

Our road-team flavor wasn't over. We beat a highly respected team from the east, too — Coach Tony Badalato's Kingston *Tigers*. With Vince Paniccia, our punishing veteran linebacker providing the leadership all season as captain, we wound up 6-2-0.

At the conclusion of the season, there were no *Division I All-Stars* as its three coaches orchestrated three-way ties at all 24 positions as a protest against *STAC*'s imbalanced scheduling which left us only each other to play. Although some criticized the coaches for our stance, we sincerely felt that, as tri-champions, each of our players was worthy of any *All-Star* team which represented the three teams. Unfortunately, the *STAC* officials didn't see it our way and rejected our recommendation. (Guess they showed us! — And our fine players!)

I've mentioned a few of our guys already. After all these years, I would feel remiss if I didn't mention Vestal's tremendous, blond-haired halfback, Dave Cook. *"Cookie"* killed us, and everyone else (EFA's only conqueror), and would eventually become an assistant coach in the area. He also "operated" on several trees (non-human variety) in the Triple Cities region, as a tree-surgeon in his family's business. I know for a fact that Dave had held a personal grudge against us (me) after our '79 game. I think he more than erased it on the scoreboard in '80 (Vestal 20, U-E 14), and again years later, in our backyard, when he helped to cut down several trees that were beginning to dwarf our house.

The *Bears* also had an outstanding linebacker, Doug Bulman. And what Ithaca fan could ever forget the *Little Red's* aggressive, hard-hitting, two-way lineman — Gary Giordano? I know that our guys picked him, unanimously, on their *All-Opponent* team. He was a dominant force all season long.

— 1981-1983

Lots of good things happened in '81 that changed the league drastically. First of all, the two Binghamton schools merged into one huge, powerful school, retaining Jud Blanchard as its coach. They would be known as the Binghamton *Patriots* and would become extremely formidable opponents.

From the west, our old pals the Elmira Free Academy *Blue Devils*, now coached by Dick Senko, and the Elmira Southside *Green Hornets*, still under the guidance of Tom Hurley, rejoined us. And they brought along a big, respected neighbor — the *Blue Raiders* of Horseheads, coached by a former CV standout, Tom Moffitt. Their rugged, rangy center, Joe Gilbert, eventually joined the football coaching fraternity as a college assistant. This would prove to provide the most stability in *Division I* thus far (although, unfortunately, EFA would beg out after four years). It was almost like the old *STC* and has basically existed since then, as of this writing.

Coach Bob Streeten's Corning East *Trojans* and the *Vikings* of Corning West, under the direction of the highly respected veteran, Arnie Northrop, joined JC and company in *Division II*, making a 7-team structure, also.

Two newcomers — Hornell and Elmira Notre Dame — joined *Division III*. This new league came about by the merger of two leagues and was called the *Southern Trails League*, retaining a single appellation from each of the former leagues.

Besides Vestal's Dave Cook, this period would supply a bunch of outstanding assistant football coaches to the Tier — all U-E *Tigers:* Brian "Juice" Jester would join the U-E staff for a brief stint before entering the business world, Larry "Hondo" Hanafin, Mark "Flinter" Flint, Marty Fisher, and John Anderson, better known as *"Tank"* (who would also make an immediate impact on the baseball scene as Vestal's head coach). Sadly, we lost an old friend and fierce competitor when Tom Hurley of ESS passed away suddenly during the pre-season of '82. (Southside eventually would build its own stadium, and name it, appropriately, in Coach Hurley's memory.)

Johnson City went on a three-year tear of an unbelievable 26 wins, and only 1 loss during the regular season. Only in '83 did it have company, as Corning West and Owego Free Academy, then coached by Al Brunetti, shared the *Division II* title with the *Wildcats* — all three with identical 3-1-0 divisional records. The *'Cats* also enjoyed these *"large school"* state rankings during this stretch: *Number Three* ('81), *Number Five* ('82), and *Number Eleven* ('83). These were all excellent football teams. Coach Fred *"Kobi"* Kobuszewski's Oneonta *Yellowjackets* had *Division III* abuzz in '81 and '82. They rolled to a combined two-year total of 15 wins, 2 losses, 1 tie, garnering the championship both years.

The *Saints* of Seton Catholic Central, under the tutelage of John Allen, burst onto the scene in '83 in *Division III*, finishing a perfect 9-0 season to claim the crown.

The wars within *Division I* during this span were keenly fought. It came down to both Elmiras flexing their muscles alongside U-E. The *Blue Devils'* aggragate record during this period, featuring swift backs and a lightning-quick defense, was an impressive 22-4-1. U-E's was 19-6-1. ESS, then coached by Ed Trexler, won the title in '83 with a 7-1-1 record. The *Hornets* had an unparalleled man-among-boys, a bona fide *All-American* two-way lineman — enormous Pete Curkendall.

Our '81 captain was Dino Dutcher. EFA won the division with a 7-1-1 record. The EFA rooters had plenty to cheer about with the likes of Tony Prettyman racking up the yards and TDs, and a staunch defense, spearheaded by Mark Seals, Lonnie Moss and Mike Reed. Other than tying the *Blue Devils* early in the season (a rare 0-0 tie), our highlight had to be playing against Liverpool in the *Carrier Dome*, the home of the Syracuse University *Orangemen*.

This was another "eleventh-hour" arrangement due to a fluke-opening in Liverpool's schedule. We still had a couple of open dates to fill, and were elated to meet someone of Liverpool's stature — at "*the Dome*." What a great opportunity and experience for *our kids!* Coach George Mangicaro's club boasted a legitimate future "*Parade All-American*," a future Syracuse University and *NFL* (Atlanta *Falcons*) force — Tim Green. Running behind him was a big, swift tailback — Henry Flournory. The *Tigers* did Endicott (and our league) proud with a superb second-half effort to win, 20-6. Among the many fans that night was my daughter, a frosh at S.U. at the time. Vaun brought several of her classmates along to give us an added cheering section — one with an "orange" personality. Ironically, Vaun and Tim Green became friends at S.U. since they not only took a few of the same English Literature classes, but also ran into each other frequently at the football office. (No, Vaun didn't play, but she did assist the football office secretary as part of her financial aid package.)

Coach Angeline with daughter, Vaun, who in 1981, was on campus at the Carrier Dome *with a contingent of Syracuse University classmates to support her high school alma mater in their hard-earned victory over future S.U. friend, Tim Green, and the Liverpool* Warriors.

Our celebration that evening was tempered by the news that Ed Folli's father, Ateo, had suffered a fatal heart attack in the stands while watching the game. The post-game interviews were very trying for me. There were more reporters than usual — they sensed my melancholy, and, to a man, were very kind and compassionate.

With the leadership of our captain-elect, Larry "Hondo" Hanafin, we shared the championship with EFA in '82 — both of us with an identical divisional record of 5-1-0. Ithaca was breathing down our necks, finishing 4-2-0.

It always intrigued me to watch a little guy grow up. Two of the seniors on this '82 team come immediately to mind:

Larry Hanafin grew up just a block away. At times I had the opportunity to observe his aggressive nature, especially when he and his other little elementary school buddies from the neighborhood would gather for some informal football or hockey at *Mersereau Park*. He became an excellent center for us. At 5 feet 9 inches, and only 187 pounds, he often had to block nose guards who were much bigger than he — especially at Elmira Southside one afternoon. I remember suggesting to him at that time that we consider giving him some *"double-team"* help to block big Pete Curkendall. His reaction? He bristled — I could tell that I had touched his pride-button. And that intangible — pride — is what allowed him to do as well, if not better than, any center in the league had done against this all-world player. I'm not surprised that Hondo Hanafin has become a very good coach.

Jason Marshall was a solid defensive starter on that '82 team. He and I had met many years before in the U-E gymnasium. It must have been inclement weather that night because we were indoors for night-practice. Jason's mom, Ernie, our affable assistant athletic director, must have opened up the gym for us and had brought little pre-school Jason along. I can still envision this little man and all his paraphernalia: He was ready for practice — he was wearing his football helmet, but his cowboy hat was in one hand, too. He had a miniature football in the other hand and a toy gun and holster set strapped on. Now there was a guy who was ready to defend his turf — *at all costs!* Many years later this tiny cowboy/gridder blossomed into a strapping 6 feet 1inch, 197 pound young man. I can assure you that he did defend his turf — and he did it very well.

Beating EFA at *Dunn Field* (27-7), mainly by keeping John Garvin in check most of the time, and by quarterback Al Pedley's *keepers* off the *counter-option*, has to rank as one of our better efforts. But, it may shock you to know that it was probably a loss that was the genuine high point of that '82 season. It took place at mid-season, and had been ballyhooed as a dream match-up.

The *Number Two*-ranked team in the state, Rome Free Academy, was about to challenge the *Number One*-ranked team, U-E...in Endicott. Both teams had some marquee players, all of whom would go on to state honors, and a few, beyond that.

Rome had a dynamite trio: A clever leader at quarterback, Chris Destito (as a relative of the owners of that great restaurant, *"The Savoy,"* he had to be good! — he would become football captain of the *U.S. Military Academy* at West Point); a slashing, shifty runner — Dan Nelson; an all-purpose player — slippery, elusive Paul Pelton.

The *Tigers* countered with their own household names: Alex Rita, who set a single game record of tackles (by a back) in that game — 29; Joe Mott, end/linebacker who, after a brilliant *Big 10* career at the University of Iowa, would earn a starting job at outside linebacker for the New York *Jets* of the *NFL* before severe injuries would abort his professional career. Our offensive fire-power was provided by Bobby Norris, who would go on to set the *"all-purpose yardage"* records at the University of Delaware.

An enthusiastic crowd, estimated at upwards of 13,000, including Syracuse University's Mac MacPherson and several other college scouts — and a large TV audience — were treated to what one reporter called, "a high school state championship football game which had all the elements of a championship boxing match — a flurry of action that was decided by who would hit quickest and latest." Rome 8, U-E 7.

In '83, although both EFA and U-E had strong teams, each posting 7-2-0 records (4-2-0 in the division), "The Sting was back," as Coach Ed Trexler (ESS) liked to say. Towering Pete Curkendall was still around for his last campaign (*whew!*) before taking his talents to Penn State. He certainly made his presence known on both sides of the ball by leading the *Hornets* to a 7-1-1 record (4-1-1 in the division) and the coveted *Division I* crown.

Led by our captain-elect, *"Tank"* Anderson, we experienced some very memorable moments in '83. I'm sure some of our players would mention the *Kingston Zoo* as one of those special moments. We had arrived at Kingston for our opener earlier than anticipated. We ate a leisurely pre-game box lunch provided by our Booster Club on picnic tables (pre-arranged). Unknown to us — but not for long — there was a zoo on the premises. We were sitting around and trying to relax — downwind. Enough said?!?

Later, as I watched the Kingston players check into their locker room before the game at *Dietz Stadium*, I was impressed with their overall size and physical maturity. In fact, Mike Miller, our JV coach, pointed out one of them who was hugging some little children at the time — I remember Mike remarking that perhaps the little tots were his (the player's) own. I can recall asking a few Kingston boosters about the Kingston ace, Parker (and he was a great one). I remarked that he could easily pass for mid-twenties (since I had seen him up close, earlier). I've never forgotten the response I received: "Oh, he's a 'P-G' (post-graduate) — just taking a few courses." I think I was too much in shock to tell this fan that "P-G's" had not been eligible in New York State since 1951.

I just responded limply, "Oh," and never did follow through on this statement. We developed a solid relationship with Kingston as the years went on. But, I'll tell you it was all we could do that night to contain Parker, and that fan's comment crossed my mind more than once as we held them off just enough to win, 27-22.

Again we had the opportunity to play "the best from the west." Although we never had the opportunity to meet any of Coach Don Quinn's excellent East Rochester clubs, we were thankful to have been able to compete against two of the top guns in the west — Sweet Home of Buffalo (*Section VI*) and Aquinas of Rochester (*Section V*). Fairport (Rochester — *Section V*) and Jamestown (*Section VI*) have become powers in the west more recently.

Buffalo's Bishop Timon Catholic generally ruled that part of the state throughout most of the 1980's. It was a thrill to just edge Coach Paul Fitzpatrick's very well-drilled powerhouse in our inaugural meeting ('83) by a score of 21-15. We would compete for seven straight years. An excellent relationship, and a mutual respect developed between our two schools. What *battles* we had! We feel fortunate to "lead" this super series by the narrowest of margins, four games to three. (Perhaps the series will be renewed someday — I'd love to see it.)

Another "high" in '83 occurred when we nipped (and I mean nipped) EFA in the last seconds. Some U-E fans had given up and resignedly left our stadium too early. But we would get back at them when we showed the game-film to the public during the following week: We turned off the projector with 66 seconds to go, inside our own 20 yard-line, and sarcastically teased our audience by commenting that anyone who wished to leave again could do so now. We didn't have any takers.

A never-say-die trio provided the heroics: Brian *"Juice"* Jester, hobbling on a bum ankle, but still throwing darts all over the field, executed the *Two-Minute Offense* (realistically a *One-Minute Offense* that night!) to perfection. His targets were Greg Prusia, performing his usual circus-catches all over the field and Joe Mott who caught the decisive, last two strikes — both on short-medium range crossing patterns, both coming off play-action — one for the TD, the other for the PAT. Final score: U-E 15, EFA 14.

Only Owego of the *Division II* tri-champions scheduled us in '83. We won, 20-0.

An individual feat probably overshadowed what was, arguably, our best effort of the '83 season — a 39-10 victory over Ithaca at home. I remember it well. It was "one of those nights" that all coaches hope to experience...often. Our tough, wiry, quick Kurt Felton set a Broome County *"Rushing Record"* (which may still stand?) of 306 yards. The amazing fact is that most of these came by the "tough" route — between the tackles — mostly on *dives* and *traps*.

Little did I know at the time (although he hinted at it when we met after the game) that this would be the last time the *Little Red's* Joe Moresco and I would ever meet on "the fields of friendly strife." This legend, this football giant would walk away from a sparkling football coaching career at the end of the season. Upon hearing the news, I had a lump in my throat. The league was losing another leader — I was losing a close friend and fierce competitor. I remember feeling alone — as if my football world were crumbling — my two old *STC* buddies were gone. Future Ithaca versus U-E clashes would continue as a natural, old rivalry, but they never held the same intensity or emotion for me.

Earlier in the season, another intense competitor and friend, Jud Blanchard, had announced his resignation. Due to the timing of the announcement, we were the unfortunate victims of this moment — at *North Field*. Many of Jud's former players had come by to wish him well that night. It was a very emotional evening for both of us...we had been doing battle for approximately fifteen years now.

The *Patriots* won that high-scoring contest, 38-34. Their diminutive package of red, white, and blue dynamite, by the name of Rick Hill, scampered for 179 yards and three hard-earned touchdowns. I think his legs are still pumping. He gave a performance that should have been an inspiration to any running back.

After congratulating Jud in our post-game chat, I whispered to him that I hoped he would reconsider his resignation — that as coaching brethren, we needed him. Although I'm sorry that we would never compete again, I'm happy to say that Jud didn't waste much time rejoining the coaching fraternity. He would take the Seton Catholic Central program to new heights in the late 1980's, and then rescue a faltering program at Susquehanna Valley in more recent years.

Post-Season *Section IV* Bowl Games

The 1980's ushered in post-season play. A *Section IV* committee decided to use *"Harbin points"* as the rating system to determine the match-ups. Since one must understand how this works, I'll try to address its main components here, without getting too technical.

Harbin points:

"First-level points" — 4 points for beating a *Class A* team (basically, a *Division I* team), 3 points for beating a *Class B* team (basically, *Division II* and some *Division III* teams), 2 points for beating a *Class C* team, and 1 point for beating a *Class D* team (basically, a few of these *Class C* and *D* teams came from *Division III*, but most came from the other leagues within the section — the *Susquenango Association* and the *Interscholastic Athletic Conference*).

"Second-level (strength of schedule) points" — All points accumulated by each of a team's victims (or half of the accumulation by a team it has tied).

Therefore, the match-ups and results of the Bowl Games (*Class A* and *B*) — 1980:

Class A: EFA 27, U-E 6
Class B: JC 34, Windsor 0

I'll be honest, I felt a little foolish as a representative in this initial play-off. After all, Vestal had beaten both of us (EFA and U-E) during the regular season, fair and square, but missed out on the basis of the point system. One can hardly blame the *Bears* for feeling somewhat miffed sitting home. I don't think that I helped our effort in that bowl game. I know that we were all down after just losing a heart-breaking finale to Vestal. I really wasn't that excited about the game, since it wouldn't lead to anything beyond. (A few of us around the state, including Senator Tarky Lombardi and Mac MacPherson from Syracuse, had been campaigning for a long time for a state play-off system.) I must admit that I didn't even understand why we agreed to play at all, and I think that our kids' performance that night reflected my attitude.

The media summarized the game well: "U-E was flatter than a pancake." I must add, however, that the *Blue Devils* were superb. Their all-everything quarterback, Blaine Fowler, a four-year starter who was destined to join the assembly line of future great *NFL* quarterbacks at Brigham Young University, certainly lived up to his advance publicity — and then some. They beat us convincingly in every department.

Match-ups and results of the Bowl Games (*Class A* and *B*) — 1981:

Class A: There was no game. One must understand the growing pains of this post-season experiment to fully appreciate what took place in '81. U-E broke the ice during the pre-season. With the full support of our superintendent, Dr. William Zimmerman and our athletic director, Dick Hover, we opted not to participate in any post-season play in '81, if we should qualify. This was not a flippant decision, I can assure you. The reason? Mainly, we saw no point in playing someone a second time (as of '81, all of the eligible *Class A* schools were in the newly formed league — in *Division I*). The other reason was the same nagging question: Where would it lead? Therefore, although we would have easily been one of the representatives when the points had been tabulated at the end of the season, we had already deferred in August. So, the next two "A" teams with the most points happened to be EFA and ESS. Since they had just met for their annual inter-city, highly emotional "war," the Elmira administrators wisely chose not to repeat the match-up one week later. (But, as you'll see, perhaps some good would come out of those deferrals.)

In the *Class B* Bowl Game, JC paid back an old debt to Chenango Forks by hammering the *Devils,* 33-8.

The Bowl format for *Class A* and *B* changed drastically from 1982 on. Influenced by the previous season's deferrals and the reasons behind them, no doubt, the *Section IV* committee decided to change the format (*i.e.*, the match-ups): From now on there would be four Bowls, depicted by Roman numerals. The *Bowl I* match-up would have a "natural attraction" (financially rewarding to the section) of the top team in the former *Class A* against the top team in the former *Class B*. *Bowl II* would consist of, basically, the top team in *Division III* against the top-ranked big team from the *Susquenango Association*. *Bowls III* and *IV* would consist of the smaller schools in the other leagues. So, although this still wasn't heading to a "next" step, the concern of playing the same team twice was virtually eliminated.

Since U-E officials appreciated the committee addressing this concern, and since we had been assured by some Albany "insiders" that a state play-off was a "live" issue (and therefore, that this was a step in that direction), we advised the committee to count us in if we should qualify. It should be noted that a few people in the *Division I* camp were not totally receptive, however. When voting on the proposed new format, I clearly remember Joe Moresco making this analogy: "If someone won't sit down at my table for dinner during the nine-week regular season, why should he be invited to the big banquet at the end?" (Approximate quote.) You'll have to admit — Joe certainly had a point.

Match-ups and results of Bowl Games (*I* and *II*) — 1982:

Bowl I: JC 24, U-E 15

Bowl II: Oneonta 20, Windsor 0

Our Bowl Game versus JC received a lot of pre-game hype. One headline, perhaps in an attempt to stir up even more emotion than already existed, blared: ***'Call U-E vs. JC the Grudge Bowl.'*** Another read, ***'Coaches' feud sparks rivalry.'*** These may have been in reference to our previous two meetings, at the close of the 70's — both one-sided victories in our favor. But they probably referred more to my well-known long-standing gripe about JC's divisional jump that began long before Chuck Gottfried had arrived. It's just that "the gripe" became magnified with Johnson City's complete dominance of the smaller schools' division and relative success whenever meeting a *Division I* school.

Actually, Chuck Gottfried and I had gone back quite a few years — back to the 1960's, as a matter of fact. His coaching ability is unquestioned, but how many know that he was one of the best college recruiters who ever came a'callin? And we had our share. (At times he would bring along his pleasant wife Betty — a nice family touch.)

I remember a lengthy discussion about our favorite subject that Chuck and I had in those days. The occasion was the annual convention of the *National Football Coaches Association*, being held in Houston, Texas. We had just run into each other in the lobby of the biggest hotel these eyes had ever seen (this was Texas — *"big country!"*). The hotel was hosting this football convention. (I feel compelled to share a bit of the lore of this hotel — although I can't remember its name — with all movie buffs: Allegedly, it had once been owned by one Jett Rink. Many will recognize the name as the sulking, cackling wrangler-turned-rich-oil-man, as portrayed by the legendary James Dean in the film, *Giant.*) Chuck was telling me that he was getting tired of spending so much time on the road, recruiting. He stated further, something like, "I'd love to have a job down there [Triple Cities] just like yours." I didn't realize how serious he was until a few years later when, to my delightful surprise, I learned about his new position at Johnson City High School.

I still chuckle every time I think of the following incident at *Golden Valley* summer football camp: Most of the coaching staff had ventured "downtown" (that's about the size of a football field in Sidney, New York) for a late-night snack. Now, some folks can't eat much late at night...then there are others. After I had finished quite a sizeable "snack," we were all sitting around, relaxing and telling "war" stories. The subject eventually evolved to food consumption. Chuck (somewhat in jest) belted out, "#*!*!#~*, Fran, you won't be eating that much when you get to be my age!"

Yes, Chuck and I had been friends a long time before "the gripe" of this 1982 Bowl Game. And we still are. However, one must realize that reporters have to sell newspapers, too. I can appreciate that.

We entered the game in an unaccustomed role of decided underdogs. One printed prediction was: "JC 22, U-E 8." (Pretty close — we "beat the line," I guess.) The outcome certainly substantiated the prediction. Chuck and I both saw a very well-played shootout. (And we didn't even get in *one punch* against each other!) It must have been exciting for the spectators. JC had a brilliant offensive game plan — the *'Cats* kept us off balance consistently with short circle patterns thrown underneath our coverage, and executed to perfection by their shifty, hard-working backs — Rich Kozak and Tim Brozovic as receivers. (Tim's wife, Theresa, now teaches at U-E, so something good came out of this!) Their talented quarterback. rangy Dick Dino (son of my '58 JC captain, Dave Lutsic) just stood tall and never threw better. These short passes complimented their rushing game very well and allowed their offense to methodically chew up both the yardage and the clock — keeping Bobby Norris and company off the field.

Since none of the other outstanding JC teams of the early 80's was on our schedule, I didn't really get to see them much. We would play some more fine JC teams in the late 80's. For the record, I wouldn't hesitate to put my money on this 1982 JC club as its best — *ever!* Such size up front, such experience, talent, cohesion, and balance! It says here that one would have to go all the way back toward the end of Eddie Butkus' impressive coaching tenure there (late 1940's - 1950) for any kind of realistic comparison. Those were some real powerhouses at this proud school, filled with tradition. However, prior to 1951, post-graduates were eligible and I don't know that it is fair to compare any modern-era team with pre-1951. But, those are the only JC teams, arguably, that could possibly have matched-up with the 1982 team overall. I told this exceptional '82 JC team as much just after the players had settled down on their bus following the award ceremony at the Bowl Game that day — and I'm glad that I had the opportunity to tell them personally.

Match-ups and results of Bowl Games (*I* and *II*) —1983:

Bowl I: JC 22, ESS 7
Bowl II: Seton CC 29, Windsor 0

ALL STARS — THE EARLY 80's (1980-1983)

1980

OFFENSE / **DEFENSE**

DIVISION I*

* *The 3 coaches submitted 3-way ties at every position. It was not officially accepted by STAC.*

DIVISION II

School	Position	Player	School	Position	Player
OFA	C	JIM KELLY	JC	L	JOHN RENO
JC	G	JEFF BRIGGS	OFA	E	JIM KELLY
JC	RB	ANDY PETERS	OFA	L	KELLY KAFKA
JC	RB	BILL McCROSSEN	OFA	DB	VINNIE KAME
BN	T	JOHN KAKUSIAN	OFA	P	PHIL CROSS
BN	G	KEN HESS	BN	E	VANCE FERRANTE
BN	QB	MIKE CONNOLLY	BN	LB	DOUG WOODRUFF
BN	RB	DOUG WOODRUFF			

DIVISION III*

* *There was no* Division III *in 1980.*

1981*

* *"ALL METRO," as selected by the* Press and Sun-Bulletin *(excludes Elmira area) — League* All-Stars *not available.*

UE	WR	AL CERUTTI	UE	LB	ALEX RITA
UE	WR	CHRIS PAVLOVICH	JC	L	DAVE DURGALA
UE	T	DINO DUTCHER	JC	LB	MIKE MORAN
UE	QB	BOB KOBAN			
JC	RB	ANDY PETERS			
ONEO	G	CHRIS SCHUSTER			
ONEO	RB	TIM PIDGEON			

1982

DIVISION I

EFA	E	MARK SEALS	EFA	T	JOHN ROSS
EFA	G	RON ROGERS	EFA	LB	RANDY RAFFERTY
IHS	C	JIM KING	IHS	T	RAY WHISBY
IHS	RB	JOHN MILES	IHS	LB	STEVE ARMSTRONG
UE	T	MARK KOHLER	IHS	DB	TOM ADDY
UE	RB	BOB NORRIS	UE	E	JOE MOTT
UE	K	DOUG MALARKEY	UE	LB	ALEX RITA
			UE	DB	TED FELTON

DIVISION II

CW	SE	PETE WOODHOUSE	CW	E	JIM GUSTIN
CW	QB	BILL PASSMORE	CW	T	CHRIS MILLER
JC	T	MARK COLLINS	CW	LB	DANA GOBLE

JC	G	RICK KOBB	JC	E	JIM MIHOK
JC	E	DAVE GRISWOLD	JC	T	JOHN WACENDAK
JC	RB	RICH KOZAK	JC	NG	TOM WOLOSZYN
JC	RB	TIM BROZOVIC	JC	LB	DAVE DURGALA
JC	K	MARK CLARK	JC	LB	MIKE MORAN

DIVISION III

ONEO	G	JIM DELELLO	ONEO	E	MIKE MARIOTTI
ONEO	C	JOHN BROE	ONEO	LB	TIM PIDGEON
ONEO	RB	TIM PIDGEON	ONEO	DB	ED HANSON
			ONEO	DB	STEVE ESCHER
			ONEO	P	ED HANSON

1983

DIVISION I

EFA	RB	JOHN GARVIN	EFA	E	ROBIN WILLIAMS
UE	E	GREG PRUSIA	EFA	T	MIKE TROCCIA
UE	G	TANK ANDERSON	EFA	LB	JIM SANFORD
ESS	T	MIKE SANZO	EFA	DB	CHRIS FOGARTY
ESS	G	PETE CURKENDALL	UE	E	JOHN MANCINI
ESS	RB	MILTON BROOKS	UE	LB	JOE MOTT
			UE	DB	GENE ROMA
			ESS	T	MIKE SANZO
			ESS	NG	PETE CURKENDALL
			SS	LB	JEFF MATTHEWS

DIVISION II

CW	T	CLAUDE TRUESDELL	CW	E	JOE FARKOS
CW	G	ERIK GATES	CW	T	JOE WOOD
CW	C	GEOFF BOBICK	CW	LB	PETE HARRINGTON
CW	RB	ED IOCCO	CW	DB	MARK McNANEY
OFA	E	TERRY DOUGHERTY	OFA	NG	SHANE KING
OFA	RB	RAY WILLIAMS	OFA	P	DAVE ZLINSKY
JC	E	RANDY FISHER	JC	E	JIM KABAT
JC	T	JOHN WACENDAK	JC	LB	BRAD BERFIELD
JC	G	ANDY ARMSTRONG	JC	DB	BUTCH SHOEMAKER
JC	QB	TIM SINICKI	JC	DB	JOHN MATYAS
JC	RB	TOM SHEREDY			
JC	K	ANDY WARD			

DIVISION III

SCC	E	CHRIS PHILLIPS	SCC	E	BOB KLEPFER
SCC	E	BOB KLEPFER	SCC	LB	DAN BOHAN
SCC	T	DAN SULLIVAN	SCC	DB	DENNIS GALLAGHER
SCC	C	JOHN McCARTHY			
SCC	QB	DAN SMITH			
SCC	RB	RANDY DeANGELO			

The 1982 Johnson City Wildcats *were undefeated under Coach Chuck Gottfried (including a* Division I *bowl win), and were quite possibly the finest team to ever represent the JC* Maroon *and* White.

If You Think You Can

"If you think you are beaten, you are,
If you think you dare not, you don't,
If you'd like to win, but you think you can't,
It's almost certain you won't.
If you think you'll lose, you've lost,
For out in the world you'll find
Success begins with a fellow's will —
It's all in the state of mind.

Full many a race is lost
Ere even a step is run,
And many a coward falls
Ere even his work's begun.
Think big, and your deeds will grow;
Think small, and you'll fall behind;
Think that you can, and you will —
It's all in the state of mind.

If you think you are out-classed, you are;
You've got to think high to rise;
You've got to be sure of yourself before
You can ever win a prize.
Life's battles don't always go
To the stronger or faster man;
But sooner or later the man who wins
Is the man who thinks he can."

— author unknown

Chapter Fourteen

"After victory, tighten the helmet straps."

— U.S. Military Academy at West Point

EVERYONE MUST PAY HIS DUES

— THE MID 80'S, 1984-1986

"Mathematical" Balance?

More juggling, leaving *Division II* with only five teams. Not to worry, however — EFA wanted out of *Division I*. (Gee, a guy could develop an inferiority complex — wasn't our toothpaste making it?) After great success in all four of its seasons in *Division I* with "the big boys" (champs in '81, '82, '84, and runner-up in '83), EFA sought admission into *Division II*. This request to shift divisions was granted. (Does that sound familiar?) If you're following all of this, the *Southern Trails League* would enjoy mathematical balance for several years — 18 teams, divided into 6 teams per division. Although we would still meet occasionally, we were sorry to lose the automatic, strong competition that the EFA *Blue Devils* always supplied. Meanwhile, *Division II* was holding its collective breath with the addition of EFA, a powerful new adversary.

Vestal's Darren Watson would return to his alma mater as an assistant coach after college. U-E graduated a couple of more fine football coaches during this era — Dan Sinclair and Jim Crunden, a lineman and fullback, respectively. EFA's smooth quarterback, Jeff Limoncelli, would do some coaching in the Elmira area (although I always thought he belonged in Hollywood with his looks). Half of *Division I* saw the debut of three coaches: Steve Deinhardt, a long-time assistant at Binghamton North and the recently merged Binghamton High, now would be elevated to the top spot. Bill Carney took over at Horseheads, and Garry Scutt at Ithaca.

Chuck Gottfried resigned from Johnson City after the '84 season. This gruff, affable guy would be missed — he had certainly left his stamp on football in this league during his all-too-brief twelve-year tenure. Cal Rucker returned to the Triple Cities scene to take over the JC football program and serve as its basketball coach, too.

— 1984: *"The President of the United States Is Coming To Town!"*

It certainly didn't take Steve Deinhardt long to establish himself as an innovative, dedicated young coach. Having had occasion to observe not only the Binghamton varsity, but the junior varsity and modified teams as well, I realized that the *Patriots* would be a dominant force for many years to come. The 1984 *Division I* honors were shared by EFA and Binghamton, each with identical overall records of 7-2-0, and divisional records of 5-1-0. (You're supposed to work into it *gradually,* Steve!) Vestal was right behind: 6-2-0 overall (4-2-0 divisional). EFA's magnificent John Garvin became the first runner in the Twin Tiers to rush for 3,000 yards. (That's plenty of real estate, by any standards!)

We had what we considered a disappointing season — a roller coaster season — and we never really threatened the leaders at all. We had decent material and experience, so we coaches must accept some of the blame. Despite early injuries to some of our key personnel, and eventually losing all three of our quarterbacks, most of our *Tiger* teams up to that point had shown that they could overcome adversity — that they could somehow hang on. Some observers, close to the situation, felt that we never quite recovered from all the unique, pre-season hoopla — the circus-like atmosphere forced upon us. (They may be right.)

Two unusual occurrences took place:

It seems as if we had just started practice under a hot August sun when we were informed that President Reagan and his entire entourage would be coming to town in a couple of weeks...and he would be using our stadium for his address. Now, putting aside for a moment your political persuasion back in '84, you'll have to admit that it was a "pretty big deal" — certainly an honor for all of us in the Southern Tier, and beyond. However, I don't know how many high school football coaches and players have tried to concentrate on practice with *Secret Service* agents swarming all over the place for several days. We were on a first-name basis with most of them eventually. We were forced to use another locker room facility. They took over our field house, moved in special wiring, and converted it into a communications center. Can you imagine the length of our players' attention span?

Eventually, our administration asked us if the entire squad would please attend this festive "rally-address," and be in uniform. They had a reserved area for us in the front-center of the crowd that swelled to 25,000, according to reports.

I'm sure there were thousands of citizens who would have gladly traded places with any of us that day. A picture of the occasion showing several of our players among the throng appeared in that November issue of *Time* magazine. Our captain, Maurice LaFuze, (with our blessing) climbed the platform and presented the President with a football jersey as a memento. (The verbiage: *"The Gipper —Number One"*). Even with all this, I'll always wonder what it cost us on the field that season. Regardless of the fact that it was a once-in-a-lifetime occasion for our athletes, IF (I hate that word!)...if we had it to do over, I know we would handle it differently.

Only two days had elapsed before we packed our bags and traveled north on Route 81 — to Liverpool — to help christen its newly built stadium. It was resplendent with impressive turf, lighting system, and a huge crowd including quite a following from Endicott. Even Bill Huther, my best buddy from our college days at Colgate University, popped in from Auburn. Well, we helped all right — we stunk up the place. It would have to rank as one of our poorest performances ever. I was actually embarrassed. We never did stop Liverpool's *All-American* man-mountain fullback/linebacker, J. J. Grant, all night long. We were shut out, 20-0.

This opener would prove portentous.

The other unusual distraction in Fall '84 took place just one week later — in our

Distractions don't get much more demanding than a presidential campaign visit and a field house full of advance security and communications.

home opener versus an underrated Owego Free Academy team. Some well-meaning fans and boosters had posted congratulatory messages on several, large portable signs, lining both sides of Main Street, and had erected a huge metal banner across our scoreboard. While concentrating on the game, I hadn't even noticed until OFA's coach, Al Brunetti, congratulated me and pointed out the writing during pre-game warm-ups. The messages on these signs and the banner were recognizing my U-E *Silver Anniversary*.

Then, just before kickoff, in a surprise pre-game ceremony, my past captains assembled in formation on the field. They were dressed in jerseys (I noticed that a few fit rather snugly — but who was I to talk?) and presented me with an autographed football. I was moved and very appreciative — but wondered if our players of '84 realized that there was also a game to be played that night (and seven more, after that). We managed to just slip past a fired-up OFA team in the 4th quarter to win, 14-9. The evening's festivities concluded with a dinner attended by my past captains, their wives and friends, my staff, and the organizers. Pat and I certainly enjoyed renewing old acquaintances — it was a pleasant surprise-dinner.

Any highlights? I suppose one highlight for us that season was our *Rushing* record of 510 yards at Elmira Southside, in a 48-18 victory. (There's that roller coaster.) I felt especially sorry for a few players who had come up through the ranks and had worked hard. Rick Hover, for instance, had been with us since he was a ball boy at a very young age. After suffering through his share of nagging injuries, he had developed into quite a defensive back. He deserved better. The '84 season wasn't a complete failure, though. I think it served as a wake-up call for many future U-E players. It was a learning experience. They learned that you don't automatically become a winner by putting on a U-E uniform — that winning comes from dedication and hard work.

Corning West High finished with flying colors in *Division II*, with a perfect 4-0-0 divisional record (4-4-1, overall). Seton Catholic Central and Oneonta High were co-champs of *Division III* with identical 4-1-0 divisional records (6-2-1, 5-4-0, overall, respectively). Coach Dick Russ's Chenango Forks *Blue Devils* shut out SCC in *Bowl II*, 27-0.

In February the community of Endicott completed celebrating my twenty-five years of service by holding a testimonial dinner. Almost everything was a complete surprise to me — especially having my son, Larry, whom I had not seen for quite a while, there. (To this day, I don't know who pulled what strings to have him released from naval duty and transported here — but I'm sure glad they did!) A huge painting, depicting the past 25 years of U-E football on canvas, was presented by the artist. Dick McLean chaired the event and Jerry Skonieczki was the Master of Ceremonies. Some coaching colleagues, fans, former players, and even my boss, Dr. Bill Zimmerman, spoke. They presented me with a VCR and other gifts. A scholarship in my name was established through the generosity of area merchants and private donations — it was introduced that night and still exists today. The evening was very emotional for me and my entire family. I will share a portion of my open "Thank You" to the community following this occasion:

> "Not even the telegram from President Reagan diminished the presence, the effort, the fellowship of so many friends. It is I who should honor you — it is I who should give a testimonial to all of you. Thank you for an evening that my family and I shall never forget."

— 1985

In Coach Deinhardt's second season, the Binghamton *Patriots* ran (and passed) roughshod over all of us, including the highly touted (nationally) Berwick, Pennsylvania team. (A side note: Berwick has never scheduled Binghamton again, as of this writing. Interesting?!?) The *Pats* dominated everybody, created tempo, completed a perfect 9-0-0 season, finished ranked Number One in the state, and 23rd nationally. I remember my exact remarks to Steve Deinhardt after just absorbing a 41-3 blowout at North Field (administered by this superlative team): "Congratulations, Steve, you have a super football team. I hope you stick around long enough...because *everybody* — *pays* — *his* — *dues* in this league."

These Binghamton athletes had it all — so *many* weapons! They get my unequivocal vote as the best team Binghamton (merged or divided) has ever had. I doubt that I would get too many arguments.

Moreover, it is my opinion that this 1985 Binghamton team belongs right up there with the all-time elite of the Southern Tier. The *Pats* capped off their history-making season by defeating a strong EFA team in *Bowl I* at Waverly, 21-12. (As I recall, the *"Mud Bowl"* would have been a more appropriate label for that one.)

The *Tigers* were runners-up with a respectable 7-2-0 overall record, (4-1-0 divisional), and the *Golden Bears* also posted an equally respectable 7-2-0 record overall, but were only 3-2-0 in the division. We were snake-bitten early.

Our "franchise" — Mike Crounse — damaged his knee severely during our pre-season scrimmage with Shenendehowa. Mike had bulked-up to a strapping 6 feet 4 inch, 260 pound specimen. He was a three-year starter as a two-way lineman, a dominant force, and more important, our leader as captain-elect. He had already been hearing from several colleges, and, at least initially, felt all of his dreams fading. The early injury-prognosis was not good — but it didn't measure this man's heart and determination. Through a strenuous rehabilitation program he made a miraculous recovery and somehow played in the last few games. Mike became, arguably, the most widely recruited athlete in U-E history — one national high school scouting service of Houston had him ranked *Number 29* from the top in the *"Blue-Chip"* silo. We even held a press conference for him so that he could make his eagerly awaited decision to all the area-media at once. He finally chose the University of Notre Dame over all other suitors. A few years later, Mike was on the brink of fulfilling his football dream as an *Irish* starter. Unfortunately, a stray bullet in downtown South Bend, Indiana, aborted his playing days by causing severe damage to his knee.

It was Mike who initially approached me about the idea of adopting the *Tiger Paw* for our logo. We've used it ever since — and I believe it has spread to most of U-E's other teams.

Considering that our only two losses came against Binghamton and Buffalo Bishop Timon, the *Number One* and *Two* ranked teams in the state, we have no complaints. We had some kids really step up and come through for us. That is what is so rewarding about this profession...kids such as Paul Munley, Jr.

I remember the day Paul had approached me in between practices on a hot, muggy August-sizzler. At the time, he was carrying what I'm sure seemed to him like the weight of the world on his shoulders. We had a lengthy discussion — it was his junior year.

Here was a great kid, a great person, who just lacked some confidence as happens with so many young men of that age. He didn't feel that he was contributing to our program, and felt that he was letting his teammates and me down. Paul was not lacking in character...nor was he lacking in courage. I pointed this out to him, and without making any promises, encouraged him to stick with it a little longer — to be fair with himself. I assured him that if he still felt the same in another week, I would not stand in his way nor would I think any the less of him. Well, he stuck around. The days passed. He kept plugging, kept learning, kept gaining confidence, and eventually won a starting job. Guys like Paul came through big-time to help fill the void created by Crounse's injury. I can't say enough about young men such as these.

Our trigger-man, Tom Pasquale, executed the *Wishbone* to perfection in our finale at Vestal that year. Tom's last night of wearing the proud *Orange and Black* will be a lasting memory, as he ran for three touchdowns and passed for another. He would continue to work his magic for the next four years for the Ithaca College *Bombers*. He would quarterback their option attack to national prominence with a couple of national titles (*NCAA — Division III*).

EFA dominated *Division II* with an undefeated divisional record of 5-0-0 (7-2-0 overall), before bowing to Binghamton in the Bowl. Corning East High was runner-up with a 4-1-0 divisional record and 7-2-0 overall.

Seton Catholic Central stood alone at the head of the class in *Division III* with an undefeated divisional record of 5-0-0 (8-1-0 overall). Chenango Forks beat them for the second straight year in *Bowl II*, 26-7.

After the season Ithaca introduced its new football coach — Ralph Boettger.

— 1986

What a fun year! Many were pointing a finger at Binghamton, with so many of its key performers returning, to repeat its amazing feats of the previous season. Everyone else, including the media, was lining up to see who would be the bridesmaid in '86. However, U-E in *Division I* and Owego in *Division II* had other ideas. These two kept going about their business quietly, methodically, and efficiently.

Why was it a fun year? — a real pleasure? Probably because I can't think of another team of ours that accomplished as much without any real headliners — any legitimate "stars." In fact, one reporter referred to our *"faceless scorers"* (I like that!), since the scoring was spread around. It marked the first time we had ever started a freshman — Paul Norris — as our corner on defense and back-up quarterback.

We had no ego problems at all on this club — no one took himself that seriously. This was a good team, no doubt about that. But its component parts caused it to become a very good team — one with character, an abundance of poise, and a burning desire to learn. It brings to mind a statement attributed to John Madden, during his heyday with the Oakland *Raiders*. Coach Madden said, "An excellent team is a group of people that play better than their parts." *How true!* I'm not surprised that these guys from '86 are still very close today — more than one might expect after a decade has passed by — including a few stints in the *Persian Gulf War*. It was an unusually tightly knit group.

Our leadership, a key ingredient, was provided by co-captains (a "first" for us) — long-time chums — Mike "Gwynes" Guarnieri, an outstanding inside linebacker and Rob "Bubba" Cole, a highly regarded defensive lineman. The elementary school children at CFJ later nicknamed Rob, *"The Fridge"* — after the *NFL Bears'* William Perry — and even built and decorated a refrigerator in his honor for our annual pep rally at their school. This nickname developed after we had inserted 6 feet 2 inch, 230 pound Rob in the backfield for a certain formation, which I'll discuss later.

So, here was the scenario for the seventh weekend of the season: All three of us (Binghamton and U-E in *Division I*; OFA in *Division II*) were still undefeated. Binghamton was bringing its 21-game winning streak, its Number One ranking in the state, its Number Nineteen national ranking, and its high-scoring machine to Endicott. The *Patriots* were exuding confidence as they stepped off their bus. I can't describe our personality that night — we had had an outstanding week of practice — it was special! (I had been fooled before...but somehow this felt different.) It was almost magical. To say that we were a decided underdog would be a gross understatement. But something amazing was taking place. We had never experienced anything like it before or since. Except for the loyal Binghamton partisans, the huge aroused crowd — from all parts of the Tier — estimated at 11,000 - 12,000, was pulling for us. I cannot explain this phenomenon to this day. Perhaps, the entire area was growing weary of reading and hearing very little in the local sports world besides *Binghamton...Binghamton...Binghamton.* I'm sure that our young men sensed this "universal" support.

For me, there are few nights during my career that could match this one. (There would be a similar one yet to come, but without the enormous, "collective" crowd support.) Therefore, please forgive me if I get slightly technical here. Beginning way back during the pre-season, we had been working diligently on perfecting *"Onside Kicks"* with our special kickoff team. We were just waiting for the "right time" to spring it. Also, two weeks before this game, we introduced our offensive squad to a brand new formation: We called it *"Top Gun,"* after the popular movie of the same name that summer. When I first introduced its concept to the staff, they were extremely receptive, to a man. (In fact, it was Tony Romeo who remarked, at the time, that the formation even looked like a "gun." I hadn't considered that, but it was true.) So, I knew that the players would like it. Actually, *they loved it!*

As a complete departure from our normal balanced *'Bone* formation, we set up an unbalanced line to our left. This side was then composed of some "prime beef" — easily the most poundage we had ever assembled in an offensive line (and still is). They were not all normal starters, but they were big and strong — not the fastest guys in the world, but then, we weren't asking them for finesse. I would guess that we averaged approximately 250 pounds per man on that four-man left side. (The rest of the linemen were more normal size.)

We lined up in a *"Power Left I"* formation in the backfield. We used our usual backfield personnel, except for one major change. We put big Bubba Cole (230 pounds) at left-halfback as our lead power-blocker. We had only one play from this formation which eliminated the necessity of a huddle. We intended to run this *"Top Gun"* attack, and eat up the clock, until they stopped it. We felt that the control of the clock would be our only chance at success.

When we first introduced the *"Top Gun"* formation, we never told the team when or why we were going to use it (and they knew enough not to ask). We had designed and practiced it with the *Patriots* in mind.

Therefore, when we lost the coin toss that night and would be kicking off to Binghamton, I made a decision. It was like the voice in the great film, *Field of Dreams,* that tells Kevin Costner, "If you build it, they will come." It was not a difficult decision. I informed the coaches and the kickoff team that this was the night — we were going to start the game with an *Onside Kick*!

I wish that someone could have captured the shocked look on the faces all around me on camera. Actually, my thinking was: Whether it worked or not, I wanted to send the *Pats* a message — and that message was, *"We're here to play."* Our talented kicker, Tino Fiori, patted me on the shoulder before heading out. He was wearing a mischievous grin and his eyes were dancing with glee. He made the perfect side-winder kick to our right (toward the Binghamton bench). Our kickoff team swarmed the ball. A little guy with a big heart wearing *Orange and Black* — by the name of Chris Rando — came up with the precious pigskin.

Wow! Our bench erupted! I jumped to the sky — and when I landed, I discovered that my glasses had been knocked off and broken in the ensuing brief melee on our sideline. Trying to regain my composure, I held the offense back and called for *"Top Gun"* personnel. The guys went ballistic for a second time — without even setting foot on the field. It was evident to me at that moment that we were on a mission that night. That we were going to have fun. That we — *were* — *going* — *to* — *do* — *it*!

I also realized, in the same moment, that Binghamton had replaced Vestal as our arch rival.

The rest is history, but let's allow the media to summarize. The headlines — some of them on the front page — jumped off the pages:

"U-E stuns Pats with 24-6 win."

"Tigers end Pats' unbeaten streak."

"Tigers Maul Patriots, 24-6."

Another reporter's editorial was under the headline. ***"Tidal wave of emotion carries U-E to victory over dazed Binghamton."*** This particular piece, perhaps, captured the moment best:

> "Union-Endicott's football team wasn't supposed to win last night's game with Binghamton. The Tigers didn't have Binghamton's speed. The Tigers didn't have Binghamton's overall talent at the skill positions. And the Tigers didn't have Binghamton's 21-game win streak, No.1 ranking in the state or No. 19 slot in the *USA TODAY* national Super 25. Know what Binghamton didn't have? Emotion. That's what the Tigers used to beat the Patriots, 24-6, before about 11,000 fans at Ty Cobb Stadium. It wasn't even close. Compared to Union-Endicott, Binghamton looked flat, almost bored. So who are those guys in orange and black who pushed the Patriots aside so easily? 'No-names' is how Union-Endicott coach Fran Angeline described them. 'Blue-collar workers,' he said. 'Talk about intensity,' Angeline said. 'This evening we stood tall.' Intensity, smarts. And poise."

The post-game celebration seemed to go on forever. So many strangers, as well as the usual loyal fans, emerged from the darkness to offer their congratulations. But, my biggest surprise came the next morning at 8 o'clock Mass at St. Ambrose, just a block away. When returning down the aisle from the communion rail, it seemed as if the whole parish was restless and still fired-up. I remember a couple of elderly ladies grinning and forming the "OK" sign with their fingers. *Wow!* I had never experienced anything quite like that (nor have I since).

It took us until post-season play, a few weeks later, to settle down. Our effort and emotion had been completely spent against Binghamton, and it almost cost us the next game. We just pulled it out with 17 seconds remaining, over an undermanned, but gallant Horseheads team. It was a divisional clash that was almost "called" due to darkness (which would have been a "first") by the officials. A late start because of national testing, an extensive injury, and an overcast November "Horseheads" day were all contributing factors.

Before the regular season ended, Vestal and Owego were also the happy "recipients" of the spent emotion from our Binghamton game. They both cashed in on the final weekend — Owego versus Binghamton and Vestal at U-E.

Our heads were never really into that wind-up game. The deep mud on our field served as a deterrent to our offense, but the sloppy conditions didn't faze Vestal's J.J. Cordi nor his inspired teammates. Coach Mac's *Bears* completely outplayed us, and made their season by knocking us off from the ranks of the undefeated, 20-6. It was one of the best officiated Vestal versus U-E games ever — especially considering the field conditions. The *Bears* posted a very respectable 3-1-1 divisional record, tying them with Binghamton for the runner-up spot. That I honestly didn't lose much sleep over the results of that game still surprises me — perhaps because I knew that we would reload for the approaching Bowl Game. Meanwhile, an excellent Owego team experienced a different type of emotion from Binghamton to finish its regular season on a very high note. The *Pats* were way down, and the *Indians* took complete advantage of it by pasting them, 41-8, to remain undefeated.

Although our Bowl Game against Owego would be anti-climactic compared with Binghamton, the challenge of meeting the only remaining undefeated team in *Divisions I* or *II* — a team that had completely annihilated Binghamton and everyone else on its schedule — was extremely enticing. It piqued our taste buds. We varied our preparation routine slightly. On Tuesday practice (with a few inches of snow on the field, as I recall) we took a few minutes for each assistant who wished to express to the squad what this particular Bowl Game meant to him, personally. Two of our coaches were especially emotionally involved since they both had strong ties with Owego: Nick (Russ Nicosia) lived there, and Fols' (Ed Folli) wife, Wendi, was an Owego Free Academy alumna whose family also resided there.

The weather was not kind to anyone all week. Realizing that the only two fields in the area that could hold up under such lousy conditions were at JC and SV, we made a strong pitch for either one. After all, we wanted optimal conditions for the players — we couldn't care less about the capacity of the stadium. After much debate, the *STAC* officials prudently made the SV stadium available to us. The game was televised for the overflow crowd — the field was in great shape — the game was a classic in every sense.

Arguably, that '86 OFA team was the best team, overall, in Owego's proud football history. Since we didn't play each other annually, I'll leave that debate up to the fine folks from Owego. However, I'll bet they would be hard-pressed to think of another one of their great teams that could match up with that kind of experience, balance, speed, size, athletic ability and fire-power. They're the best we ever saw, for sure.

There were many big plays made by these two evenly matched teams all day long. It all came down to the kicking game — specifically, to our special kickoff return team. In the fourth quarter, the *Indians* scored with a Field Goal, putting them ahead 15-14 in this seesaw battle. They were just lining up for their fourth kickoff of the game. We noticed that all day they had been intentionally kicking off short, line-drive-grounders. (Apparently, they were unwilling to kick to our deep safeties.) We inserted our regular tight end, Deron Bowman, on the receiving team — not for his speed (he'd be the first one to admit that), but for his good hands. Furthermore, we played him up fairly close just in case they might still kick short. Boy, did *that* pay off! Unlikely return candidate Bowman scooped up the final short kick — broke toward the middle — and sprinted 76 yards, *untouched,* for the decisive points. We then held on for dear life. Our defense stiffened and we came away with the "W", 21-15.

I'm happy we only had to meet that OFA team once!

In *Bowl II* action, Chenango Forks owned Seton Catholic Central, as they whipped the *Saints* for the third year in a row, 10-7. It was a great season all around, and it would appear that everyone had, indeed, paid — his — dues.

ALL STARS — THE MID 80's (1984-1986)

1984

OFFENSE School	Position	Player	DEFENSE School	Position	Player
DIVISION I					
VHS	QB	MARK CARR	VHS	L	JOHN BOUSA
VHS	K	ROB KURST	VHS	L	BOB HEUMANN
EFA	E	JAMES SANFORD	EFA	LB	ERIC SKINNER
EFA	G	JEFF STREETER	EFA	LB	JAMES SANFORD
EFA	RB	JOHN GARVIN	EFA	DB	RANDY BROOKS
BHS	T	JOE NATALE	BHS	L	SCOTT KLEMPKA
BHS	G	MIKE BALZHISER	BHS	LB	LaFAYETTE WOODEN
BHS	RB	KING RICE	BHS	DB	RICK COLEMAN
BHS	C	BILL DIAMANTOKOS			
DIVISION II					
ME	C	CHRIS CONKLIN	ME	LB	JAMIE McGUIRE
CW	E	JOHN WOOD	ME	DB	VINCE OKUN
CW	RB	CHRIS PETERS	ME	P	JAMIE McGUIRE
CW	T	CLAUDE TRUESDALE	CW	L	CHRIS SWANSON
CW	WB	JERRY STILLWELL	CW	L	KEITH BURGIO
CW	K	CHRIS HOGUE	CW	LB	RICH KIMBALL
DIVISION III					
ONEO	T	JIM KONSTANTY	ONEO	L	JIM KONSTANTY
ONEO	RB	VINCE TOSCANO	ONEO	LB	VINCE TOSCANO
SCC	T	DAN SULLIVAN	SCC	L	DAN SULLIVAN
SCC	K	JOHN WALTERS	SCC	LB	ADAM VanZANDT
			SCC	DB	MIKE KILUK

1985

School	Position	Player	School	Position	Player
DIVISION I					
UE	G	MIKE STOUT	UE	E	MARK WESTCOTT
VHS	T	MARTY JOHNSON	UE	L	ROB COLE
VHS	RB	J.J. CORDI	UE	L	MIKE CROUNSE
VHS	K	ROB KURST	UE	LB	MIKE GUARNIERI
BHS	E	CHRIS TOLERSON	UE	DB	DAVE MOHL
BHS	E	WENDELL MACK	BHS	E	TOM CAMPOS
BHS	T	MARK POMPI	BHS	L	MIKE SCOTT
BHS	G	PETE REGULSKI	BHS	LB	PETE REGULSKI
BHS	C	BILL DIAMANTOKOS	BHS	DB	RICK COLEMAN
BHS	QB	MARK OLMSTEAD	BHS	DB	WENDELL MACK
BHS	RB	RICK COLEMAN	BHS	P	CHRIS TOLERSON
BHS	RB	KING RICE			

DIVISION II

EFA	E	ALFIE BROOKS	EFA	L	MIKE HARPER
EFA	T	TRACEY WOODRUFF	EFA	L	KELVIN LAUREY
EFA	C	DUKE HARRIGAN	EFA	L	CHARLES ROBINSON
CE	E	JOHN ROSSETTIE	EFA	LB	JON BRADLEY
CE	T	SEAN ROCK	EFA	DB	JOE ZAPARZYNSKI
CE	QB	BRIAN LeBARON	CE	L	GREG TAFT
CE	RB	TONY PAVLIK	CE	LB	BRIAN LeBARON
			CE	DB	BRIAN KENT

DIVISION III

SCC	E	JOHN BOBURKA	SCC	T	REB RUSSELL
SCC	T	REB RUSSELL	SCC	LB	ANDY MICHALAK
SCC	C	RAY BIEBER	SCC	LB	ANDRE DuQUELLA
SCC	RB	ANDY MICHALAK	SCC	DB	JIM CALLAHAN

1986

DIVISION I

VHS	G	CHRIS HARTLEY	VHS	E	CARL BOEHLERT
VHS	RB	J.J. CORDI	VHS	LB	CHRIS CHESMORE
BHS	E	CHRIS TOLERSON	VHS	P	ROB KURST
BHS	E	WENDELL MACK	BHS	T	MIKE SCOTT
BHS	T	MATT REGULSKI	BHS	DB	WENDELL MACK
BHS	RB	JERRY LYNCH	UE	E	CHRIS BUCINELL
UE	T	ED CIOTOLI	UE	T	ROB COLE
UE	G	STEVE HOVER	UE	LB	MIKE GUARNIERI
UE	C	TOM VILLANTI	UE	DB	DAVE O'HARA
UE	RB	JOE HOPKO			
UE	K	TINO FIORI			

DIVISION II

JC	T	CHRIS LOZINAK	JC	L	JOE MIKALAJUNAS
JC	RB	GEORGE KOLBA	JC	LB	RANDY BELAUS
OFA	G	SCOTT FARGNOLI	JC	DB	MATT STEINFORT
OFA	G	STEVE BRADY	OFA	L	PAT O'ROURKE
OFA	C	TED McDONALD	OFA	L	JIM PRICE
OFA	T	CHRIS CHARLIER	OFA	DB	TERRY FOOS
OFA	RB	JOE PALLADINO	OFA	P	KEVIN SCHUTT
OFA	K	RICK KUKLISH			

DIVISION III

NOR	G	STEVE CLARK	NOR	S	TERRY HAGENBUCH
NOR	RB	STEVE SCHUTT	SCC	E	ANDY SMITH
SCC	T	REB RUSSELL	SCC	T	REB RUSSELL
SCC	C	ZACK PERLICK	SCC	LB	ANDRE DuQUELLA
SCC	QB	JIM CALLAHAN	SCC	DB	RON SMITH
SCC	RB	ANDRE DuQUELLA			
SCC	RB	LUKE VanZANDT			
SCC	K	CHRIS DUNN			

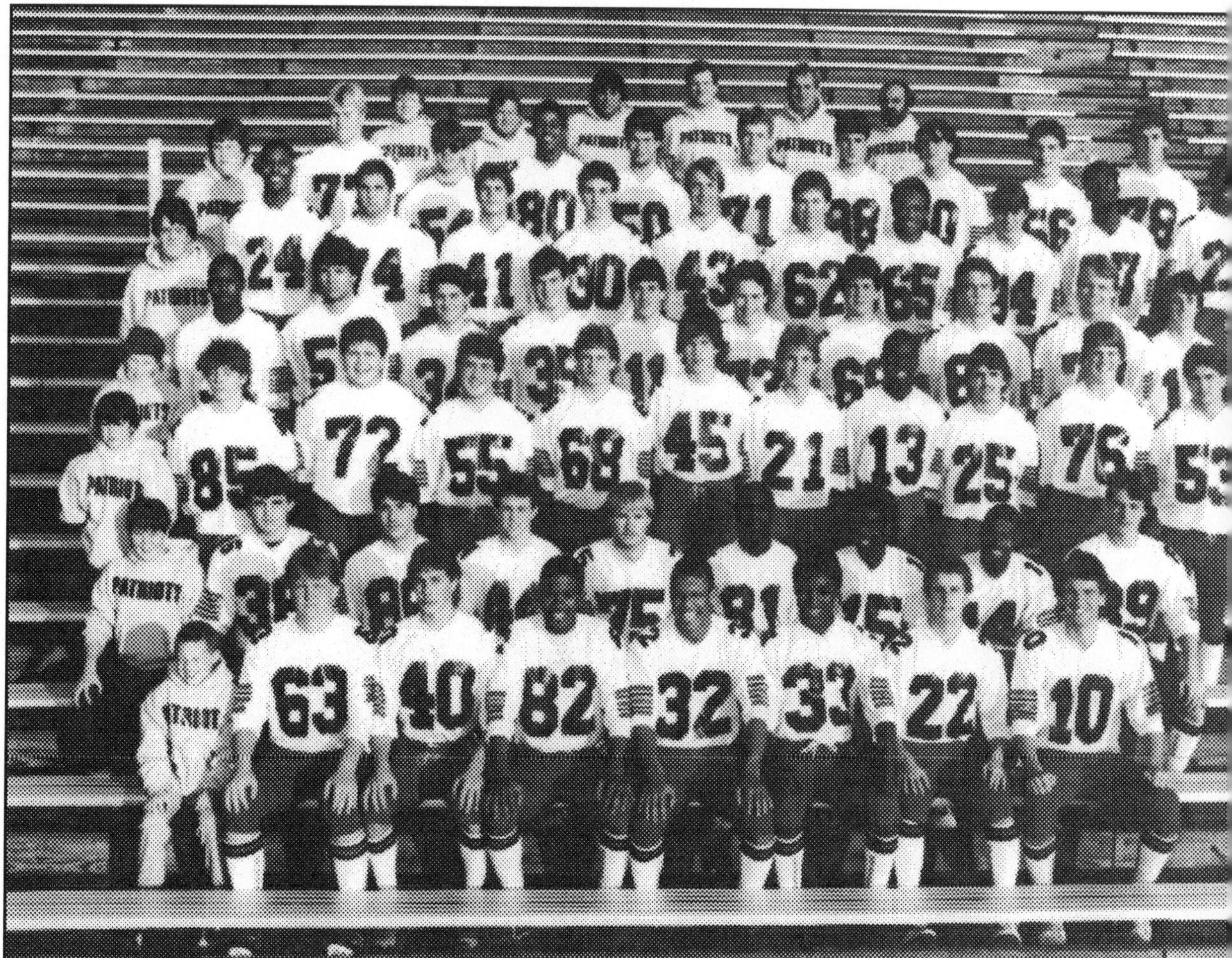

The 1985 Binghamton* Patriots *are thought to be the best team ever raised in the City of Binghamton — finishing undefeated — ranked* Number One *in the state and 23rd nationally.

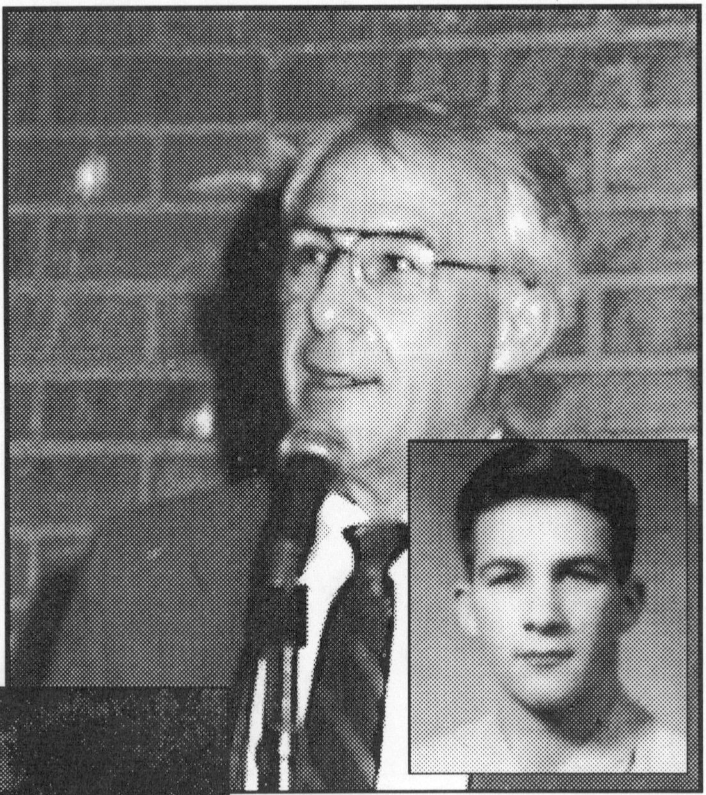

Chapter Fifteen

"I sometimes wonder whether those of us who love football fully appreciate its great lessons: That dedication, discipline, and teamwork are necessary to success. We take it for granted that the players will spare no sacrifice to become alert, strong, and skilled — that they will give their best on the field. This is as it should be, and we must never expect less, but I am extremely anxious that its implications not be lost on us."

— President John F. Kennedy

HOOVER and MORESCO

— Role Models

Dedicated. Competitive. Indefatigable. Proud. Loyal. Fair. There aren't enough adjectives to describe Dick Hoover and Joe Moresco — two men who played such a major role in my professional life as well as in the lives of an indeterminate number of fortunate students and athletes.

My initial introduction to Dick Hoover (other than as an opposing player) was a unique one:

As the 1951 season had come to an end, we were notified, separately, that we had both been selected for post-season honors — Dick, as *"Triple Cities Coach of the Year,"* and I, as *"Triple Cities Player of the Year,"* I believe. I readily accepted Dick's kind invitation for a ride up to Binghamton to accept our awards in front of the cameras. Dick came over to pick up this wide-eyed 17-year-old, at his Church Street home. He introduced himself to my parents, and was extremely engaging. We had a pleasant conversation up and back, and he wished me well in my college pursuits. I was immediately impressed, and haven't stopped yet.

Joe Moresco and I first met on the field at Johnson City during my rookie coaching season of 1957.

We really became much better acquainted a couple of years later as the opposing head coaches of the *Optimist East-West All-Star Game* in the summer of 1959. We were scheduled for a live interview at a TV studio in Binghamton, as part of the pregame hype. Since I realized that we would both be driving into town from our respective camps (at opposite ends of the boondocks) for this mid-week interview, and since I (a bachelor, then) had planned to have a late meal with my parents, I figured that Joe, too, might enjoy some of "Mama" Angeline's home cookin'. (One can handle only so much of that institutionalized camp food, you know — we were both ready for some solid pasta.) Joe jumped at the invitation. My mom enjoyed doing "her thing," and my dad loved listening to the two of us "talk shop." Mom put out her usual delicious spread with the accustomed, Italian-sized servings. Joe and I had found our common ground, and have been good friends ever since. I have always held him in the highest regard.

You couldn't find two more fierce competitors than Hoover and Moresco. Their teams were always prepared. You'd better come buckled-up against Hoover's *Golden Bears* and Moresco's *Little Red*, or you might as well stay home. The battles involving either of their teams were not meant for the meek. One had to be prepared for anything: Watch out for that little Vestal scat-back who is drifting off at half- speed, feigning nonchalance and indifference, because *HE HAS THE BALL!* (Their deceptive, famous "*Razzle-Dazzle*" play.) If you don't attack an Ithaca linebacker first, *HIS BIG FOREARM MIGHT BE ENGRAVED ON YOUR CHEST!* If you possessed personnel anywhere near their equal, it was always an enticing challenge to try to match *strategies* with these men. And you'd better be *as prepared* as they, too — because they were the measuring stick. They were master organizers, motivators, and obviously a couple of guys who paid attention to detail.

The intensity level of the rivalries that once existed between the Vestal *Golden Bears*, the Ithaca *Little Red*, and the U-E *Tigers* was as high as it can get on the high school level. Unless you have actually played or coached in one of these Vestal versus U-E, Ithaca versus Vestal, or Ithaca versus U-E games, it is impossible to entirely comprehend what happens on the field. Whether these games determined first place or last, each team considered it a winning season if it had beaten the others.

You could always look these men squarely in the eye before, as well as after, the game. And they would look you squarely in the eye. Each one would congratulate the winner without malice and then, with a determined, silent resolve, vow to even the score next time around. I have never heard either man whine, invent some lame excuse for losing, or blame someone else for falling short. Neither man felt that he needed to use profanity to get a point across. Both were humble in victory and magnanimous in defeat.

In the midst of all this intensity and competitiveness, we had our light moments, too.

Dick and I really became solid friends while coaching side-by-side — each summer for years — at the *Golden Valley Football Camp* in Sidney, New York. He always marveled at my prowess with knife, fork, and spoon. He loves to relate a couple of camp stories about this. One of his favorites occurred long after the "kiddies" had been tucked in for the night. We decided to go into town to grab a snack. (His idea — I just went along to be "sociable.") Dick ordered a pizza, while I ordered a "couple" of things. After eating only one or two pieces, he offered me the rest. He claims that I initially refused — said I was too full already — but would try just one slice — and proceeded to devour the whole thing. I'm afraid that is a true story, since I do remember his quip as we were leaving the restaurant: "Gee, Fran, I'm sure glad you weren't *really* hungry."

I have a similar camp story about Dick, however. Realizing that a future evening meal would feature spaghetti and meatballs on the camp menu, I approached the camp owner, *"Soddy"* Mirabito, and, more specifically, his congenial wife, *"Carmie."* (One would have to search far and wide to find better people.) I made a proposition to

Carmie about a possible slight adjustment in the menu, since she was renowned in culinary skills: If I would buy the clams, would she consider preparing pasta with clam sauce for the coaches, as a special treat? She readily agreed, insisted on buying the clams herself, and put on a fantastic "banquet" at the residence — replete with crunchy garlic bread and all the fixin's. Now, how does Coach Hoover fit into this story, you ask? When I informed him about the special menu and forthcoming treat, he said that he couldn't really handle clams — but would "try." Well, let me tell you about his "try": It must have been the aromatic Italian cuisine that wafted throughout the area that got to him — he had at least two servings, and maybe more (but who's counting?) He continued to rave about that meal long afterwards. We agreed that it was one of the most delicious Italian meals we had ever had. And so this growing friendship was further sealed over a sumptuous meal in the great Italian tradition.

Dick and I also became quite a formidable tennis doubles team at football camp. (We always said that a *Bear* plus a *Tiger* would be quite a potent combo in any athletic endeavor.) We never turned down any challenges, but our usual opponents were a couple more coaches — Bobby Campbell and Bob Naso (Rutgers University, at the time). Ask them about it. (I had plenty of incentive — it was the only chance I had of repaying Bobby for making our life so miserable in the early 60's.) In all fairness, I should mention, at this point, that I probably had much more tennis experience than all three of them combined. But, Dick was the key. His competitive nature would emerge out there — he was all over the court. We had many laughs. (How Dick relished pounding an overhead at Bobby!) If my memory serves me correctly, no matter how many *"ringers"* were imported to *"knock us off the hill,"* this doubles team of ours remained unscathed for all the years at camp. It was a lot of fun — camaraderie at its finest.

Because of distance, Joe Moresco and I saw each other less during the off season, but I don't remember one spring passing by, over all those years, when Joe didn't make a point of visiting with me at courtside whenever I'd take our U-E tennis team to Ithaca — even after hanging up his whistle. While we don't have any camp stories, I'm sure that Joe will remember one incident in particular. It was an unusual happening: We were well into one of our accustomed Ithaca versus U-E clashes at *Bredbenner Field* when one of our U-E players was injured. The medics didn't dare move the boy at first (always a wise precaution if any doubt exists). Quite an amount of time elapsed — perhaps as much as a half hour, or so — before they finally transported the boy to the hospital by ambulance. Other than periodically checking on the injured player, what do you suppose Joe and I, these two fierce rivals, were doing? We stayed out on the field and, removing ourselves from the players and medics, we discussed many topics including injuries, mutual problems, officials (always) — but mostly, our wives and families.

As I have already mentioned, I experienced a great void when Dick and Joe stepped away from football. Shortly after Dick retired in 1976, I felt doubly honored to be asked by the Vestal folks not only to serve on the planning committee for the *Dick Hoover Testimonial Dinner*, but also to speak at it, as well. Of course, I accepted. The Morescos and the Angelines sat together at the *Fountains Pavilion* in Johnson City for that January event. Both Joe and I appreciated having the opportunity to honor and pay tribute to Dick and Mary with a few words.

After Joe bowed out in 1983, Dick and I were both honored to be invited by the Ithaca people to say a few words at Joe's testimonial that winter. We readily accepted, and decided to travel up together, accompanied by our lovely ladies. When *"Joe Moresco Night"* finally took place — at *The Party Box* in Ithaca — we learned from one of his old childhood buddies that Joe used to be called, *"Jesse,"* around the neighborhood. We found the explanation for this nickname interesting: It seems that Joe's little playmates had a difficult time pronouncing the Italian version of Joe — Giuseppe. We certainly enjoyed reminiscing, breaking bread, and paying tribute to *"Jesse"* and Shirley that night.

It came as no surprise to me that so many people attended both functions. That fact in itself is testimony to the esteem the guests had for these men. Fellowship, affection, and respect were in abundance on both occasions. I really enjoyed renewing some former acquaintances — former "enemy" fans, boosters, parents — and introducing Pat to them. I was especially elated when some of their former players — young adults now — reintroduced themselves to me. The names conjured up images of some classic gridiron battles. How could I ever forget these former wearers of the *Green and Gold*, and the *Red and Gold*? I was extremely impressed with these young men, many with beautiful families now. I couldn't help thinking that they were reflections of the example set, not only by their parents in their homes, but also by their coaches on their fields.

One gleans from the speakers and from conversations with various guests and former players at these affairs, that these two combatants had much more in common than their humble Pennsylvania roots. Dave Rossie, Associate Editor of the *Press and Sun-Bulletin*, once wrote a column about Dick Hoover upon his retirement. Dave told us that Dick wasn't just a coach — he was a teacher. The same could be said of Joe Moresco. These men were educators. They were father-figures to many. The youngsters who knew them as coaches and mentors came away with something that doesn't show up on transcripts and report cards, but may be more valuable in the final analysis. Dick and Joe were character-builders in the truest sense of the phrase — and not just during a rare losing season, as the sports cliche goes. They were disciplinarians. Their promise was good. They were loving and caring husbands and fathers. Anyone whose lives they touched along the way is richer for it. They have done so much for high school football.

I've known many outstanding people in and out of football, and Dick and Joe are two of my most treasured friends. I learned a great deal from both of them. I've admired and respected them for many years. They are my heroes — my champions. I fear that they are two of a vanishing breed. I doubt that we'll ever see another Dick Hoover or Joe Moresco.

Chapter Sixteen

"They laugh at scars,
those that have never felt a wound."

COACHING ADVERSARIES

Here are the men we have competed against over my 36-year span (1957-1992). Why include them? ... Why not? They are actually a vital part of this book, and we learned something from each one of them. (My apologies to anyone who has been inadvertently omitted.) Alphabetically:

BADALATO, TONY — Kingston

BAKER, BILL — Susquehanna Valley

BAKER, LLOYD — Oneonta

BARNABA, GARY — Syracuse CBA

BEERS, REGAN — Maine-Endwell

BLANCHARD, JUD — Binghamton North & Binghamton H.S.

BOETTGER, RALPH — Ithaca

BRAMANTE, JOE — Maine-Endwell

BRUNETTI, AL — Owego Free Academy

CANOSA, MARSH — Pine Bush

CARNEY, BILL — Horseheads

CASHMAN, JACK — Chenango Valley

CIPP, JOE — Bellport

CLAUSI, RICK — Kingston

COBB, TY — Union-Endicott

CORNICK, JOHN — Owego Free Academy

COSTELLO, BOB — Chenango Valley

CROOKS, GARY — Johnson City

CUZZOLA, JOE — Erie East (Pennsylvania)

D'ALISO, PAT — Monroe-Woodbury

DECKER, MARK — Owego Free Academy

DEINHARDT, STEVE — Binghamton H.S.

DEYO, BUD — Binghamton Central

DILLER, HANK — Johnson City

DiNUNZIO, NICK — Union-Endicott

FAZIO, FRANK — Ithaca

FERRIS, ABE — Elmira Southside

FITZPATRICK, PAUL — Buffalo Bishop Timon

FORNAL, RIP — Newburgh

FUREY, JOHN — Maine—Endwell

GOTTFRIED, CHUCK — Johnson City

GRAY, TOM — Owego Free Academy

HARRIGAN, MARTY — Elmira Free Academy

HOKE, TOM — Rome Free Academy

HOLDEN, RANDY — Corning East

HOLLY, JOE — Binghamton Central

HOLMES, TONY — Elmira Free Academy

HOOVER, DICK — Vestal

HURLEY, JERRY — Maine-Endwell

HURLEY, TOM — Elmira Southside

KAUFMAN, NORM — Norwich

KIBLER, CARDIN — Binghamton North

KINEK, GEORGE — Allentown Catholic (Pennsylvania)

LALLA, DICK — Binghamton Central

LOVUOLO, FRANK — Bing. Central & Catholic Central

MAHON, STEVE — Vestal

MANGICARO, GEORGE — Liverpool

MARKS, TONY — Elmira Southside

MATEJKA, JOE — Horseheads

McGUIRE, BILL — Vestal

MOFFITT, TOM — Horseheads

MORESCO, JOE — Ithaca

MUNLEY, PAUL — Johnson City

NORRIS, MIKE — Homer

O'REILLY, GORDIE — Binghamton North

PACE, PETE — Utica Proctor

PALAZZI, LOU — Norwich

PARADISE, DOM — Auburn

PARSONS, DOUG — Oneonta

PASKE, JOHN — Chenango Valley

PERRY, GENE — Catholic Central

PLIMPTON, BILL — Elmira Free Academy

POLICARE, TONY — Vestal

PUSHKAR, ED — Oneonta

RADZAVICZ, JACK — Cortland

SENKO, DICK — Elmira Free Academy

ROWE, LARRY — Binghamton Central

RYDER, NICK — Maine-Endwell

RUCKDESCHEL, BOB — Newburgh

RUCKER, CAL — Susquehanna Valley & Johnson City

RUSHIN, JERRY — Elmira Free Academy

RYAN, JOE — Susan B. Wagner (Staten Island)

SAMMON, DAVE — Vestal

SCUTT, GARRY — Ithaca

SHIFFLET, JOE — Buffalo Sweet Home

SKIDMORE, TOM — Horseheads

STEUERWALD, BRENT — Shenendehowa

TETA, NICK — Rochester Aquinas Institute

TOUHEY, JACK — Maine-Endwell

TRAVIS, DICK — Chenango Valley

TREXLER, ED — Elmira Southside

VALENTINI, MARIO — Mount Saint Michael (New York City)

VIGLIONE, JOE — Warwick

WAITE, HAROLD — Elmira Free Academy

WEINMAN, JIM — Binghamton North

WHEATON, DICK — Owego Free Academy

WHITEHEAD, JOHN — Middletown

WOLSLAYER, DICK — Middletown

ZUR, RANDY — Binghamton Central

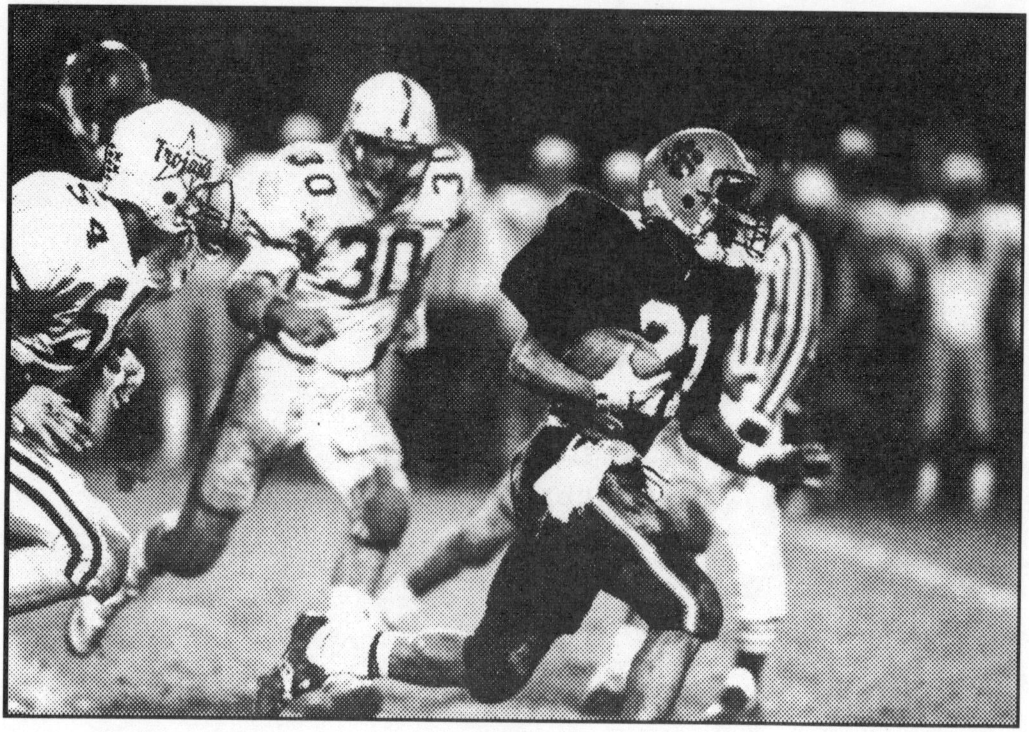

By the end of the 80's, the* Tiger Game *was up and running full out across the Southern Tier.

Chapter Seventeen

"The moon with his trifling whims
Importunes the night as always, again
To join him in some prankish game
But night demures for one less tame
Slinking away in her inky cloak
She delights in the grisly joke
Where one beast, alone, magnificent stood
With thews rigid as he supped the blood
of one less awesome, perhaps more tame
Then night slipped away from the Tiger-Game."

— Vaun Angeline, *Syracuse University, '86*

THE TIGER-GAME

— *THE LATE 80'S* ***1987-1989***

There were multiple coaching changes as the late 80's rolled around. Tony Marks took over at Elmira Southside. Up from New Jersey in '87 came a couple more Tonys: Tony Policare brought his passing game, riding on the golden arm of his son, young Tony "Air Policare," back to his alma mater in Vestal. My former U-E quarterback, Dave Sammon, became Tony's successor at Vestal in '89. In *Division II*, Randy Holden took the reins at Corning East and Owego tapped Mark Decker for its top spot. Jud Blanchard returned to the coaching fraternity by heading up Seton Catholic Central's football program.

This era marked the beginning of the *Section IV Football Conference*, containing over 40 teams. It was divided into multiple divisions, essentially still retaining the same teams in *Divisions I, II, III*, as before. Basically, we shall continue to deal here with only these three divisions. This conference, and its original structure, remains almost the same today.

Dick *"Mac"* MacPherson of Syracuse University and I co-hosted a meeting of coaches at the annual Binghamton Football Coaches' Clinic as the late 80's approached. We spearheaded a concerted effort to inaugurate high school state football championship playoffs in New York. A major step toward this long-awaited end took place in 1988: An eleventh game was added to post-season play. It would be called *"Regionals"* and would pit the top teams in four classifications (*A,B,C,D*) from one section against another. (We'll deal here with mostly *Class A* and *B* results.) These were exciting times. We could see that a dream-come-true (i.e., state playoffs) was finally on the horizon!

On a personal note, I lost a very close friend and colleague. I remember receiving the call from Auburn, telling me that Bob Adams' days were numbered by cancer. I was shocked. "Beef" was the first assistant we had hired at U-E back in 1960. He became my right arm and was instrumental in helping to lay the groundwork for U-E's gradual rise, before he left to build his own Auburn machine. At least we all had a chance for a last good-bye at an outdoor Testimonial Roast for Coach Adams. I spoke with him briefly, by telephone, close to the end. It wasn't easy. Bob was a great coach, and an even greater person.

White Hair? — 1987

Ever see a coach go from gray hair to white hair in just one season? Big Steve Hover was our captain in '87 and gave us solid, quiet leadership. Here's a guy I had known ever since he was a little pup. As he became our ball boy later on, I remember some of our players calling him "*the Little Professor*" — he seemed so studious with his glasses and quiet demeanor. In the home opener, we lost our sophomore sensation, Paul Norris, to a freak knee injury for the season. We had had some big plans for Paul, so we had to juggle and adjust. We became a really come-from-behind team for most of the season. In six out of our eight wins, we pulled them out in the fourth quarter. One of our rival coaches even remarked toward the end of the season that he didn't know how I could stand it, week in and week out. (I have news for him: It wasn't easy!) One reporter called this team of ours "*a cast of relative unknowns.*" They sure didn't put up very big numbers, but they had big hearts. All season long, they had to scratch and claw their way to survive — but they knew how to win.

Look at these scores of our 1987 "*Cardiac Kids*" and you'll see what we're talking about. In sequence: U-E 7, Buffalo Bishop Timon 3; U-E 7, Mount St. Michael of the Bronx 0; U-E 26, JC 22.

The Johnson City game was won on our last offensive play, with 39 ticks left on the clock, and a long way to go. Our rookie reserve quarterback, sophomore Chris *"Muddy"* Waters, was inserted to pass. That was his forte, and everyone in the stadium knew it. You think a "*Hail Mary*" pass is coming, but not really. Muddy was forced out of the pocket, rolled to his right to avoid a flock of Wildcat linemen, and hit his classmate, Dave Adamson, with a perfect strike — just behind the JC secondary — at about the 10-yard line. Adamson found the end zone in a hurry from there — his third trip into paydirt that afternoon at *Green Field*. (Adamson had stepped into the starting line-up after Norris had gone down — a rather auspicious start!) I can still see Hover's reaction on that play: He lay supinely on the ground, beat his chest (Tarzan-style) and pumped his burly legs like a bicycle for what seemed like an eternity. I think my hair turned to white that afternoon — and we still had two-thirds of the season to go.

U-E 19, Horseheads 15; then Binghamton.

In the previous four contests, we had allowed only one second-half score, but the Binghamton *Patriots,* still smarting from the previous season, changed that in a hurry. They put three TD's on the scoreboard after intermission to hand us our only defeat, 32-15, and establish themselves as the top team around.

Then it continued: U-E 16, Corning East 13; U-E 19, ESS 6; U-E 28, Ithaca 12; U-E 29, Vestal 12. Whew!

Binghamton went undefeated in *Division I* (5-0-0), and 7-2-0, overall. U-E was right behind, having lost only to Binghamton for a 4-1-0 divisional and 8-1-0 overall record.

The *Pats* also beat a strong JC team in *Bowl I*, 46-29. *Divisions II* and *III* ended up quite similarly: Rucker's JC team was undefeated in *Division II* (5-0-0), and 8-1-0 overall. Owego was runner-up, finishing 4-1-0 in *Division II* and 8-1-0 overall.

Chenango Forks made plenty of noise during its inaugural season in the conference by also going undefeated in *Division III* with a 5-0-0 mark, and 5-3-1 overall.

The *Cardinals* of Newark Valley upset Forks in *Bowl II*, 8-0. Coach Jeff Ward's *Cardinals* might have set a single-game record for the number of punts that day. As I recall, the field conditions at Forks were sub-par after the rains had hit. The *Cardinals* were quite content to keep controlling the clock, punting the ball, playing field-position, and playing tough, relentless defense all day long.

An Unusual Year — 1988

I don't think anyone in his wildest dreams would have predicted a 3-way tie in *Division I*, and co-champions in *Division II* in 1988. *Unbelievable!* I know with our 1-3 start that we were totally dismissed from the picture. But, watch out for a *cornered tiger!* We may have the distinction of being the only *Division I* champion to ever finish a season with four losses on its record. And as anyone from *Division II* will be happy to tell you (I can't blame them), two of those losses came against *Division II* teams. Our overall record in '88 was 5-4-0.

We were smaller than usual (one reporter referred to us as "*Tiny Tigers*"), and struggled in '88. About the only bright spot for us in the first half of the season was a record-setting 95-yard kickoff return for a TD against Mount St. Michael. This was, perhaps, the first time that the league sat up and took notice of our very promising sophomore halfback, Jarvis Shields. He didn't see too many more balls kicked anywhere near him for the rest of his career. (In '90, Kingston inadvertently "slipped" — kicked off to Jarvis — same result — i.e., TD.) Jarvis is the fastest athlete we've ever had. In time, the U-E crowd would start to "oooh" and "aaah" every time he touched the ball out in the open. I don't ever remember any reaction like that before, or since. Jarvis was a great talent, and an even greater young man.

We hit a low point by mid-season. First, Cal Rucker's JC *Wildcats,* and then Bill Carney's *Blue Raiders* from Horseheads showed us how the game should be played by completely outclassing us in every department. Horseheads shut us out, 17-0.

But, you know, sometimes in this great sport of ours, one sees a little glimmer in defeat. We had been looking for a noseman all season. We tried almost every single defensive lineman against Horseheads in that vital position, as they continued to butcher us up the middle for the entire first half. So, we decided to give a senior who had been working hard, but who could never seem to advance beyond third string, an opportunity. We were desperate. We had nothing to lose at that point. Why not? Some players are late-bloomers — some know how to make the most of an opportunity — others just watch it pass them by. After the half, Chuck *"Chuckie Cheese"* Louden jumped in there at the nose and did a whale of a job. Horseheads did not score in the entire second half. We had finally found our noseman...as Binghamton was about to discover.

Fortunately, another plus for us was great leadership that season. Our captain was Kerry Pedley, the last in a long line of Pedleys, all outstanding young men with superb character and work ethic. Kerry's cool and intelligence (one of my prize Latin students) helped a lot, too. We also had our first exchange student, Ben Tarbox, from Down Under. Naturally, our guys dubbed this Aussie, *"Dundee."* Ben was extremely outgoing and provided us with some light moments (unintentionally) during some tough times. He had some experience with *"Australian Football,"* but our version was quite new to him. I remember Ben making a picture-perfect tackle during practice one day. He was elated! He thought he had done very well — until we pointed out to him that, as an offensive lineman, it was illegal to *"tackle"* your opponent. He took it all in good stride. We learned from each other and had a lot of fun. He was a great kid — a real credit to his country.

One of our *"Tiny Tigers"* was a defensive tackle, Dave Machalek. At 6 feet even and 185 pounds soaking wet, he epitomized our superlative defensive effort against much bigger people. Our climb out from the depths really started when another state-ranked Binghamton team came to town. Remember, we had already lost three out of four games. Actually, we didn't belong on the same field with the *Pats*. To add to our troubles, our starting quarterback, Muddy Waters, went down with an injury early in the second quarter. Steve Loposky, who had been working hard day after day, replaced him. Just before halftime, Steve lofted a perfect spiral to Ben Prusia down the sideline — 41 yards and a touchdown — for what proved to be the only points of the game. Loposky...another young man to seize the opportunity and be ready when called upon.

As outstanding as this play and others by Loposky were, one reporter captured the real story in the first sentence of his post-game summary: "Union-Endicott's defense silenced the whispers and answered its critics." That's because guys like *"Chuckie Cheese"* Louden, Machalek, and their defensive teammates came through — against all odds. This same reporter's last line read: "There was joy in Tigertown." *Wow, I'll say!*

Mentioning young Loposky here reminds me of a rather unique sidelight in U-E football blood lines. Steve was the last of two sets of brothers who would perform admirably for us, and whose lives were intertwined: The Loposkys — Mark and Steve; the Weskos — Mike and Chuck. Their fathers, Joe Loposky and Mike Wesko, Sr., grew up together near the En-Joie Golf Course. They became football teammates, golf partners, and best friends. Eventually Joe married Mike's sister, Joanne. From the offspring of the two families came four football-playing cousins who spanned two decades: the young Weskos in the 1970's, the young Loposkys in the 1980's. It wasn't until the youngest cousin, Steve Loposky, had played that I realized this unusual twist: Mike Wesko, Sr., had been a smooth quarterback in his high school days, whereas his future brother-in-law, Joe Loposky, had been a fine center. Their sons played the same exact skill positions — a fairly common occurrence among fathers and sons. No one can say that these cousins were *"chips off the old block,"* however. Each set of brothers mastered their uncle's skill: Mike and Chuck Wesko became centers for us, whereas Mark and Steve Loposky became quarterbacks. I know that their dads were very proud of them. From my end of it, having known both Mike and Joe, their sterling character, competitive nature and work ethic when we were all growing up together in the same neighborhood, I was very happy to be entrusted with a young Wesko or Loposky — at any position.

Often the outcome of one highly emotional game can affect the direction a team takes, depending on the team's personality. Unlike the unprecedented (because of circumstances) Binghamton game of '86, after which we were completely drained for a couple of weeks, this '88 upset of Binghamton served as a springboard, a catalyst for the rest of the season. We really cranked it up several notches and defeated the rest of our Division I opponents. So, Binghamton, Horseheads, and U-E shared the championship — each with identical 4-1-0 divisional records, having knocked off each other. Although both Binghamton and Horseheads finished with 7-2-0 records overall, Binghamton was the *Division I* representative in *Bowl I* in 1988.

For those who are really into the Bowl-thing, here's a wild scenario as described by the media and easily forgotten by now: If Mount St. Michael (one of our five victims) had not lost an overtime squeaker in its championship downstate, we would have edged out both Binghamton and Horseheads as the *Division I* representative on the basis of *Harbin Points*. Obviously, this would have been on the basis of *"secondary" Harbin Points*. Mount St. Michael was at least twice our size in enrollment, and had had an extraordinary season against competition of similar size — so we would have received all of their accumulated points. It almost happened. *That would have been one for the books!* Although U-E was only 5-4-0, we certainly would not have apologized for being the representative, and would have been more than happy to meet our next door neighbor, Maine-Endwell, in *Bowl I*.

Jack Touhey's M-E *Spartans* came out of nowhere to share the *Division II* honors with JC, each with identical 4-1-0 divisional and 7-2-0 overall records. M-E, as the *Division II* representative, then went on to put another feather in *Division II*'s cap by nipping the *Patriots* in *Bowl I*, 29-28. In my opinion, 1988 was probably the most legitimate year for *Division II* to have bragging rights over *Division I*, due to the overall results of the entire season, as well as the bowl results.

Jud Blanchard's Seton Catholic Central *Saints* went on an undefeated tear — smashing everyone and everything in sight, finishing with a 5-0-0 divisional and 9-0-0 overall record. In *Bowl II* action, they completely outclassed Windsor, 40-6.

Our *Section IV* representatives did us all proud in the inaugural *"Regionals"* in '88, which matched *Section IV* with *Section II* from the Albany area at Cornell's *Schoellkopf Field*. This planning by the *Section IV* committee, as host, proved fortuitous to the participants, because a steady, all-day rain — quite heavy at times — didn't detract from the footing on Cornell's artificial turf. Both Maine-Endwell and Seton Catholic Central dominated their foes from *Section II*. *Class A*: M-E 13, Colonie 0. *Class B*: Seton CC 36, Johnstown 6. The *Spartans* wound up '88 with a very impressive 9-2-0 record, while the *Saints* enjoyed an unprecedented season with a perfect eleven wins and no losses against stiff competition.

Unfortunately, three of our biggest benefactors, all of whom had been loyal, staunch supporters, were not around anymore to see these U-E teams, including another one that would achieve national prominence soon. No request was ever too big for these magnanimous individuals:

Fred Zappia's wit was matched only by his generosity.

I have never forgotten Bill Gargano — not only raising the money in record time from area merchants to purchase high quality championship jackets for our entire squad back in 1964 — but also delivering them, in person, as well.

My first experience with Joe Pisani, the restaurateur, was when he visited our locker room when I was a nervous, rookie-underclassman. I was about to start my first game with the U-E varsity alongside all those post-graduates. This kindly man took me aside and gave me a few pointers on defensive end-play. The instructional distraction had a very soothing effect on me.

These three men would have been very proud of their *Tigers* yet to come.

Sadly, some other U-E folks, all loyal supporters, weren't around to share in our soon-to-be powerhouse. Three of my former "building-bosses," all former U-E principals, had passed on:

Mary L. Pitkin had been principal when I was a student, also.

Marty Bortnick was also gifted at the bridge-table, not only in the bid, but in the play of the cards.

Vito Popelka (has to be the most nattily dressed high school principal to ever grace any halls) was my high school football, basketball, and track coach, also.

Frederica *"Fritz"* Hollister had been the head of the language department at U-E for over 30 years. She was also a terrific Latin teacher. She always took great pride in telling all of her colleagues about "her boy" — with a unique combination of Latin and football. During her declining years, I would take her for a spin in her wheelchair around the halls at the hospital. She loved to admonish all the doctors, nurses, and orderlies with, "*Step aside!* I have my bodyguard with me today, and you don't want to *mess* with him!"

Frank Pollard and I had been playing tennis almost every day in the summer since he first came to town in the early 1950's. I always considered him as "U-E family." Eventually, we added indoor-tennis to our winter recreation. Frank was the extremely popular, outgoing tennis coach at SUNY Binghamton. This fierce competitor (he used to love to win even the *"toss"*) was one of the kindest, most considerate, most upbeat guys I have ever known. His broad grin, shiny dome, and sparkling blue eyes could light up any room. He was like a big brother to me. I was devastated when he suffered a sudden, massive, fatal stroke.

I can assure you that these people would have been very proud of these *Tigers* who were about to make some big noise.

How Good Are They? — 1989

"Four things come not back:
the spoken word;
the sped arrow; time past;
the neglected opportunity."

— Omar Iban

Where does this U-E team rank? This was a very popular question raised by several fans and reporters as the '89 season began to wind down. Kevin Stevens, the very knowledgeable sports writer from the *Press and Sun-Bulletin*, who had grown up in Binghamton, devoted an entire page to the ongoing debate after the eighth weekend of competition. The headline of his article read: ***'Excellence comes again for Tigers — Eras, teams different, but similar.'***

A few excerpts from that article follow:

> "Football teams of different eras, some say, cannot be compared with any sensible degree of accuracy. But in the case of U-E's teams of '79 and '89 such examination cannot be avoided. This season's backfield — quarterback Chris Waters, halfbacks Dave Adamson (also, Markus Wilson, often filling in admirably for an injury-plagued Adamson — author's note) and Jarvis Shields, and fullback Paul Norris — compares favorably in striking potential to the '79 team. Add receiver Ben Prusia and Shields, the most frequent recipients of Waters' throws, and the pass-run balance is there to keep overzealous defenders honest. The '79 team might have been the premier defensive unit in Southern Tier history. The front line, including Steve Villanti, Ken Tatko, Larry Angeline and Armie George, was the backbone of a team that kept six of nine opponents scoreless. Said Dick Hoover, long-time Vestal coach: 'They talk a lot about Shields, but this kid Waters, he's as good an option quarterback as has come down the pike. He comes out of that option with Shields as the trailer and, I'll tell you what, that's a purdy tough combination to defend.' Gary Beddoe, a flanker in '79, said of a '79 versus '89 matchup: 'Usually, what makes or breaks a football team are the offensive and defensive lines. And if I had to make an analysis, I'd have to say that our offensive line was better than their ('89) defensive line, and that our defensive line was better than their offensive line.'Angeline, who is winding down his 30th season as head coach, doesn't go for year-to-year comparisons, such as stacking his '79 team against this season's squad."

Let's go back to the pre-season which saw four coaches make their debut after lengthy stints as assistants: at Vestal, Dave Sammon (my first *Tiger* captain); at Maine-Endwell, Regan Beers; at Norwich, John Pluta; at Corning West, Jim Oman.

Except for Todd *"The Load"* Kehley, our valuable center/noseman at 6 feet 2 inches and 235 pounds, we were not unusually big. We had some solid experience returning, especially in the offensive backfield. What we knew we had, from the start, was overall speed — definitely the most we had ever had. We also had Paul Norris — the youngest of the great Norris family — all talented athletes in addition to being outstanding people with exemplary character.

It seems like just yesterday when little Paul used to wander down on his bicycle to football-practice at the time his older brothers, Carl and Bobby, were with us. (Even then, as an elementary school child, Paul could field punts as well as some of our guys.) After becoming the first freshman to ever start for us in 1986, a severe injury sidelined him for most of his sophomore season. Although he never regained those natural moves and speed again, Paul was an athlete — and he was determined. He became very strong and powerful. Running straight away, no one could match him. He was now 6 feet 1 inch and 205 pounds as a senior...and he hit like a ton.

Paul became a very punishing load to bring down — as several opponents discovered. It was not unusual to see a small defensive back *"make it look good,"* but wisely step aside as he came roaring through. Every *Tiger* on our bench (some of the U-E fans eventually caught on and would join in) would start making the sound of a train when it was *"Paul's time"* — blasting away for short yardage, or in possession and clock-management situations. But more than all of these physical attributes, Paul was a natural leader and exemplary captain-elect. He kept everyone down-to-earth. He kept everyone together. And, he harnessed any egos that might have begun to grow.

Before we get into all the records shattered by this amazing '89 U-E team, let's review the season in sequence by taking the various media's capsule-summaries. First the headline, then the summary:

'Opener a breeze for U-E.'

"Union-Endicott's football team must have forgotten that its season opener was Saturday night. The Tigers conducted a full-scale workout instead, pounding visiting Kingston, 40-20, in a non-league game. The final score was deceiving. U-E led, 40-0, in the third quarter before coach Fran Angeline removed most of his starters." It was an unusually muggy night. I'm still amazed that both squads performed as well as they did. We had to constantly remind our boys to pump lots of liquids into their bodies all week long. We knew they'd all be sweating several pounds off that night — and they did.

'Union-Endicott crushes Buffalo foe, 60-7.'

"For 12 minutes Saturday night, Union-Endicott and Buffalo Bishop Timon played good football. Thereafter it was just Union- Endicott. The Tigers scored three touchdowns in the last 4:39 of the second quarter and went on to maul Timon, 60-7. 'They've got my vote for No. 1 in the state,' said Timon coach Paul Fitzpatrick." This was the second game in a row, played in the sweltering heat. It was the only lop-sided game in our extremely competitive, seven-game series. Every single runnng back on our squad contributed that night to a new U-E (possibly league and beyond, as well) one-game rushing record of 525 yards.

'Unbeaten U-E rolls past EFA.'

"So much for the adage about the head that wears the crown lying uneasily. That is, at least in Union-Endicott quarters. The Tigers, playing their first game since being rated atop New York's Class A football teams, waltzed away from an early deficit to score a 32-14 victory over visiting Elmira Free Academy Saturday night. As is typical of these 1989 Tigers, their offensive output included three big scoring plays plus an overpowering ground game." This was a good one for us, since it proved that we could come from behind.

'Tigers' speed kills Patriots.'

"It was a football game that couldn't possibly live up to its advance billing — but did — before 6,000-plus fans at Binghamton's North Field. Union-Endicott 35, Binghamton 26. The Tigers dashed past Binghamton quicker than the Patriots could say 'Jarvis Shields,' only to have the Pats match them virtually score for score for more than three quarters. But it was the speed of the Cheetahs — 'er, Tigers — the Patriots could not contain. 'I think they're faster than they were in '79,' said Binghamton coach Steve Deinhardt, 'and faster than we were in '85.'" Let's face it — this was the crucial game in our season — the one that we had to have.

'Bang, bang, got ya - U-E's guns blast JC, 49-6.'

"Union-Endicott already possesses Uzi-like firepower. The last thing it needs is for its prey to stumble in the heat of battle. That's what Johnson City did Saturday afternoon. The Wildcats bungled two punt attempts, committed 10 penalties and lost two fumbles as undefeated U-E rolled to a 49-6 non-league triumph."

'Sluggish start, same old U-E finish.'

"Union-Endicott started a bit off key Saturday night, but the beat went on. The Tigers drummed Elmira Southside, 54-0, at Ty Cobb Stadium to improve to 7-0 overall, 3-0 in Division I of the Section 4 Football Conference."

'Top-ranked U-E rolls over IHS.'

"It was just a matter of time. 'The first quarter we played well, but that happens a lot with U-E, because everybody's gunning for them,' said Ithaca coach Ralph Boettger. In the end, however, it was simple. Talent won out. U-E 40, Ithaca 13."

As I recall, there were a couple of bizarre things, unrelated to football, going on out there that night. It was very uncharacteristic of the Ithaca versus U-E rivalry. I thought our kids showed a lot of poise. A few days later, I received a letter of apology from an Ithaca fan who was embarrassed by these incidents. That considerate gesture stands high in my memory.

It was at about this time of the season when the veteran Sports Editor of the Press and Sun-Bulletin, John Fox, felt that U-E had an exceptional team. This sports guru of the Southern Tier (and beyond) wrote a very complimentary article about his impression, under the heading: ***'U-E football deserves dose of national ink.'*** A few excerpts from John's article follow:

> "I'm not my brother's keeper, and certainly not Big Brother's. But someone should inform USA TODAY that when it comes to high school football teams of renown inhabiting the north shore of the Susquehanna River, there's more than one of them.

(The reference here was to the annual lofty national recognition accorded Berwick, Pennsylvania, already a Binghamton victim in '85 — *author's note.*)

> "U-E's eight weekly demonstrations of thunder and lightning have kept it No. 1 since day one of the New York State Sports Writers Association 1989 rankings. U-E hasn't yet received even honorable mention in USA TODAY. Never has, in the 'Super 25's' eight-year history."

The indefatigable Mr. Fox even went out of his way to personally contact Big Brother, Dave Krider, the Sports Editor of the LaPorte, Indiana, Herald-Argus, near South Bend. Some of their conversation is related in the same article:

> "Krider said, 'I don't look for New York teams if they're not already in the rankings — but tell me about this Union-Endicott team — is there a hyphen in there? How many Division I players do they have?...' I told him I'm no expert on that, only on recognizing clothed lightning."

Krider, too, must have been impressed with John's keen eye and tenacity, since I remember Krider contacting me by telephone each Sunday for the rest of the season. U-E broke into the national picture shortly thereafter. Regardless of the quality of teams here in the Northeast, a team would usually have to have a respected advocate to receive that kind of national exposure. This entire area was fortunate indeed, to have had the dedication of just such an exemplary advocate in John Fox.

Back to the summaries:

'U-E wins ugly, stays perfect.'

"Union-Endicott continued its drive toward a state championship Friday night, while Vestal's comeback season concluded with perhaps its grittiest effort. The Tigers defeated arch-rival Vestal, 23-6, before over 6,000 fans at Hoover Memorial Stadium."

(The Vestal Stadium had recently been named, appropriately, in honor of Dick Hoover's years of dedicated service — *author's note.*)

Things did get "ugly" in this game toward the end. There was an excess of jawing going on by everybody — players on both sides, and even some of the officials. I remember entering the verbal fray in the middle of the field — an automatic 15-yard penalty under ordinary circumstances — but all I received from the referee was what I considered a circuitous, evasive (at best) explanation of what in hell was going on. Unfortunately, the whole situation could have and should have been snuffed out before emotions were allowed to escalate. It severely detracted from a superlative effort by the Vestal kids and a fine performance by our guys.

This completed our first perfect season in a while with a 5-0-0 divisional and 9-0-0 overall record. Binghamton was runner-up in *Division I* with a 4-1-0 divisional and 8-1-0 overall record.

Division II experienced plenty of balance at the top with three outstanding teams: Randy Holden's Corning East *Trojans* emerged as a power to join EFA and JC as tri-champions, each with identical 4-1-0 divisional records. Their overall records were all different, however: Corning East, 8-1-0; EFA, 7-2-0; JC, 6-3-0. Obviously, Corning East would be the *Division II* representative in *Bowl I*.

Bob Zanot's Chenango Valley *Warriors* ruled *Division III* with an unblemished 5-0-0 divisional, and a 7-2-0 overall record. CV went on to defeat Elmira Notre Dame in *Bowl II*, 20-7. The *Warriors* then lost a heartbreaker in the *Regionals* at Cornell in *Class B* action against Onteora of *Section IX* in the Middletown/Kingston area: Onteora 20, CV 18.

Back to the *Tiger-Game*. In our *Bowl I* game preparation, we tried to tell our troops that we would have our hands full against a big, talented, tough Corning East team that had knocked us off the previous year. Moreover, we pointed to our results against a common foe, EFA. We had experienced a struggle for most of that game before finally subduing the *Blue Devils,* 32-14. By comparison, however, Corning East was just coming off a thorough destruction of this same Academy team, to the tune of a 42-0 drubbing. Surprisingly, Corning was much more excited about this bowl game than our guys were. Go figure. Corning brought a huge group of loyal supporters to Endicott. The Elmira/Corning media account follows:

'East hangs tough with powerful U-E.'

"Two points. A couple of missed tackles. A botched up pitch on a two-point conversion try. Those are all that will keep the Corning East Trojans off the plush astroturf at Cornell University's Schoellkopf Field next week. The underdog Trojans gave Union-Endicott, the state's top-ranked team, the battle of its life in the Section 4 Bowl I Game Saturday

> before dropping a 21-19 decision as a crowd estimated at 6,500 looked on. The unbeaten Tigers amassed 195 of their 266 total yards on just four plays, three of which resulted in touchdowns — a 61-yard run by Markus Wilson, a 77-yarder by Jarvis Shields, and a 28-yarder by fullback Paul Norris. For the rest of the contest, East's defense simply turned the Tigers aside."

We coaches had felt going in, that East would present our stiffest challenge of the season — we were worried. The *Trojans* gave us everything we expected — and then some. They played an outstanding game. Fortunately, *Tiger* poise was in evidence all night long.

Now the scene was set for the *Class A Regional* game at Cornell University. It was scheduled for the nightcap of a busy, unprecedented Sunday slate against coach Pat D'Aliso's high profile Monroe-Woodbury team from *Section IX* downstate in the Middletown/Kingston area.

From the moment we arrived that night, I was filled with nostalgia. In my Colgate days, we had played at Cornell three times — all pleasant memories. The beautiful campus, the locker room, the *"Crescent"*...all so familiar...got to me long before game time. I had to search for a "hiding place" to collect my thoughts. A recessed corner outside the locker room, engulfed in shadow and ivy, provided the solace I needed. For several minutes, I conjured up images of sunny September afternoons, the breathtakingly exquisite panoramic hues made possible by autumn's magic paintbrush — images of my Colgate teammates in our *Maroon* and *White* colliding with the *Big Red*. I could almost hear the "grunts" and "groans;" the "ooohs" and "aaahs" of the usual capacity crowd. Finally, these lights, the chill of the night, and the snow and sleet shook me out of my reverie. Suddenly Pat and the kids, and the past 30 seasons of Union-Endicott football flashed before me. It was then that I realized that it was time again for, possibly, the biggest *Tiger-Game* to date. We were on a mission — we had a job to do. I wouldn't have traded places with anyone in the world at that moment in time. *What an opportunity!*

Despite over an inch of snow and sleet causing extremely slippery conditions elsewhere, the carpet over *Schoellkopf Field* provided solid footing for the players. We didn't know that much about Monroe-Woodbury, other than the fact that it had at least two outstanding athletes — a pro-size, strong-armed quarterback — J.C. Jones, and an all-purpose, exceptional talent — Julian Bastarrechea. I made a point of seeking out and conversing with one particular opponent during pre-game warm-ups — a fine sophomore starting linebacker, by the name of Devin Hoover. The surname should sound familiar — he is Dick Hoover's grandson, and former Vestal quarterback, Glenn Hoover's son. It was a mighty proud Hoover contingent at Cornell that day, braving the elements for the early game as well where former Vestal fullback, Jim Hoover's dynamite Walton team (clad in orange and black, I might add) convincingly whipped Red Hook High in the *Class C Regional* matchup: Walton 34, Red Hook 0.

I don't remember whether it was Paul Norris' idea or mine — nor does it matter — but, to the best of my knowledge, this marked the first time any team sent all 18 seniors out for the pre-game ceremonial coin-toss. (As far out, at least, as the officials would allow them.) They weren't out there hootin' and hollerin,' either. They were clasping each other's hands as one, unified battle line. The press account:

'U-E rout caps season of perfection.'

"Quarterback Chris Waters scored four touchdowns and threw a 53-yard scoring pass as Union-Endicott completed a perfect season with a 54-13 romp over Monroe-Woodbury at Cornell University's Schoellkopf Field on Sunday night."

Afterwards, the stands poured forth. Everyone was milling around on the field for what seemed like an eternity. Although it was freezing (this is when I had acknowledged that fact), no one wanted to leave...each one wanted to savor the moment. We finally separated our players from their legions of fans, families, and girl friends, and shooed them into a well-earned warm shower.

Before deciding how this U-E machine compares, and where it fits in, here are the offensive records set by these '89 *Tigers:*

RUSHING YARDS, ONE SEASON	3,685
TOTAL YARDS, ONE SEASON	5,340
FIRST DOWNS, ONE SEASON	194
TOTAL POINTS, ONE SEASON	457
RUSHING YARDS, ONE GAME (Bishop Timon)	525

(Some of the above records might be league marks, as well.)

Six *Tigers* were chosen as *All-State*: Linemen and linebackers — Matt Beers, Billy Carlini, Tony Valachovic; receiver — Ben Prusia; running back — Jarvis Shields; quarterback — Chris Waters. Also, a couple of seniors set a few individual U-E records:

TD PASSES, CAREER	19	CHRIS WATERS
TD PASSES, SEASON	14	CHRIS WATERS
TD RECEPTIONS, SEASON	10	BEN PRUSIA
TACKLES (linebacker), CAREER	492	BILLY CARLINI
TACKLES (linebacker), SEASON	217	BILLY CARLINI
QUARTERBACK SACKS, SEASON	22	TONY VALACHOVIC

The 1989 *Tigers* were the first U-E team to win 11 games in one season. They achieved the *Number One* ranking in New York State. They were ranked as high as *Number 17* in the nation by *USA TODAY* at one point in the season, and finished at *Number 19*. These *Tigers* were further recognized and honored by the Broome County Legislature, the Mayor and Board of the Village of Endicott, the U-E Board of Education, the school, and the community.

But all the tangible accolades, honors and proclamations aside, and much appreciated, I love to relate the following special anecdote:

Shortly after the team had completed its season, I was stopped on Washington Avenue by an elderly gentleman I had never met before. He explained to me, in halting English, that he had come to this country from Italy only a few years earlier. (I get goose bumps each time I think of what ensued.) He grabbed my hand and told me haltingly, "Coach, tanka you team very much for whata you do for all.... I prouda I Endicott." I shall never forget that poignant moment of sincere civic pride. *That* is what it's all about!

Who was the best of all time? I'd be the first one to tell you that we've been blessed with more than one great team in Endicott. We have also had the opportunity to compete against the great ones, not only from the Tier, but from other sections of the state, as well. I shall defer all comparisons, judgments and superlatives to the ages...and also to the street corners, barber shops, and local watering holes....

"...then night slipped away from the Tiger-Game."

ALL STARS — THE LATE 80'S (1987-1989)

1987

OFFENSE School	Position	Player	DEFENSE School	Position	Player
DIVISION I					
UE	RB	DAVE ADAMSON	UE	DB	BARRY DOYLE
UE	G	STEVE HOVER	UE	T	JOE SANGIULIANO
UE	RB	STEVE HORN	UE	LB	MATT SWEENEY
BHS	QB	RAY STANTON	BHS	S	MIKE KURTY
BHS	G	MIKE BEAM	BHS	LB	JERRY McKAN
BHS	TE	DAN DAVIS	BHS	T	JOE MOHR
BHS	SE	RON BLAIR	BHS	DB	TIM WOLFE
DIVISION II					
OFA	RB	JOE PALLADINO	OFA	LB	GEORGE IGNASZAK
OFA	C	TED McDONALD	OFA	LB	MIKE TULSEY
OFA	TE	GREG ASH	OFA	T	DAVE KOSZTYO
OFA	G	STEVE BUNDY	JC	DB	MATT STEINFORT
JC	QB	JOE KATUSHA	JC	LB	CHRIS DRIMAK
JC	C	BRENDON CASEY	JC	T	MIKE SLATER
JC	T	CHRIS LOZINAK	JC	T	JOHN FRANEY
JC	RB	STEVE FARR	JC	DB	DAN FARRELL
DIVISION III					
CF	QB	TOM McCOY	CF	NG	JIM SHEAR
CF	RB	TOM ZAWERTON	CF	LB	GENE BARTLOW
CF	SE	TODD CHELAK	CF	DB	JOHN WORDEN
CF	TE	DAVE WARPUS	CF	T	RICK FINCH
SCC	G	GREG WILLIAMS	CF	LB	KEVIN TRAVIS
SCC	TE	JOE McGUIGAN	SCC	G	MATT GEISER
SCC	QB	RON SMITH	SCC	E	STEVE COUTANT
SCC	RB	JOSH WIGGINS	SCC	LB	MARK SPEICHER

1988

DIVISION I					
HH	T	DAN GROSS	HH	LB	BERT CONKLIN
HH	T	JIM JANESKI	HH	E	MIKE DOMINIKOSKI
HH	T	JEFF PURVIS	HH	E	BUB KENNEDY
HH	G	JOE REIS	HH	NG	JOHN McKRACKEN
BHS	QB	RAY STANTON	BHS	T	CHRIS LoVUOLO
BHS	FB	KEVIN McHUGH	BHS	T	DYLAN MENDELSON
BHS	WR	RON BLAIR	BHS	LB	DARRELL PARKER
BHS	TE	DAN DAVIS	BHS	S	ADAM BARNETT
UE	FB	PAUL NORRIS	UE	LB	BILL CARLINI
UE	HB	JARVIS SHIELDS	UE	S	ED MAGUR
UE	T	JIM BALLAM	UE	T	TONY RANDESI

UE	WR	MIKE TIDICK	UE	T	JEREMY TERWILLIGER

DIVISION II

ME	RB	J.J. SHIVELL	ME	L	JOHN CANESTARO
ME	QB	GARY GAETANO	ME	L	DARIN MOODY
ME	WR	RUSTY KNAPP	ME	DB	JAY ZUNIC
ME	C	TOM WALLS	ME	DB	TROY SMITH
JC	RB	JOHN NANNERY	JC	L	MIKE MIKALAJUNAS
JC	QB	JOE KATUSHA	JC	L	MIKE VANCA
JC	RB	JOE CHAPMAN	JC	DB	JOE CAMP
JC	C	DAVE KAHN	JC	L	STEVE BANOVIC

DIVISION III

NOR	RB	STEVE YU	NOR	LB	JIM KAUFMAN
NOR	RB	DAVE WHITE	NOR	DB	MATT BEADLE
NOR	C	CHRIS TURNER	NOR	DB	PETE DeRENSIS
NOR	QB	PAT DOWDALL	SCC	LB	MARK PHELAN
SCC	QB	RON SMITH	SCC	LB	GERRY WARD
SCC	TB	MATT SPEICHER	SCC	L	SEAN MURRAY
SCC	SE	JOE McGUIGAN	SCC	L	RICH PETRISKO
SCC	L	MATT GEISER	SCC	L	GREG YESENSKY

1989

DIVISION I

BHS	TB	CHRIS WILLIAMS	BHS	T	MIKE HOLLY
BHS	QB	NATE O'NEIL	BHS	DB	BASCO SPIVEY
BHS	FB	GARY McBRIDE	BHS	G	JOHN CALLOWAY
UE	HB	DAVE ADAMSON	BHS	LB	D.J. MILLER
UE	HB	JARVIS SHIELDS	UE	LB	BILL CARLINI
UE	FB	PAUL NORRIS	UE	NG	TODD KEHLEY
UE	QB	CHRIS WATERS	UE	SS	BEN PRUSIA
UE	G	JOHN YOEST	UE	E	TONY VALACHOVIC

DIVISION II

CE	FB	DUKE KIMBALL	CE	E	TONY RUOCCO
CE	QB	FRANK OLMES	CE	FS	DOM DINARDO
CE	RB	DAN PARILLO	CE	G	JOE MORGAN
CE	T	COREY COLYER	CE	E	MIKE HENKE
EFA	RB	JOHN COOK	EFA	L	KEVIN MURPHY
EFA	RB	TRACY McGEE	EFA	L	TRACY BARCHET
EFA	QB	JEFF GRANGER	EFA	E	JOHN CLEARY
EFA	WR	SEAN FOGARTY	EFA	E	GARY WELLS
JC	FB	PERRY GREEN	JC	E	JEFF BERDINE
JC	G	STEVE BANOVIC	JC	E	CHAD VanKUREN
JC	T	RENNY SPENCER	JC	DB	DAVE KABAT
JC	QB	D.J. SABLICH	JC	G	JON DAVIS

DIVISION III

CV	QB	SCOTT KLEIN	CV	LB	STEVE LUCAS
CV	C	MIKE TURNA	CV	E	KYLE TURNER
CV	T	RICH DAVIS	CV	E	JOE HUNTER
CV	TE	JAY HOPE	CV	S	SCOTT DONALDSON
CV	FL	MARK WILSON	CF	E	JOE WALKER
CF	L	JOE VREDENBURGH	CF	LB	MIKE THOMPSON
CF	L	JIM AUKEMA	CF	LB	B.J. HANLY
CF	L	JASON MILLER			

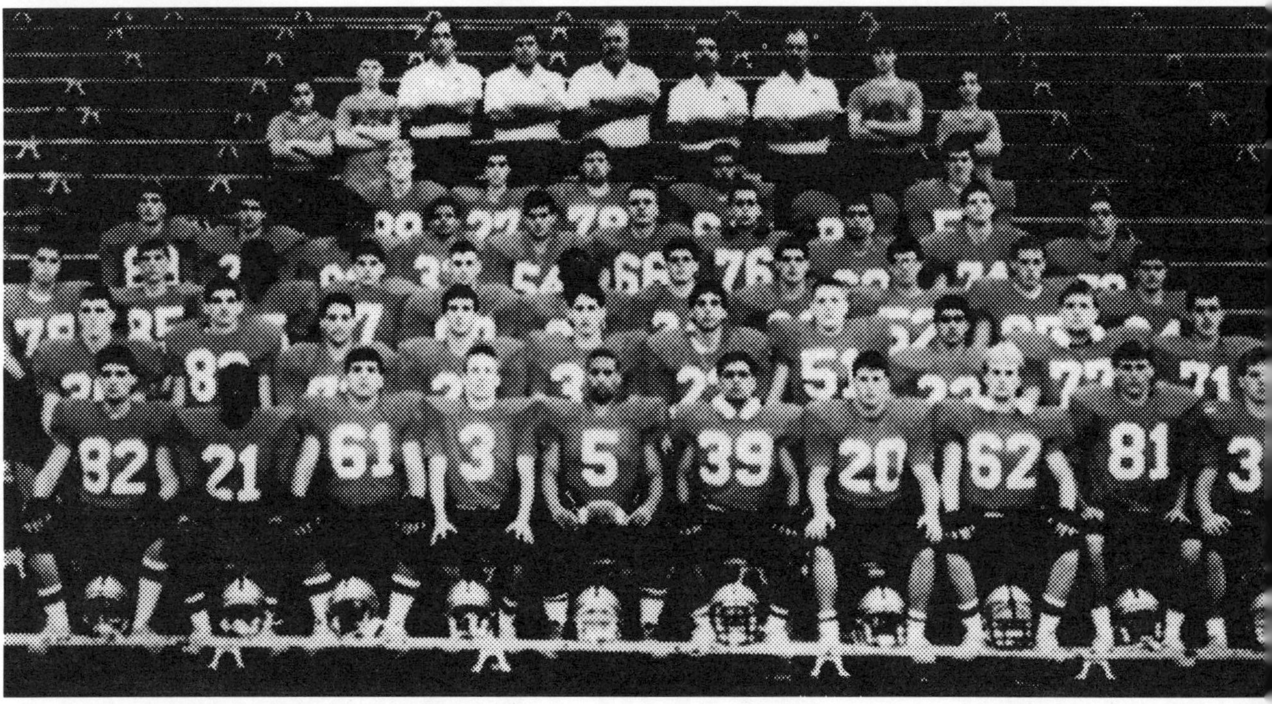

The 1989 Union Endicott Tigers *were masters of the* Tiger-Game *with an 11-0-0 record and finished* Number One *in* STAC, Number One *in the state, and* Number 19 *in the nation (*USA TODAY*).*

Following the 1990 season, Coach Angeline and wife, Pat, shared the appreciation of school and community with a once-in-a-lifetime trip to Hawaii. If only all those many friends could have tagged along....

Chapter Eighteen

"The purest treasure mortal times afford is spotless REPUTATION; that away, men are but guilded loam or painted clay. A jewel in a ten-times barr'd up chest is a bold spirit in a loyal breast. Mine honour is my life; both grow in one; take honour from me, and my life is done."

— William Shakespeare

"ALEA IACTA EST"

("The Die Is Cast") -Julius Caesar

— THE EARLY 90'S, 1990-1992

The Eye of the Tiger — 1990

B-r-r-i-i-n-n-g-g-g.

"Hello, Fran, this is Joe Cipp," the caller said. "I'd like to bring my Bellport team to Endicott for a game."

What a rarity this call was. It could well have been the only time in my entire career that a potential opponent initiated contact with us for a game. Joe was very much up front. He explained that his team had ended up as runner-up to us in the 1989 state rankings, that he was loaded, and that he had three big-time, *"Blue-Chip"* (i.e., potential *Division I* college level) players. Naturally, we readily accepted and booked them for our home opener.

The local football world was shocked to learn of Vestal coach Dave Sammon's sudden, untimely death as the school year was almost over. Thousands gathered at the memorial service, held at *Hoover Stadium*, to mourn this popular young man. Among others, Dick Hoover, Steve Mahon (who would be Dave's successor) and I gave brief eulogies. Standing there on that field to say good-bye to our old pal was very emotional for me, and I'm sure, for the others as well.

On the eve of the first practice in mid-August, my mother, Lea, passed away after a long illness. Even if it's expected, perhaps many of us think that our moms will go on forever. She had certainly attended to her sons' every need during our growing years, and was our Number One fan. The Angeline family was deeply touched when the entire football squad attended the funeral service in lieu of practice that morning.

Several coaches made their debut in 1990. Half of the coaches in *Division I* alone, were new: Joe Matejka at Horseheads; Frank Fazio at Ithaca; Steve Mahon at Vestal. In *Division II*, Regan Beers took over at M-E after a lengthy apprenticeship. In '91 at JC, I would line up opposite another former player — Gary Crooks.

I always felt that it was a special honor and privilege to have sons of rival coaches who lived in our school district entrusted to us. Such was the case with the Munleys. Two of them — Paul, Jr. and Kevin — played some inspiring football for us during the mid 80's. (Incidentally, their two brothers, John and Brian, became two of my tennis aces, too.) Regan Beers' (M-E) oldest son, Matt, was a premier offensive lineman for three big years ('88, '89, '90). Mark Decker's (OFA) older son, Rob, after missing his entire sophomore season due to injury, surely made up for it as a starting fullback/tight end, and defensive end in '91 and '92. Having observed these four characters at the table often during pre-season camp and on the road, I still don't know how Bette Munley, Carol Beers and Kathi Decker kept up with their appetites. (Decker was easily the most "eager eater" of the four — perhaps that's why he played so many different positions!)

U-E had the rare distinction of opening and closing its 1990 season far from home — on the banks of the Hudson River at *Dietz Field* in Kingston. In between, we would travel to the hostile environs of *Dunn Field* in Elmira three times. We repeated as champs and remained undefeated within our division. However, it wasn't all downhill as our overall record of 7-2-0 might indicate. Binghamton was right behind us, with a 3-1-1 divisional and 6-2-1 overall record.

We had graduated some key personnel from that record-setting '89 club. However, we felt that we still had enough solid experience and talent, including some veterans at the skill positions, to make a run for the flag again in '90. On paper our defense was a seasoned crew, for the most part, led by captain-elect Tony Valachovic at strong safety. Frankly, our main concern was with a green offensive line. Only Matt Beers was returning, and unfortunately, we could only use Matt in one of seven spots....

We were still optimistic, however. In fact, I'm afraid I got a little carried away soon after the '89 season, by making a very uncharacteristic prediction...on record: "You think we were good ('89)? *Wait 'til you see us next year!*" (I should have known better than to think it, let alone say it.) I know that our veterans felt that way, too, because a few of them thought that all they had to do was "show up" when the season unfolded. Our concern about inexperience in the offensive line was well-founded. It was obvious that this would take some time...and patience. This factor, coupled with the mindset of a few of our veterans, caused us to really struggle in our early games.

Kingston boasted a brand new facility and the potential of a highly ranked powerhouse. We were happy to have the opportunity to help christen the glistening artificial turf at refurbished *Dietz Field*. What an exquisite high school stadium! They would prove to be the best Kingston team we had ever faced, and...*it was hot*. We managed to win, 24-12, but it was really a lot closer than that. Our special teams' play and our physical conditioning were probably the main differences in the score. Kingston's Joe Davis proved to be one of the best receiver/defensive backs we ever faced.

Remember the phone call from Bellport, Long Island? Coach Cipp certainly can't be accused of "blowing smoke." He had advised us that they were loaded — *and they were!* He promised that they had three legitimate, big-time players — *and did they ever!* Their quarterback/safety Antonio O'Ferral, center/linebacker Jeff Cipp (Joe's son), and mammoth Matt Neuss, their exceptional two-way lineman, would all eventually accept full *NCAA* scholarships to the University of Kentucky and the University of Georgia, I believe. These three were surrounded by a cast of good, solid players who knew how to play and how to win. Filled with confidence (understandably so), Joe had done an unusual amount of advance public-relations work. The media from the Big Apple was there, in force. They say that reporters from the *New York Times, New York Newsday*, and the *New York Daily News* made the upstate trip. Since Joe would only agree to a one year contract, this was definitely going to be a winner-take-all deal. It didn't take us long to find out why. His predominantly senior-laden team treated its decent-sized contingent of fans to a 30-7 demolition in our own backyard, and a legitimate claim to the *Number One* spot in the state. They were terrific — I'm glad we played them.

It had been a long time since our guys had lost — a couple of years, in fact. How would they react? Each group reacts differently under various circumstances.

The drums in the west had been beating loudly since even before pre-season. This was reputed to be the best team in EFA's storied football history. So, when we ventured west on Route 17 the third weekend of the season, we found out in a hurry why Chemung country was all abuzz. They were the biggest team we had ever faced — including a bruising fullback, 6 feet 2 inches and 220 pounds, with sprinter-credentials — John Michael Cook. They handed us a deceiving second defeat in a row, 39-20. Deceiving because it wasn't even that close. Worse yet, they had beaten us up physically and, perhaps, had dented our pride. The word around the Tier was out then, loud and clear: "U-E is human, is vulnerable, and *can be had.*"

What to do? We could sense a little element of doubt and possibly some whining creeping in. Some of the veterans were beginning to hang their heads and feel sorry for themselves. We held a fairly lengthy meeting on the following Monday — just the veterans and coaches present. We asked them if they had ever considered in August that they'd be facing the possibility of losing three games in a row. This had now become a distinct possibility. Our first divisional battle was coming up — against our prime challengers — the Binghamton *Patriots*.

We opened it up for two-way dialogue. It was, arguably, the most productive meeting we ever held. Sure, there were some mental adjustments that had to be made, and, sure, we stepped on a few egos. We even discussed their interpretation of "*The Eye of the Tiger*" (the popular theme from the film, *Rocky*), and what it really meant. We agreed that perhaps we didn't have "*the eye*" yet in '90 — that perhaps we weren't as hungry as we had been in our previous quest for supremacy.

We tried to point out that our defense had not lived up to expectations, and that our offensive line needed their support. We stressed that the offensive linemen were willing to learn and had already come "miles" since August...although it might not be showing up on the scoreboard yet. We also told them that we had probably played the two best teams we'd be facing all year and that we could still do some great things — could still be a force. Before parting, we told them, in no uncertain terms, to quit their whining and begin leading by example, starting that moment. The main message in the dialogue was that we still believed in this team. It also became obvious that they believed in us.

What a turnaround! These boys became men that week. A favored Binghamton team didn't have a chance! Two relatively obscure running backs, neither of whom was exactly a burner — quarterback John Piester, and sometime-fullback Steve Erle (better known for his linebacking) — together collected 279 of our 331 rushing yards that night at home. About 9,000 spectators had shown up. This was a surprise — perhaps the numbers had swelled this particular time with outsiders who had come to see the *Tigers* get de-clawed and de-throned. The *Tigers* got neither.

Afterwards, the media stated, "Without question, this ballgame is sure to find a prominent spot on the ever-growing list of Patriots-Tigers football classics." We won, 34-28. But, more importantly — we persevered — we believed.

From that moment on, we felt as if we had begun a new season — and, in a sense, we had! It pumped some new life into every single player. At that point, it became obvious to us that, if we could continue to improve, who knew? That became our bible — our goal: *Improve*.

And were our guys ever willing and attentive! We had some very intense, spirited practices — not always an easy thing. The remaining teams on our schedule didn't have a prayer. We had our chin-straps buckled-up and ready every time we took the field: U-E 34, Horseheads 15; U-E 37, JC 16; U-E 54, ESS 6; U-E 35, Ithaca 0.

I must comment about Ithaca. Their field was a quagmire. In fact, Bill Bryant, Ithaca's outstanding athletic director, advised us toward the end of the week about the adverse field conditions and gave us the option of postponing. (That's the type of solid relationship we've always enjoyed with the *Little Red*.) We decided to play, anyway.

Bill wasn't exaggerating about the field conditions. I remember going out on the field to check on an injured player and having a very difficult time getting back to the sideline because of the deep mud. I recall that one of my shoes was sucked down, came off, and embarrassingly, had to be *pulled out!* What still amazes me, though, is how Jarvis Shields and Markus Wilson, our premier, fleet halfbacks, skipped around, juked, and sprinted on top of that mud as if it were a dry carpet. (Of course, they both weighed considerably *less* than their coach!)

Frankly, we had been concentrating so hard on our goal to improve week after week that we didn't even realize that we might be involved in post-season play. We scouted EFA just once toward the end when that possibility became a reality. "Hey, men, we might get another shot at EFA if this keeps up!" Our last regular season game: U-E 48, Vestal 7.

Bowl I was now set for *Dunn Field*: U-E versus EFA. What an opportunity — they were undefeated — had never been tested all season — had butchered us badly early in the season — and were ranked *Number One* in the state, *Class B*!

However, I knew a couple of things about this amazing, regenerated team of ours that Elmira didn't know. First, it was true that we were missing a couple of key people, due to injury, in our earlier encounter. We hadn't advertised that fact before or after that game. (Either way, it would have sounded like an excuse.) The other thing the Elmirans couldn't possibly have known was that I had observed three potent intangibles in our men during the past several weeks: they had been developing character, pride, and, most recently, confidence. I don't know that I've ever felt more confident as a decided underdog. My assistants will tell you that they thought I was crazy when I advised them at our Sunday (EFA preparation) staff-meeting to "*pack your bags*." They knew exactly what I meant, of course — that we were going right on to the *Regionals* after taking care of mighty EFA. We were on a roll — I just knew that we were going to shock Academy — *guaranteed!*

At Monday's practice I asked our players if there were any volunteers to play against the *Blue Devils*. The rules stipulated that we had to have a minimum number of players (about twenty) in uniform. After all, we were a bunch of tall, skinny guys up front, and tiny in the back end. We were being asked to go up against those behemoths who had already kicked the snot out of us once...and I was responsible for our physical well-being....

What a response I got! *Wow!*...There wasn't any looking around (you know — to see how your buddy is reacting). On the contrary, to a man. they raised their arms (fast!), accompanied by one collective, *unrehearsed shout!* Their pride had been challenged. I was convinced then and there, by the intense, determined look in their eyes, that the Elmira juggernaut would not be meeting the same team that it had annihilated a couple of months before. I knew that we were going to play well. Very well.

As expected, there was an abundance of pre-game hype all week long. The Binghamton and Elmira media, as well as both coaches, had contrasting approaches to this "biggie." The Binghamton media declared, "Tigers better prepared for rematch with EFA." I tried to keep it low-key, and would only say on record, "We're not going up there just for the ride, I'll guarantee you that."

The Elmira media had much to say about what they touted as a ***"Super Bowl"***:

> "Elmira Free Academy will put its 11-game streak on the line, along with its No. 1 state ranking, against Union-Endicott. The Blue Devils have been dominating all year and blasted Union-Endicott in week 3, 39-20. Although EFA is clearly the best Section 4 team U-E has faced, Blue Devil Coach Dick Senko also pointed out another reason why the Blue Devils had handled the Tigers, while U-E beat Binghamton High by six points, then blew out Horseheads, Johnson City, Elmira Southside, Ithaca and Vestal in succession. 'We match up with them,' he said. 'We've got the speed to cover their two pitch men (Jarvis Shields and Markus Wilson). These other teams don't have that. And we can match up with them size-wise.'"

(*This last comment was the epitome of understatement....*)

The timing of a column by Deron Snyder, a sports writer with the *Press and Sun-Bulletin* was ironic — it appeared that Wednesday. It was a general interview, not dealing with the game, but rather a "*Q and A*" format dealing with my reflections on three-plus decades of U-E football. The big print said, ***'Trying to achieve the maximum.'*** The very first question Deron asked was, "What do you enjoy most about coaching?"

My answer: "The thing that I get the biggest kick out of is trying to get the maximum, have each athlete achieve his maximum potential. That's a kind of mini-goal with each individual. By the same token we try to maximize that into a team, a cohesive unit, and maybe have them play better than their parts. Also, I truly enjoy what happens to them after they leave here, as adults and young men."

Perhaps some Elmirans saw this. If they did, and if they thought about the initial question and most of the response, they might have considered it portentous...at least in retrospect.

I remember our last words to the team before leaving the locker room for the field. After reminding them about "*The Eye of the Tiger*," and its true meaning, we told them to go out there and have some fun. We also instructed them, "If it's wearing blue, and it so much as quivers, *HIT IT!*" The night was bleak, cold, and damp, as I recall. *Dunn Field* was just recovering from a recent snowfall of several inches. Jim Runyan, Elmira's dedicated athletic director, and his field crew had done a masterful job in getting their field ready for play.

I don't remember why, but I was later than usual getting out to the field. The national anthem had just started when I reached the goal posts. Our cheerleaders, always the very best under the watchful eye of their unparalleled coach, Felicia Putrino, were there in the end zone. I stopped in my tracks and joined them in singing (a "first" for me, although Felicia and I had been singing together at holiday-time for years). I felt great — I mused about some words of wisdom a colleague had shared with me many years before: *"Each day is another day in which to excel."* How true.

There weren't that many spectators there. I can only speculate that the combination of lousy, iffy weather, TV coverage, plus EFA's total dominance of everyone (including us) had kept several fans from Endicott and the Triple Cities home — fans who would have been there under better circumstances. Those *Tiger* supporters who did venture forth on that dismal night — bundled up in blankets, gloves, and winter apparel— were treated to one of the finest efforts by any *Tiger* team...ever.

Wow! ...What a night!

The post-game media headlines:

'Revenge-minded U-E romps'; ***'Tigers stuff EFA with defense, 30-7'***; ***'Tigers trounce EFA in Bowl I, 30-7'***; ***'Done in at Dunn — U-E rushes for 267 yards, tops EFA, 30-7.'***

A few excerpts follow:

> "Jarvis Shields rushed for 118 yards and the Union-Endicott defense totally shut down Elmira Free Academy as the Tigers came away with a 30-7 win at Dunn Field in Section 4 Bowl Game I."

Another:

> "Improvement! All season Union-Endicott football coach Fran Angeline said that his goal for the season was for the team to improve from week to week. Saturday at Dunn Field in Elmira, the Tigers showed exactly how much they have improved since the third week of the season, when they were defeated 39-20 by Elmira Free Academy. The formerly undefeated EFA was beaten black and blue — or rather black and orange — 30-7 by the new and improved U-E team."

And yet another:

> "And here are the nuts and bolts of just how U-E earned that 11th-week berth: The Tigers' defense manhandled EFA throughout. The team that had seven weeks earlier scored 39 points against U-E this time could muster just a single first down before halftime; With Jarvis Shields' 118 yards showing the way, U-E busted through EFA for 267 rushing yards. The Blue Devils could answer with just 72 yards of their own; The Tigers scored on their final two possessions, led 20-0 at half-time, and floored EFA with an 11-play, 82-yard touchdown drive on their opening second- half possession. That made it 27-0. 'They had a mission, they had a goal in mind,' said Angeline, describing his squad's mindset when it took the field."

The events of this game will be engraved in my mind forever. We had decided to take our "*Top Gun*" formation out of mothballs. Our opponents hadn't seen it since we had initially unveiled it versus Binghamton four years ago. Perhaps, subconsciously, I was making comparisons between these two teams (Binghamton of '86, and EFA of '90), and the circumstances surrounding both games — especially our vast underdog role in both — when I decided to reactivate "*Gun*" for this special occasion. The conditions for its use were ideal: We had completely dominated the first-half, had cashed in on almost every opportunity, had a comfortable 20-0 lead, perhaps had our opponents somewhat demoralized and reeling — and we would be receiving the kickoff to start the second-half. Without repeating the mechanics of this special formation (see Binghamton, '86), suffice to remind you that its main elements were to position the biggest bodies available, including some non-starters, in an unbalanced alignment and to use the best running back on one play — off tackle. The philosophy behind it was threefold: first, the element of surprise; then, clock management (*i.e., "milking the clock"*); and finally score (the least priority). Well, we accomplished all three — especially clock management — eating up most of the third quarter on our initial drive.

However, I must share a humorous incident that took place on the field, during this drive, if you can believe it. Yes, in the midst of all this intensity — and it was intense, believe me — a couple of our players, both great kids, neither one a starter, but both in the *Top Gun* line-up, unintentionally provided us with an unrehearsed "*sit-com*". This comical incident couldn't possibly have been discerned from the stands. Every single man on the squad, including the managers and ball boys, knew our exact offensive game plan as the whistle blew to open the second-half.

We returned the kickoff to our 18-yard line. We then assembled the *Top Gun* personnel on the sideline and reminded them one last time: "Men, we're going to take it right at 'em with *Top Gun* — we're going to take our time and go straight down the field — and we're going to keep using it until they stop it — any questions?...*Then let's go!*"

Man, did that eleven-man crew ever fly out there as they lined up over the ball with no huddle! Two of these "new" linemen, both real big guys, had seen very little playing time all year (except for field goal protection). There they were, side by side, doing a great job as our first play from scrimmage went better than expected. Shields took it for about 17 yards, and almost broke it all the way, as I recall. *Our bench exploded!*

But...what was this? Those two big rookies, apparently excited by their initial success, came sprinting off the field, whooping and jumping up and down, while the remaining nine were lining up over the ball. I'll bet you can guess our initial reaction....We were angry and had to use a time-out. Our reprimands and frowns quickly changed to smiles and chuckling, however. You should have seen the look on their faces. They finally realized what all the fuss was about — they were supposed to stay out there, pounding away.

We all lightened up over this "first". It was good for all of us, as we sent our two embarrassed "delinquents" on a U-turn. That's one screw-up that probably had a positive result. We seemed to play with even more intensity, but were totally loose for the remainder of the game.

That special night at *Dunn Field* has to rank right up there alongside our 1986 Binghamton game for intensity and effort against a heavily favored foe in a major game. The only difference in the two games, I suppose, was the great disparity in attendance. (The Binghamton game must have drawn at least three times as many spectators.) As I shook hands after the game with Coach Senko, I couldn't help thinking of the quotation (and its connotation) from the outstanding, award-winning Ken Burns' documentary on the Civil War — the TV miniseries — *"Looks like bottom rail on top now."* I didn't say it, of course, but I sure was thinking it. Dick didn't make any excuses — I like that. He was quoted afterwards in print: "We just got beat by a good team tonight. They were very prepared and it just wasn't our night."

Although I didn't realize it at the time, this would be my last visit to *Dunn Field* with its brown-shirted security guards. I had entered the stadium that night standing 5 feet and 11 inches.... I left standing *twelve feet tall!*

I may be wrong, but I think many fans have the misconception that all opponents (including their entourages) are "the enemy" — and "hate" each other — especially in big games. Actually, nothing could be further from the truth. A vignette from after the 1990 EFA game helps to demonstrate the kind of relationship and mutual respect competitors can have for each other. I spent much time after the game consoling EFA's great back, John Michael Cook. Here was a first-class gladiator who had been knocked down. He was devastated, but I knew that he would rise again. And he did.

Later, when a few of us were standing around — the Cook family and Dana Carpenter, Senko's right-hand man — the subject of pasta came up. To make a long story short, the Cooks, Linnette and John, Sr., asked if Pat and I would like to come up for a real Italian feast sometime. Naturally, I told them I was "easy" — and readily accepted. We joined the whole EFA staff that winter at the Cook residence. The Cooks were the perfect hosts. Linnette (of Italian decent, I discovered — I might have known!) put out a scrumptious Italian spread, as promised. I lost track of the number of courses and the variety of pasta. The fellowship was outstanding. It was easy to see how young John Michael possessed his fine intangible qualities, as one became better acquainted with his parents. Dana Carpenter, John Michael Cook, and I vied for honors (consumption) that Sunday afternoon. (Coach Senko ate more intelligently — or perhaps he was on his best behavior because his lovely wife was there.) It was a beautiful day all around. This camaraderie is what true competition is all about. All of us still keep in touch today.

In all fairness, and taking nothing away from a very good Warwick team, the

Regional game was anticlimatic. It pitted us against the best from *Section IX* at Kingston's *Dietz Field* on Friday night. A couple of reporters wanted to draw attention to the fact that between the two coaches, Warwick's Joe Viglione and myself, "more than 400 victories and 60 years of coaching experience come to a head." I think I deflated that angle by going on record with this rejoinder: "All it means is that two old timers will be going out there with two excellent teams."

We decided to make a real big-league trip out of it. Unlike our last trip to Kingston, back in early September, we wanted our players to be rested and to get used to the artificial surface. We felt that they had "earned" it. Our administration co-operated and consented to our overnight stay. What a *royal reception* Kingston gave us throughout our entire visit! Tony Badalato and Rick Clausi, Kingston's athletic director and football coach, respectively, couldn't do enough. In fact, it seemed as if the entire city of Kingston embraced us as its own and really "*rolled out the carpet*" in every way. We worked out at the stadium, under the lights, on Thursday night, and conducted a final walk-through session on Friday morning. Many spectators from town, Mike Ferraro and Joe Davis (Kingston's prolific passing and receiving combo), and some of their teammates whom we had faced back in September, showed up at our night practice. I think we were all surprised that there was this much interest in a practice, but it provided us with the opportunity to become reacquainted with the Kingston players and to meet some of the nicest people anywhere.

We decided to make an educational trip out of this, too. We felt that we owed it to the boys to expand their horizons. Our first move toward this end was to make room assignments as diversified as possible: The closest buddies found themselves intentionally split up; seniors were mixed in with underclassmen; and minorities were intentionally split up and mixed in. On game-day we took the squad on a mini-tour of Kingston. We spent a good portion of that afternoon discussing all aspects of college: applications, admission procedures, scholarship possibilities, recruiting, and related topics. We feel that we accomplished a great deal, and perhaps more than made up for the day and a half of instruction that our student/athletes had missed back at "*The University of Endicott*," as some of our overly zealous fans began referring to U-E. (I'm not sure that all of our teachers and administrators shared these fans' enthusiasm for this innocent moniker.)

Quite a following from Endicott showed up. Felicia Putrino's vibrant cheerleaders and our spirited marching band, "*The Tigers' Pride*," under the direction of Barry Peters, made the long trip to lend their support and glitter. (Don't ever let a few macho statements fool you — it always meant a lot to both players and coaches to have this great backing — especially when so far from home.) A Warwick teacher/coach who was in attendance would write me an extremely complimentary note afterwards — in praise of the entire Union-Endicott "spectacular show" — not just the team, but the cheerleaders, band, and fans as well. I accepted it

proudly as a reflection of our exemplary school district and community.

The post-game headlines summarized the action well.

From Kingston: ***'U-E dismantles Warwick'***; from Binghamton: ***'U-E too tough for Warwick — Quick start gives Tigers 28-7 victory.'***

Joe Viglione, Warwick's outstanding veteran coach, was magnanimous in defeat with these words: "No one was going to beat them tonight. They played the best game I have seen anyone play all season. They were aggressive, came out hitting and moved the football." I felt that we had defeated a really good football team — one that was disciplined and well-coached and had some outstanding athletes at a few of the skill positions. Incidentally, our two staffs became acquainted quickly. We all broke bread together at a local restaurant when they came up here for the annual *Binghamton Football Clinic* that spring.

The Southern Tier enjoyed its first all-star game in more than thirty seasons. Some of us had been campaigning tenaciously for this, for several years. It was called "*The Ernie Davis Exceptional Senior Classic*" and took place in Endicott on *Thanksgiving* morning. It was most appropriate that the *Section IV* football committee agreed to incorporate Ernie's name in the title. He had performed in the very first all-star game, way back in 1958. (In an earlier chapter, I discussed this favorite *Section IV* son who was taken suddenly from our midst in what would have been his prime — this young man who exemplified the best traits of not only athleticism, but of character as well.) The inaugural game in 1990 featured the top one hundred (approximately) players in the entire section, divided into two teams. It has become an annual event.

That winter I received a couple of letters from former players who were then on duty in the *Persian Gulf War*. It's amazing how they both related to their football days. I was reminded of the influence we coaches have on our charges, and what an awesome responsibility that is. One, a Marine, promised that he would "keep the eye of the tiger keen in all operations." The other, from the *Airborne Division*, made detailed analogies between the Strike Forces over there and special teams here, between the Infantry and linemen, and so on. I shared these letters with both our players and staff. Perhaps it was a confirmation to all of us that there were lessons to be learned on our field. These guys were thanking me for all the training, discipline, and attitude — when it is I who should have been thanking them. Both Pat and I sent them brief notes — that's the least we could do. I was very proud of them, and had the opportunity to express that pride and the gratitude of all of us to them, personally, when they returned home and paid us a visit.

For the second year in a row, our team was honored by the school, the U-E Board of Education, the Village of Endicott, and the community. I received the gift of gifts at one of the team banquets, which took place at "*Kelly's*." Gene LaBare, a '67 grad who had done some great things for us on the field (our trainer, "*Hammy*," used to refer to him as the "*Money Player*"), summoned me forth at the end of this banquet. He informed me that he "represented the community and had something to give me from a very appreciative community." At first he teased me with a "hint." He produced a pineapple. My taste buds were stimulated at the sight — I love fruit. Then Gene presented me with a flight bag, brochure, airline tickets, hotel reservations — a week-long trip to Hawaii for Pat and me. *Wow!* I was absolutely stunned — and *speechless!* As I burst into the house afterwards, I could tell by the look on Pat's face that she had known about it all along, and had been sitting on top of it for a couple of months. We had never been west of Buffalo together unless we count one quick trip to Ohio. Hawaii was truly paradise, as advertised. This was a once-in-a-lifetime venture, and certainly one which neither of us will ever forget.

JC wound up as runner-up to EFA in *Division II* with a 4-1-0 divisional and 5-4-0 overall record.

Division III was a horse race with Seton CC edging CV for the honors, with a 4-0-1 divisional and 6-2-1 overall record. CV's divisional record was 4-1-0, and 6-3-0 overall. In *Bowl II* action, coach Mike D'Aloisio's fine Elmira Notre Dame team beat Seton, 20-16. The *Crusaders* then went on in *Class B Regional* play and dominated *Section IX* Saugerties at *Dietz Field*, Kingston, 32-13.

Our coaching fraternity was saddened to lose Dick Wheaton from OFA. Dick had certainly produced some exciting *Red* and *Blue* teams.

The *Patriots* Rule — 1991

Binghamton came on like gang busters in '91. No one could topple big Brad Bess, a fast, powerful 6 feet 1 inch and 230 pound battering ram. He was enjoying his third year in a row as a starter — and only a junior. Brad was just as effective on the defensive side of the ball. He has to be one of the best power backs the Tier has ever produced. The *Pats* ripped through everyone, going 4-0-0 in the division and 9-0-0 overall. They kept their record unblemished by winning both post-season contests — *Bowl I*: Binghamton 37, Elmira Free Academy 12; *Class A Regionals* at Cornell: Binghamton 15, Pine Bush (*Section IX*) 12.

The storm clouds up on Cayuga's waters began to rumble again after a lengthy quiet spell. Coach Fazio was turning things around up in *Little Red* country. Ithaca lost only to Binghamton within the division, 3-1-0, and finished with a 6-2-1 record overall.

In case one wonders why the *Division I* records are one game short, Elmira Southside had been allowed to compete in *Division II* for this year only.

EFA ruled the roost again in *Division II* with back-to-back perfect divisional seasons. What teams these guys produced year after year! The *Blue Devils* posted 5-0-0 divisional and 7-2-0 overall records, before losing to the Binghamton machine during the post-season. ESS made the most out of its one-year stint in *Division II*, losing only to Academy in posting a 4-1-0 divisional, and very respectable 7-2-0 overall, record.

Norwich and M-E were nip and tuck in *Division III*, but Norwich emerged undefeated within the division and was 7-1-1 overall. M-E finished with a 2-1-1 divisional and 6-2-1 overall mark in this, its only season in *Division III* before moving back to *Division II*. Coach Dan Hodack's Windsor *Black Knights* then beat Norwich in *Bowl II*, 27-8, before losing to *Section IX* Warwick in the *Class B Regionals* at Cornell, 16-7. Coach John Pluta's *Purple Tornado* of Norwich served notice to the entire league that it had an extremely talented sophomore class, one that very soon would emerge as a real power in both football and basketball.

We were saddened with the passing of four more coaches. They all conjure up pleasant memories:

Nick DiNunzio was a dedicated member of the U-E football staff (through 1959) and its golf coach. Nick was a real character, especially with his crooked little finger. Once he took a couple of us, both high school seniors at the time, to the spring football game at his alma mater, Syracuse University. He drove right up to a prime, "reserved" parking spot. When stopped by the official on duty, Nick barked out, without any hesitation whatsoever, "Chancellor's party."...

"*Yes, sir.*"... And in we went. My coaches might readily tell you that this lesson of so many years ago would serve us well in scouting excursions, especially with a tight schedule, to many stadiums over the years.

Maurice "*Hammy*" Hamilton was our long-time football trainer and baseball coach (through 1972). Many in the Endicott-Endwell area, including Pat, knew him as an excellent swimming instructor. Hammy loved popcorn — and used to try to hide his indulgence from me during pre-game warm-ups at times. He never knew...that I knew.

Francis Mullins, affectionately known as "*Moon*," was the veteran Elmira Southside and Johnson City football coach. As my predecessor at JC, we became fast friends. I visited this little Irish elf with the dancing eyes throughout his final bout with Advanced Alzheimer's. It's difficult to be positive about how much he grasped during these visits, but his eyes would always light up as he seemed to relish my reminding him of the time that he and I, together, physically "removed" the mayor of Johnson City, our teaching colleague, Jim McCabe, from the faculty room at JCHS. Poor Jim was just sitting and relaxing in an easy chair when we hoisted the chair (with Jim in it) and deposited both out in the hall.

Vic Impeciato was Elmira Free Academy's football coach during my high school playing days (early 50's). Vic moved to Atlanta, Georgia, after the 50's and became a well-known restaurateur there. While I was attending a national football convention there in the 80's, we hooked up. It gave me an opportunity to thank him personally for the complimentary remarks that he had made some thirty years earlier — remarks about this opposing player (me). His comments certainly didn't hurt my chances in attaining a college scholarship.

A couple of veteran fans, good pals and very close to our "U-E football family," passed away — "*Horky*" Dove and Lou Morris. It didn't seem the same without Horky's automatic, annual pre-season phone call in which he would offer his personal observation and assessment of our new personnel. Lou and I go back much further — he had been my coach during my junior year of high school when I was playing in a basketball league. Many years later, Lou was one of the speakers at my surprise "*Silver Anniversary Testimonial Dinner*," and made some very kind remarks. We missed seeing these two loyal fans during their declining years. They had been "regulars" at our first practice each year for as long as I can remember. (In fact, they were late once, and I "*fined*" them!)

We had a mediocre year in '91. Although we never seriously threatened our division with only three veterans, we might have exceeded our realistic expectations overall. Even finishing '91 with an overall record of 5-4-0 it may have been one of our "best" seasons. Who can judge?

We were led by our darling veteran scat-back, Markus Wilson. He did a great job as captain-elect, but didn't have the supporting cast of the previous two years — far from it.

We definitely had a couple of highlights that season, although the record might not sound that way. I was very proud to "square off" with another former student that year — Gary Crooks — who had just been handed the reins at JC. Markus set a U-E punt return record against Kingston — a 93-yard touchdown. Our greatest effort that season, arguably, came at the end, in defeating the *Golden Bears*, 37-15. Markus was absolutely scintillating over there that night. The headlines the next morning blared, ***'U-E senior puts on a show.'*** *I'll say!*

Markus broke open a fairly tight game in the fourth quarter — like a man possessed. He executed one of the most spectacular runs these eyes have ever seen. One reporter's version: "On third-and-3 from the U-E 27, three plays after Vestal's score, Wilson broke free from five tacklers and turned what should have been perhaps a first down at best into a marvelous 73-yard touchdown." He followed this on his last carry of the night (and of his high school career) with a 40-yard TD sprint up our sideline. Steve Miller, a premier defensive back/wide receiver, also gave us a consistent, high quality performance all season long.

"Is That All There Is?" — 1992

My knees were shot. Many point to football as the culprit, but I don't think football had anything to do with it. I'm convinced that it was a culmination of years of abuse on the courts — tennis (especially hard surface) and basketball — that finally took its toll. (Of course, a few extra pounds didn't help matters.) My coaches, all avid golfers, had secured a used golf cart. Although its original intent was to facilitate the transportation of small equipment, training supplies and water jugs to all areas of the practice fields, they insisted that I take advantage of it, too...for my knees' sake. I had found myself demonstrating less and less over the past couple of seasons, and that bothered me more than one might realize (including my coaches). I didn't really enjoy "riding" out to practice in '92, but I didn't want to hobble out either. I found that these old knees were having a difficult time making it through the rigors of double sessions in the pre-season.

Although Pat and I had broached the subject of the possibility of giving up football upon occasion during the past few seasons, she sensed that this time, when I brought it up during August, I was more serious than usual.

Binghamton and Ithaca were co-champions of *Division I* with identical 4-1-0 divisional records. Binghamton finished the regular season at 7-2-0 overall, and Ithaca finished at 8-1-0. U-E was breathing down their necks (especially Ithaca's), and counted two highly touted teams from *Section IX* — Middletown and Pine Bush — among its victims in posting a 7-2-0 season.

U-E's two losses, unfortunately, came at the hands of Ithaca and Binghamton. The *Pats* retained a solid nucleus from their '91 championship team — and they also had a seasoned Brad Bess for his fourth and final (*whew!*) year. Brad had bulked up to a solid 250 pounds, well distributed over his frame of 6 feet 2 inches — a "man among boys." I felt at the time (and still do) that Brad could have helped a couple of struggling *NFL* clubs. Ithaca returned almost all of its key performers from a strong '91 runner-up squad. The *Little Red* boasted some great athletes in their number.

Division II was also closely contested in '92. Both JC and M-E would share the spotlight with identical 4-1-0 divisional and 6-3-0 overall marks. Norwich dominated *Division III* with a perfect 5-0-0 divisional, and a very impressive 8-1-0 record overall.

Although I wouldn't be on the sideline to enjoy it, a dream-come-true was finally on the front burners. Albany announced that, beginning in 1993, New York State would have post-season playoffs, and crown a champion at the *Carrier Dome* in Syracuse. That is something toward which a few of us around the state had worked and campaigned tenaciously for what seemed like a lifetime. So all of the trials and tribulations a handful of us had experienced were at last coming to fruition. *We were ecstatic!*

To accommodate this state playoff tournament, our section wisely adjusted its post-season Bowl format in '92: *Bowl I*, now called *Class A*, would pit the top two teams in *Division I* against each other (a rematch). *Bowl II*, now called *Class B*, would match the top team from *Division II* against the best from *Division III*. Following are the 1992 post-season match-ups and results:

Section IV Bowls:

Class A: Binghamton 38, Ithaca 12

Class B: Norwich 26, Johnson City 0

Regionals — Section IV versus Section V *(Rochester):*

Class A: Fairport 40, Binghamton 32

Class B: Norwich 28, Hilton 14

We were a bona fide "road team" in '92. The timing of this rugged schedule couldn't have been worse because, due to financial belt-tightening by our district, we were forced to travel great distances by the "*yellow hounds*" (*i.e.,* school buses), rather than by our usual commodious charter buses with their ample leg room, air conditioning, and reclining seats. We should have invited our superintendent, board of education members, and a few tax payers to join us on our excursions. They would have quickly discovered that it's one thing to travel within the Triple Cities by school bus, but it's quite another to travel in cramped conditions, on consecutive weekends, to Shenendehowa (Clifton Park/Schenectady), Middletown, Pine Bush (Middletown area), and Elmira Southside. Someone figured out that we (including our knees) had already logged over 1,000 miles on the road — all via "*yellow hound*" — before ever getting a break to play at home.

Willie Nelson's popular vocal, "*On the Road Again*," took on a special meaning for us. Some began greeting each other with a few of its lyrics quite often during the first half of that season. Ed *"Fols"* Folli, who was just recovering from a major knee operation the previous spring, and I must have been a strange sight up in the front of these buses. The two of us, because of our knee problems, needed the entire front row of four seats, and the aisle, too. We tried to sit side-saddle to facilitate stretching our legs toward each other by forming a "bridge" over the "spacious" aisle between us for most of each journey.... It was interesting, to say the least.

The timing of the '92 autumn heat wave coincided with these first four trips also.

The term, "*greenhouse effect*," had recently become the popular description for it, coined by the ever-increasing number of meteorologists appearing regularly on our TV screens. Anyone who thinks that we had the luxury of air conditioning on these "outings" is extremely naive — or perhaps a little dense — or both. *What an experience!*

...But, we survived.

The administration at Liberty High School was kind to make their facilities available to us for our first two games. Liberty was enroute and approximately two-thirds of our final destination both times. This provided us with an opportunity to eat a light, pregame box-lunch, to stretch our legs (and knees), and to take a little "down time" before moving on. Led by our 6 feet 5 inches and 213 pound captain, Jeff Pilarcek, the entire squad walked all around the Liberty campus to help work out the kinks.

Coach Dick Wolslayer's Middletown *Middies* (not to be confused with "*Iddy-biddies*") were ready for us at their spacious stadium in the opener. Our two schools hadn't met since splitting a pair of games in the early 60's. The area media, including at least one TV crew, were there in force — usually a clue as to the quality of the hosts. These *Middies* were, arguably, even bigger than that EFA team in '90. Their outstanding tight end played both ways (a plus for us, as things developed on this hot, sticky night). He was 6 feet 5 inches and 335 pounds of man playing a boys' game. We'll never forget him — Miguel Dolson.

Pilarcek was our offensive gun that night, mostly on short option-keepers. We were trying desperately to develop some vastly inexperienced running backs. Jeff rushed for 87 yards on 26 carries, and they were all tough, hard-earned yards in this defensive struggle. "That quarterback was very strong, and very tough," Wolslayer said of Pilarcek. "We hit him with everything but the goalpost and he kept coming at us." The *Tigers* were very happy to come away with a 6-0 victory that night, as they set their sights on Middletown's rival from the same general area of the state — Pine Bush.

The game at Pine Bush marked the first time our two schools had ever met on the gridiron (and last time, as of this writing). After repeating our Middletown itinerary almost entirely the following Friday (we might as well have just stayed down there for the week), we arrived at Pine Bush's stadium. (In the short trek between Middletown and Pine Bush we passed some of the most sleek and beautiful horses that we had ever seen, as they were grazing in abundant fields.)

From almost the moment we unloaded we thought we detected an atmosphere, a certain hard-to-describe air of superiority. I'm sure that the *Bushmen* had their reasons — after all, they returned some of the key personnel that had come within a whisker of beating Binghamton in the regional *Class A* game at Cornell the previous year. They featured a very swift and talented 6 feet, 3 inch, 212 pound running back by the name of Eugene Jones, as well as a big, *All-American* two-way tackle. They must have thought that they were really going to hammer us.

Well, they didn't. As a matter of fact, I think our guys sensed this aura of invincibility down there, and did a little hammering themselves...to the tune of 38-29. (The score was very deceiving, since 14 of their points were scored quickly when our reserves had taken over for most of the fourth quarter.)

A rare sidelight occurred during these two downstate games, played on consecutive weekends: Our starting safety, senior Rob *"Horny"* VanHorn, was also our reserve quarterback. Because of the heat, he had spelled Pilarcek for a few plays. He owned these offensive statistics after the Middletown and Pine Bush games: 2 carries (one in each game) for 101 yards and 2 touchdowns. In fact, on his lone carry against Pine Bush, we were just trying to eat up the clock with a quarterback sneak. Horny ate up the clock all right — and a disheartened, tired *Bushmen* defense, too — as he "sneaked" for an 88-yard TD.

When we traveled to Elmira Southside next (played at Elmira Notre Dame's stadium), it was almost like playing at home. The 50-mile drive was "*cake*." We were gaining some confidence and momentum after those first two games against quality people downstate, and our backs were beginning to run with more authority. Rob Decker's 94-yard touchdown sprint just before halftime broke a 7-7 tie and became a big part of 350 yards of offense...all on the ground. We beat a game *Hornet* squad, 23-7.

Our fourth game was at home. *Can you believe it?!* It was such a rarity that we almost felt like visitors in our own house. This was a neighborhood battle against a veteran, undefeated Maine-Endwell team that had made some extremely lofty predictions. They were on record during the pre-season, and again as part of the pre-game hype. A huge following from M-E was on hand — this was going to be their year — they smelled blood! The halftime score was 7-7. Then the *Tigers* went *wild*! They set a U-E one-quarter scoring record by going on a 35-point explosion in the third quarter. (This may be a far-reaching record, as well.) One reporter stated that this period took almost an hour to complete. After he had related this to me, I supposedly said, "We weren't in any rush." Obviously, the defense also rose to the occasion in a big way. Final score: U-E 42, M-E 7.

"*On the road again ....*" Our defense and kicking game continued to improve as we achieved consistently great field position, and really shocked a good Horseheads team in its own stable, 33-0.

When Corning East came to town for the first time in a few years, we reminded the troops about what almost happened the last time these *Trojans* had come to Endicott as decided underdogs ('89). Perhaps we shouldn't have mentioned it. We had our first flat half of the season, and East played very well to find itself down by only a point in two lackluster periods, 7-6. We came out of the locker room door a little more like hungry *Tigers* in the second half and convincingly rolled up our sixth victory, 30-6.

The two-thirds mark of our season was an exciting time. Both Ithaca and U-E were about to enter the seventh weekend with identical and unblemished 6-0 records. The two of us, the oldest rivals on the books, hadn't met under these same circumstances for almost thirty years (1964). Ithaca had already established itself as the front runner, a result of its early season lopsided victory over Binghamton. U-E and Binghamton were both coming on strong. The *Tigers* were facing the teeth of their schedule — at Ithaca — then with Binghamton and Vestal at home.

The media didn't waste much time building up the approaching Ithaca versus U-E clash. The early week headlines read, ***'Tigers erasing thoughts of '91 — U-E back, with a vengeance.'*** An excerpt: "The goal, as stated by Coach Fran Angeline back in early September, was 'a return to the hunt.' 'This is the peak of the hunt,' Angeline said."

I liked what the Middletown coach had to say when he was contacted about us. (The *Middies* had lost only to us, and had beaten a couple of king-pins by then — Monsignor Farrell of Staten Island and Newburgh.) "Farrell looked outstanding, and Newburgh had all the personnel, yet U-E wins," Wolslayer said. "To say they have an outstanding this or that, they don't. But they execute, and they win." The only coach to have already faced both of us at this stage, Tony Marks of ESS, talked about us as two contrasting styles: "Raw talent [Ithaca] versus execution [U-E]. Creativity [Ithaca] versus discipline [U-E]." We were really looking forward to the challenge. We had a great practice week. This promised to be the pivotal game of the season.

They say it was the biggest crowd *Bredbenner Field* had seen since the early 70's and the Steve Webster era. The game was vintage Ithaca versus U-E. Except for a few mental lapses (including one that proved very costly), we played well. Ithaca played even better, and secured a well-earned 16-14 victory. My heart bled for these proud young warriors of ours — and for my coaches, too. It was a devastating defeat — easily one of the most devastating ever. We felt totally empty — totally spent on the long ride home. In retrospect, sure there are a couple of things we could have, and probably should have, done differently. But, "*could'a*" and "*should'a*" don't get it done on the field. We just ran out of time. Ithaca won — fair and square.

The post-game headline said it all: ***'U-E suffers first defeat.'***

A little over two months had passed since I had discussed the possibility of giving up coaching with Pat. It had been on my mind all this time. I had become more convinced with each passing practice; each passing game. Before the weekend was over, and after much soul-searching and anguish, I made a final decision. Since I didn't want it to drag on much longer, and since the district might want to start thinking about a successor, I handed in a letter of resignation (effective at the conclusion of the season) at the beginning of Binghamton week. My only request was that the district not make any formal announcement until after the Binghamton game. I felt that this would give me time to make sure that my children, staff and team hear it from me before reading or hearing about it elsewhere. This request was honored.

Pat knew, of course. I didn't have any experience with anything like this. There's no way one can prepare for it. It is, without doubt, the most difficult singular thing I've ever had to do through all the trials and tribulations of a lifetime. How do I tell these people — all "family" to me? And when do I tell them? These were heart-wrenching decisions, believe me.

I decided not to tell the squad until right after the Binghamton game. I did not want to burden them with any additional pressure beyond what they were already feeling after the loss at Ithaca.

Late in the week, I called each of my children. It's difficult to gauge one's reaction by phone. I remember that initially it seemed like an eternity of silence before, perhaps, disbelief. They were terrific in their support and love, however.... It meant a lot to me.

I informed my immediate staff (varsity) in the privacy of our office just before we took the field for pre-game warm-ups. Initial shock became hugs and tears — hey, we had been together for a long time — we had been through peaks and valleys together — we were family. It wasn't easy.

We had a pretty solid week of preparation for Binghamton — we were in focus. And our traditional *Halloween* week ritual came off without a hitch:

On a pre-determined practice session, for as many years as I can remember, I slipped into the locker room toward the end of practice to get into my "costume." My assistants always divided the squad into two groups after practice — rookies and veterans. (Of course, the veterans now realized what was happening and were sent to the far end zone, lest their knowing snickers might tip off the unsuspecting rookies.) The coaches then invented different types of end zone contests for the rookies. They would send the individual winner of each brief contest into the locker room. Of course, unknown to most of them, I was lurking just inside the door with my black cape and mask (alternated between *Darth Vader* or a *Werewolf*). Since the entire charade was organized so that the rookies left the field one-at-a-time, they entered the locker room alone. As each one would enter, not noticing that the room was a little darker than usual, and eerily quiet, I would use one of two tactics — either jumping out at each one with some blood-curdling scream, or wait until he had taken a few steps before confronting him with a gentle, "Good evening."

We never scared all of them, but there were always a few "special" ones each year who jumped or recoiled with terrified expressions. (The coaches and veterans would always try to guess who they might be in advance.) Afterwards I presented each of the "tricked" with a little "treat." The veterans and coaches couldn't wait to come in as a group to learn who had "won" (*i.e.*, who had been the most frightened), and, of course, to see me in a rare role.... And to get their little goodie.... Lots of fun!

This was always a special time of year for me. I always looked forward to taking my own little hobgoblins around the neighborhood for tricks or treats, and was sorry to see it end when they "outgrew" it. Over the years, several players visited the Angeline residence on the official night. They showed up in some very clever and creative costumes. The Angelines always enjoyed their originality. A few candid pictures of these *Halloween* visitors have become a part of my memorabilia.

Binghamton was not the same team that Ithaca had so convincingly destroyed in the beginning of the season — not by a long shot. There were two reasons for its transformation: Steve Deinhardt and his coaches had been doing a great job in getting their players to believe in themselves, to not hang their heads, and to want to improve. The other factor was the return of their best, biggest, strongest, and most experienced lineman — 6 feet 3 inches and 275 pounds — Tom Kaminsky. A pre-season injury had put Tom on the shelf up to this point. This was a big, talented, confident team that entered our stadium on that bright, sunny *Halloween* afternoon. (Dr. Dennis Sweeney, our superintendent, had changed the game time to 2 P.M., citing "Halloween activities around town," as the reason.) Here was the team that had beaten everyone...except the *Little Red* of Ithaca.

The *Patriots* had devised a brilliant offensive game plan against us built around the return of Kaminsky. They lined him up at tight end, rather than at his expected tackle position. We were not prepared for it. Tom was overpowering. Let me tell you something: When you run Bess, *"The Bull,"* at 250 pounds, behind Kaminsky, *"The House,"* at 275 pounds, and then you mix in a clever athlete like quarterback Mel Daniels to keep an opponent "honest"— you are virtually unstoppable — as we (and Ithaca in the subsequent Bowl rematch) were about to find out.

The *Pats'* new alignment up front definitely caught us off guard. We tried hard to adjust, but did not have the defensive personnel to match up with that kind of strength and firepower. Our men still displayed an abundance of courage, poise, and pride, however, and the *Tigers* had their moments. They brought the crowd to its feet on three big plays, all resulting in touchdowns.

In the first half, our only score came on a most unusual play when Ricky Whatman and Charles Green, two very promising sophomore backs, teamed up for an 86-yard kickoff return — Whatman pitching the ball to Green while being tackled near mid field, and Green sprinted it in from there. On the first play of the second half Green started off tackle and zipped 65 yards for a second TD. Then, six Binghamton plays later, Horny VanHorn received a punt at his own 18 and racing and weaving through traffic, behind a wall of picture-perfect blocking, took it all the way in. All of a sudden, we found ourselves on top, 21-20!

But it was short lived. Binghamton wore us down, and eventually won, 31-21. Anyone who was there would tell you that the final score was not really indicative of the game. The *Patriots* had thoroughly dominated throughout, and had controlled the clock very well. The effect of the switch in game time, on either team, would be pure conjecture. We would have loved another shot at Ithaca in a Bowl rematch, but I honestly don't think that either of us could have matched up with the "new" Binghamton — day or night.

In the locker room afterwards, the first thing I did was congratulate the boys for their effort against what I felt was a superior team. I had sent out word to make sure that my entire staff (JV and modified coaches included) was in that room at the same time, and then asked someone to secure all doors (to avoid any possible interruptions). A few of them probably sensed that "something was up." It was a trying experience for me. I broke the news to all of them — the last of my "family" — all at once. I assured them that they were not responsible for my decision in any way. Our recent two losses, our only two, had nothing to do with my retirement — in fact, this had been decided earlier in the week. My words took only a minute or two.... The silence in that room was deafening.... The ensuing bonding, love and fellowship are indescribable. Many kept hanging around for a long time after showering. I felt somewhat relieved — my decision and announcement to my entire "family" were behind me now — *the die had been cast* — there was no turning back....

I had crossed *my* Rubicon.

There was one last piece of unfinished business, however — the *Golden Bears*. The media had picked up the scent of my resignation before the weekend was over. At midweek, I was surprised to read about it in *USA TODAY*. I remember thinking at the time how thankful I was that I had already informed my children, who were scattered all over the country, before that particular issue had hit the newsstands.

The entire Vestal week was peppered with several phone calls from well-wishers and visits to the field by former players and fans. Although I certainly appreciated their sincerity, I was somewhat concerned that all of this, plus an unusual amount of media attention, might serve as a distraction to our preparation. The pre-game hype in the media seemed to be focusing more on my retirement than on the game itself, a game about to be played by some of our nation's finest young men from two of its finest public high schools. I worried about that a lot.

Toward the end of the week, I began to relax a little. The Charles F. Johnson Elementary School put on a rousing pep-rally for the squad, and the little folks (and big ones, too) presented me with several mementos that I shall always treasure. Practice for our traditional senior-parent ceremony went especially well. I wound up the week by treating my staff to our traditional Vestal-week dinner, known simply as *"The Annual."* Camaraderie was overflowing.

Saturday dawned with a start. I was fairly composed until I perused the morning paper over a cup of coffee. The headline of, ***'Fran's last stand,'*** caused me a little stir. However, another article jumped off the page and begged my attention: ***'Football or not, dad's little girl loves the coach'*** — by Vaun Angeline.

Completely unknown to me, Vaun, who was 3,000 miles away in L.A. and unable to share this evening with me, had chosen this way (with the cooperation of Charlie Jaworski, Executive Sports Editor of the *Press and Sun-Bulletin*) to pay tribute to her dad. *Wow!* I was deeply moved — and apparently I wasn't alone, judging by the many, many people who remarked about it. Even months later strangers from the area would stop me to relate how they had teared-up when reading it that morning. It summons up my emotions even today when I think of it.

I was anxious, antsy, and wanted to be alone. Impossible. I realized that I wouldn't be able to remain cooped up all day, so I treated myself to breakfast at a local restaurant. Mistake. One of our favorite waitresses became quite emotional. I tried the solitude of church — but became too itchy there.

Pat's best girlhood friend and fellow U-E graduate, Angela Monaco McCarthy, had travelled from Buffalo to share the weekend with her. This helped take the edge off, a little. I finally decided to do what I usually do — see a few games. And anyway, I needed the fresh air. I attended the U-E JV game at Vestal in the late morning and the JC at M-E game in the afternoon. There were many well-wishers — they were terrific! They said some very kind things — I don't know if I was deserving of all of them. Most people must have sensed that I needed some space that day and allowed me that.

I had a little popcorn.... Had some deep thoughts.... Would game time ever come?

I was relaxed during our pre-game work-out. Lots of nice folks, even including some from the "other side" of the river, "dropped by the end zone" to wish me well. I will never forget one fan in particular — a staunch, loyal, long-time U-E supporter. He grabbed my hand and uttered two words: "Thank you." I really appreciated that.

The pre-game parent-senior ceremony went off without a hitch. Dr. Sweeney surprised me by presenting me with a plaque of "*appreciation from the district*" in a brief ceremony on the field. Hovie Hover had arranged for Pat and our sons to be there at my side. It was a nice touch — I certainly enjoyed having them there.

Then it was time to tee it up. My adrenaline was flowing.... I was really *pumped!* All of my concerns about possible distractions during the circus-like atmosphere of the recent days were about to disappear. It became obvious to me from the opening whistle that our *Tiger* team had had their eyes on the prize all week. Vestal was the recipient of their full, undivided focus. The *Tigers* were absolutely vibrant and magnificent!

For me, this final game conjures up so many pleasant memories and mixed emotions that even now I am reluctant to review them. I'll let the media retell it:

'Fran out with a rout.'

> "'Farewell Fran' night was, for the most part, business as usual. Time ran out on Fran Angeline's 311th and final game as a high school football coach on Saturday night, two hours after its 7:30 kickoff, with Union-Endicott enjoying a 42-8 command of Vestal. 'What just happened, I think, was they were trying to make a statement,' Angeline said, speaking of U-E players who had racked up a 35-0 halftime spread. 'I was very concerned with all the hoopla. But I would say they really got down to business.'" Another account: 'One last crushing defeat.' "It was one of the coldest nights of high school football at Endicott's Ty Cobb stadium, a field of battle hovering only yards above the ice-cold Susquehanna River. But the 42-8 Union-Endicott victory over archrival Vestal provided the current year's crop of Tigers with their most heartwarming contest of the year. But though the Tigers turned in a resounding performance that generated enough heat to ease the chill, at least a bit, of the frosty November 7 night, the stadium witnessed no mere football game. This was indeed the end of an era. It was a heart-pounding, moist-eyed farewell from an entire team, an entire community to the only head U-E football coach many of them had ever known. Post-season bowl berth or not, Fran Angeline and the 1992 Tigers went out the way they wanted to."

Our gag rule was relaxed and everyone realized it — a few of the players were quoted afterwards:

"We worked very hard all week for him, to win this for him." — Jeff Pilarcek, quarterback and captain.

"We wanted to win, send him out a winner. He loves this game, works harder at it than we do. That was as much as we could do to repay him." — Walter Scott, fullback.

"It was very emotional. It was our privilege to send him off that way. We wanted to send Mr. Angeline out with a bang." — Joe Osiecki, defensive back.

The fact is, our young men chalked up 383 yards of total offense — 331 of them on the ground. Our defense was equally impressive — allowing Vestal one touchdown, 117 rushing yards and 45 passing yards.

I recall briefly "losing it" for just the last minute or so of the game — my mind was not on the game, nor even on our players doing battle. It was on the hundreds of young men who had worn the *Orange and Black* so proudly over the years. I was very proud to have been associated with every single one of them, along with these last forty-five from '92.

After what seemed like hours of on-field hugs, handshakes, tears, and then, good-byes to the squad and staff, post-game interviews and a most relaxing hot shower, I remember vividly walking alone out into the now still night and thinking about the song and lyrics popularized by the vocal legend, Peggy Lee — "*Is That All There Is?*"

In December, Pat and I took the entire staff, their wives and guests out to dinner. It was our way of thanking them. Those rascals turned it into a party for us, though — and showered us with all kinds of gifts.

That February, the community of Endicott held a farewell testimonial dinner for me. The morning paper announced it was a "sell-out." I'm sorry that some people were turned away at the door (I found out later), but it was an exciting, emotional evening for the Angeline clan. My entire family, including most of my in-laws (the Hanley crew) were there. My favorite vocalist had flown in from Los Angeles, and with a few of her former local band members, treated her dad and guests to some great jazz renditions during cocktail hour. Dick *"Mac"* McLean, our former superintendent of schools, did a superlative job as emcee. My old "sparring partners," Dick Hoover, Joe Moresco and Paul Munley spoke, as did Ed *"Fols"* Folli, representing the staff, and Jerry Hanley, my brother-in-law and former captain. Bob Gallagher, our colleague and close friend, read a very touching poem he had written. Mac introduced a newly engaged couple that evening — our Chris and Kathleen Duffy (also a former *Tiger*). My entire staff, most of the Binghamton staff and several others in the coaching fraternity were there. So many colleagues, former players and students, parents, neighbors, fans and boosters were there — even a few former classmates and teammates. Several guests had driven a considerable distance, in lousy weather (a Nor'easter had hit that day), to attend. What more could a guy ask? Everything was just perfect. They overwhelmed me with more gifts, proclamations, and memorabilia. It was an evening that my family and I shall cherish forever.

My closing remarks on that special night are still appropriate now:

> "What does one say to so many? While I am very appreciative of such generosity, please know that your fellowship and contact diminish everything else. These shall endure forever. As I reflect, I realize that I have been associated with this great game of ours, as both a player and coach, for almost forty-five years. That's almost a lifetime! But, it's now time for me to move on. I do not know what the future holds. I want you to know, however, that I'll miss all of you. And wherever I am, when the leaves begin to fall and there's a slight chill in the air, my finest thoughts will always be of the *Orange and the Black.*"

On a sad note, Dick McLean passed away before the year was over. Without any-one's knowledge, he must have been suffering when he undertook the tedious job of heading up the program for "my" evening. He was called by many the quintessential volunteer for his indefatigable, countless, selfless efforts of service to our community over the years. He was an exemplary educator — an educator who championed ath-letics, as well as academics. He was an ideal boss; he was our friend. We miss you, Mac.

From the experiences of this odyssey, let me say:

To that youngster out there who has a burning desire to play this great game, but who thinks or has been told that he is too small, too slow, too clumsy — *give it a shot anyway.*

To that parent, athlete, student, fan, booster out there whose world has seemingly collapsed over a loss — *there will be other games.*

To every wife or mother out there who has tried to run a household, to act as secretary, to absorb insults about her child and/or husband, and to keep supper warm — *thank you.*

To every coach out there who has shed some tears, has experienced anxieties, has wondered whether it is all worth it or not — the answer is, *"YES."*

It's difficult to speak for my staff, the team and the U-E community. However, we would like to think that we have helped to shape high school football in the Southern Tier and, perhaps, beyond. Although we feel that we have received far more than we have given, we have attempted to impart the finest ideals of sportsmanship, competition, fellowship, prestige, and PRIDE. This has been our creed, our bible, and, we hope...our legacy.

The 1990 Elmira Free Academy Blue Devils *plagued the entire league with their size and talent. (This photo belies the size of these guys!) This was quite possibly their best squad ever.*

ALL STARS — THE EARLY 90'S (1990-1992)

1990

OFFENSE School	Position	Player	DEFENSE School	Position	Player
DIVISION I					
BHS	QB	ROB BAXTER	BHS	L	JOHN JURASKA
BHS	TE	JOEL DAVIS	BHS	L	CHRIS KUMPON
BHS	C	ANDY RUSSELL	BHS	DB	BASCO SPIVEY
BHS	FB	BRAD BESS	UE	SS	BEN PRUSIA
UE	T	MATT BEERS	UE	LB	STEVE ERLE
UE	C	PETE CANNAVINO	UE	LB	JEFF LONG
UE	HB	MARKUS WILSON	UE	DB	ERIC HOTTENSTEIN
UE	HB	JARVIS SHIELDS	UE	L	JOHN RANDESI
DIVISION II					
JC	T	RENNY SPRNCER	JC	LB	PERRY GREEN
JC	HB	RASHINE HARRIS	JC	DB	DAVE KABAT
JC	G	MATT BENNETT	JC	L	JOHN GAUGHAN
JC	C	TONY RUSSO	EFA	L	MATT CONE
EFA	QB	JASON THOMAS	EFA	K	JAMAAL IRVIN
EFA	RB	JOHN M. COOK	EFA	L	FELIX WHITE
EFA	WR	JEREMY THOMAS	EFA	DB	BRYAN FRENCH
EFA	L	TRACY BARCHET	EFA	LB	D'ANDRE FULMER
DIVISION III					
CV	RB	SCOTT DONALDSON	CV	L	BARRETT OUIMETTE
CV	C	TODD WHEELAND	CV	DB	ADAM POLGREEN
CV	QB	CRAIG EHRIE	CV	L	PAUL McDANIELS
CV	FL	JEREME MACIAK	SCC	E	JIM RICCI
SCC	E	CHRIS CUMMISKEY	SCC	L	BILL FISHBACK
SCC	L	BUTCH DelREAL	SCC	LB	JOE HULL
SCC	L	BOB LALOR	SCC	DB	MARTY MARGHERIO
SCC	QB	ADRIAN LOLLIE	SCC	DB	MARK VIERA

1991

OFFENSE School	Position	Player	DEFENSE School	Position	Player
DIVISION I					
UE	HB	MARKUS WILSON	UE	LB	JEFF DuBRAVA
UE	L	JOE GASIOR	UE	LB	DAVE WALKER
IHS	QB	DOM AMICI	UE	DB	STEVE MILLER
IHS	E	TERRY ROACH	IHS	E	STEVE KILEY
IHS	WR	COREY PARZIALE	IHS	LB	PEREZ DINKINS
IHS	HB	STAN HOUSE	IHS	LB	DARIN STRONG
BHS	RB	MARK McBRIDE	BHS	L	JASON KECHAK
BHS	FB	BRAD BESS	BHS	L	BILL CAHILL
BHS	L	CHRIS KUMPON	BHS	E	TOM CIOTOLI
BHS	WR	SEAN BEERS	BHS	DB	DAN PRATT
BHS	L	ANDY MILLER			

DIVISION II

ESS	E	RYAN WOODWARD	ESS	L	PHIL CLARK
ESS	QB	MARK RICHARDS	ESS	LB	ANDY RICE
ESS	RB	TONY FISHER	ESS	L	DAVE WILBERT
EFA	QB	JASON THOMAS	EFA	L	FELIX WHITE
EFA	RB	JEREMY THOMAS	EFA	DB	BRYAN FRENCH
EFA	L	ED STOWELL	EFA	DB	SEAN MOUNTAIN
EFA	L	MICKEY PIROZZOLLO			

DIVISION III

ME	RB	NATE KOFIRA	ME	L	SHAWN NALEPA
ME	E	TOM BEATTY	ME	DB	DAVE POCANGAL
ME	L	JOE ZUNIC	ME	L	TIM AHRENS
NOR	RB	JASON MORRIS	NOR	L	RAY BLISS
NOR	RB	SEAN RYAN	NOR	L	MIKE BLENIS
NOR	E	PETE BURTON	NOR	L	TOM STODDARD
NOR	L	DAN JENNINGS			

1992

DIVISION I

UE	QB	JEFF PILARCEK	UE	LB	JEFF DuBRAVA
UE	TE	BRENDAN WALSH	UE	NG	PAT RUSSO
UE	FB	ROB DECKER	UE	S	ROB VanHORN
IHS	FB	PEREZ DINKINS	IHS	L	SEN SOGAH
IHS	E	TERRY ROACH	IHS	LB	MARSHALL JOHNSTON
IHS	RB	STAN HOUSE	IHS	L	ROGER RUMSEY
IHS	L	STEVE KILEY	IHS	LB	GABE SMITH
BHS	WR	SEAN BEERS	BHS	T	MATT STONER
BHS	C	MATT SEXTON	BHS	L	BARRY WOOLFOLK
BHS	QB	MEL DANIELS	BHS	LB	JON PENNA
BHS	FB	BRAD BESS	BHS	S	TOM PRATT

DIVISION II

ME	RB	RANDY MOREY	ME	LB	PETE AHRENS
ME	WR	GEORGE RUTKOWSKI	ME	E	SCOTT THOMPSON
ME	QB	SCOTT PINKER	ME	L	ANTHONY ADAMS
ME	C	JOE ZUNIC	ME	L	GREG CAMERA
JC	RB	A.J. BRUNETTI	JC	NG	TODD PLACE
JC	L	MIKE CIPAR	JC	LB	CHRIS JONES
JC	WR	MIKE VAVRA	JC	S	JEROLD LOWERY
JC	P	DAVE COLGAN	JC	DB	ROB FARRELL

DIVISION III

CV	RB	JOSH HUBBARD	CV	S	MATT AURELIO
CV	C	MIKE BURNS	CV	E	JEFF RINKER
CV	E	MATT TURNER	CV	LB	DAVE WILKINS
NOR	C	DAN JENNINGS	CV	LB	BRANDON GENDRON
NOR	TE	PETE BURTON	NOR	E	JEREMY FRINK
NOR	QB	CHRIS MAYNARD	NOR	E	RAY BLISS
NOR	RB	SEAN RYAN	NOR	NG	TOM STODDARD
NOR	RB	JOSH MORRIS	NOR	LB	JASON JAMES

To Try Is To Win In Itself

"Yes, I love the youthful winner,
With the medal and the mark;
He has gained the prize sought for,
He is joyous as a lark.
He is on the honor list;
Everyone will haste to praise him.
I've a tender thought, my friends,
For the one who tried and missed.
One? Ah, me! They count by the thousands
Those who have not gained the race.
Though they did their best and fairest,
Striving for the winner's place.
Only few can reach the laurel;
Many see their chances flit by.
I've a tender thought, my friends,
For the earnest band who try.
'Tis the trying that is noble,
If you're made of sterner stuff
Than the laggards who are daunted
When the bit of road is rough.
All will praise the happy winners;
But when they have hurried by,
I've a song to cheer, my friends,
The great company who try."

— author unknown

EPILOGUE

*"Achievement...
A time for looking back with pride,
for looking ahead with joy."*

"Do you miss it?"

I can't begin to fathom a guess on how often I have been asked this question since I left football. Tell me: Wouldn't you miss something in which you had invested body, soul, and love for most of a lifetime? ...*Of course I miss it!* Especially missed is the unique bond and camaraderie with my coaches and players. The actual on-the-field coaching. The fall hunts. And the preparation and strategy of each one. And I miss the little things such as the *Halloween* tradition and popcorn. This was a true labor of love.

A few people, whose opinions I respect, have suggested that my retirement from football was premature — that I was just arriving at my peak. Whether this is true or not, is conjecture. Frankly, I haven't given it much thought, one way or the other — I've never been one to second-guess myself or to peek over my shoulder. But I must say, *my knees have been elated!*

My decision has allowed me to expand my horizons — something I always encouraged my children, students and athletes to do. So, I'm satisfied with that decision.

For one thing, I've not only been able to see, but also to *actually enjoy* autumn's vivid foliage.

During the 1993 season, this free time also gave me an opportunity to experience the world of television as WBNG-TV sportscaster Paul Devlin's co-host for a weekly show entitled, *"The Point After."* It was an extremely educational experience for me. It was a lot of fun — and, a lot of work. (Not unlike coaching.) Although I worked mainly with Paul, I observed the work ethic of sportscaster Chris Maathuis and others at the studio. I developed a newly found respect for these television people — their behind-the-scenes hustle and bustle, their preparation, sweat, and dedication. Believe me, they earn their salaries.

And (subject to debate) I've taken up golf. (Is there ever going to be a light at the end of *that* tunnel?)

I have also had time to pursue what has always been an interest of mine — writing. Although I've written a few articles over the years, this is my first attempt at a book. I have found that it has given me a chance to reflect...to reminisce. Through it, I've learned I wouldn't trade this journey or these memories with anyone — I've enjoyed every single minute of the trip.

What happens next?

For one, a miraculous event has blessed us during “retirement”: the birth of our first grandson: Ryley Francis Angeline. Baby Ryley and his parents, Chris and Kathleen, have taken things right in stride. Grandpa Angeline, however, has been walking on clouds ever since receiving the joyous news from Trappe, Pennsylvania near Philadelphia. Only a grandparent can appreciate the exhilaration — it is unlike any other. So, I’m sure you know how Pat and I are spending a lot of our time.

Someday, perhaps, Ryley will come up for a visit during the fall. I intend to take him to the top of *Ty Cobb Stadium* when he is old enough to comprehend its scope. I will point down at the arena of earth and grass, and say to him:

“This is where your daddy played, Ryley.... Your uncles, Larry [Angeline], and Pat [Duffy].... Your great-uncles, Rick [Angeline], and Jerry [Hanley]....

Your grandpa Fran...

Your great-grandpa Frank [Angeline]....”

“And this, Ryley, is where your aunt Vaun sang the national anthem....

Where your grandma Pat co-captained the cheerleaders....”

“This is where your grandpa Fran lived and breathed football for most of his life....”

Then I’ll take him down to the practice field, where he can experience first-hand the clash of pads — the grunts, groans, and growls of the players.

And when he asks, “Grandpa, what are those noises?” — I’ll tell him: “It means the *Tigers* are getting ready, little Ryley....”

“They are getting ready to play!”

BIBLIOGRAPHY

Illustrations, pages 27, 69, 191, by Larry Angeline, are courtesy of Dave Archer, Beyond the X's and O's, 1980, and with permission of the artist.

Illustration, page 124, from Johnny Hart and Jack Caprio, is from the author's collection and with permission of the artist.

Photographs, pages viii, 5, 34, 77, 99, 164 and the back cover are shown through the courtesy of the *Press & Sun Bulletin*.

Photographs, front cover and page 116, by Steve Appel.

Photograph, page 210, by Ed Aswad.

Other photographs, clippings, and memorabilia, including championship teams, are from the author's collection or from the schools represented.

Other journalistic photographs and editorial references are taken from various publications and identified in the text when known, including:

The Binghamton Press

The Binghamton Sun

The Buffalo News

The Colgate Scene

The Corning Leader

The Daily Bulletin (Endicott)

The Elmira Star Gazette

The Evening Press (Binghamton)

The Ithaca Journal

The Johnson City Journal

The Kingston Freeman

Lombardi, Vince. *Vince Lombardi on Football*. James J. Walsh; New York. 1973.

The Middletown Times-Herald Record

The Newburgh News

1958 East-West All Star Game program *(Section IV)*

The Press & Sun-Bulletin (Binghamton)

The Rome Daily Sentinel

Slawta, Roger. *Triple Cities Football*. 1992.

Southern Tier Sports World. Frank C. Maus; Binghamton, New York. 1974.

The Sun-Bulletin (Binghamton)

The Sunday Press (Binghamton)

The Sunday Press & Sun-Bulletin (Binghamton)

Super Prep Football

The Syracuse Post Standard

The Tempo of the Towns (Endicott)

USA TODAY

The Valley News (Vestal)